Real-World Next.js

Build scalable, high-performance, and modern web
applications using Next.js, the React framework
for production

Michele Riva

BIRMINGHAM—MUMBAI

Real-World Next.js

Group Product Manager: Pavan Ramchandani

Publishing Product Manager: Aaron Tanna

Senior Editor: Aamir Ahmed

Content Development Editor: Feza Shaikh

Technical Editor: Simran Udasi

Copy Editor: Safis Editing

Project Coordinator: Manthan Patel

Proofreader: Safis Editing

Indexer: Manju Arasan

Production Designer: Roshan Kawale

Marketing Coordinator: Anamika Singh

First published: January 2022

Production reference: 1310122

Published by Packt Publishing Ltd.

Livery Place

35 Livery Street

Birmingham

B3 2PB, UK.

ISBN 978-1-80107-349-3

www.packt.com

I want to dedicate this book to Alice. It wouldn't have been possible without your patience, support, and love

- Michele Riva

Contributors

About the author

Michele Riva is a passionate and experienced software architect and Google Developer Expert from Milan, Italy. Over the years, he has contributed to many open source projects from big companies and foundations in many different programming languages and paradigms, including Haskell, Elixir, Go, and TypeScript. He has also written dozens of public domain articles on a broad range of topics and given many talks at international conferences and meetups.

While writing this book, he worked as a senior software engineer in the architecture team of ViacomCBS, building a multi-tenant Node.js application at the heart of their streaming websites and networks.

Currently, he's employed as a senior software architect at NearForm.

About the reviewers

Alberto Schiabel (@jkomyno) is a software engineer from Venice who sold his first apps in his teenage years. He obtained a master's degree in computer science from the University of Padua and has collaborated with other universities in Europe. Alberto has worked in several product and consulting software companies, but he has also worked as a freelancer and start-up cofounder. He enjoys mentoring colleagues and learning something new every day. Alberto discovered Node.js and React.js in 2015 and has worked with these technologies ever since, also as an open source maintainer. He's now primarily interested in distributed backend architectures and strongly typed functional programming, but he's amazed by the beauty of Next.js nonetheless.

Christian Sarnataro is a software engineer with more than 15 years of experience in web development. He is always trying to keep up to date with the latest technologies and best practices with a specific focus, in the last few years, on frontend development.

He is currently a senior SW engineer at Arduino, an open source hardware and software company well known for its electronic prototyping and IoT platforms.

In the past, he has worked for mid-to-large companies as a web architect, mobile developer, and teacher.

Table of Contents

3
Next.js Basics and Built-In Components

Part 2: Hands-On Next.js

4
Organizing the Code Base and Fetching Data in Next.js

5
Managing Local and Global States in Next.js

10
Working with SEO and Managing Performance

11
Different Deployment Platforms

Part 3: Next.js by Examples

12
Managing Authentication and User Sessions

13
Building an E-Commerce Website with Next.js and GraphCMS

14
Example Projects and Next Steps for Learning More

Index

Other Books You May Enjoy

Preface

Next.js is a scalable and high-performance React.js framework for modern web development. It provides a large set of features, such as hybrid rendering, route prefetching, automatic image optimization, and internationalization, out of the box.

Next.js is an exciting technology that can be used for many purposes. If you (or your company) want to create an e-commerce platform, a blog, or a simple website, with this book, you can learn how to do it without compromising on performance, user experience, or developer happiness. Starting from the basics of Next.js, you will understand how the framework can help you reach your goals, and you will realize how versatile Next.js is by building real-world applications with step-by-step explanations. You will learn how to choose the proper rendering methodology for your website, how to secure it, and how to deploy it to different providers. We'll always keep a focus on performance and developer happiness.

By the end of this book, you will be able to design, build, and deploy beautiful and modern architectures using Next.js with any headless CMS or data source.

Who this book is for

This book is for web developers who want to improve their React skills by building scalable and maintainable full-stack applications using a modern web framework – Next.js. Intermediate-level knowledge of ES6+, React, Node.js, and REST is assumed.

What this book covers

Chapter 1, *A Brief Introduction to Next.js*, serves as an introduction to the framework, showing how to set up a new project, customize its configurations, and (if needed) how to adopt TypeScript as the primary programming language for Next.js development.

Chapter 2, *Exploring Different Rendering Strategies*, dives into rendering methods, teaching the differences between server-side rendering, static site generation, incremental static regeneration, and more.

Chapter 3, Next.js Basics and Built-In Components, provides a complete explanation of the Next.js routing system and essential built-in components, focusing on search engine optimization and performance.

Chapter 4, Organizing the Code Base and Fetching Data in Next.js, covers some helpful tips about organizing a Next.js project and fetching data on both the server and client side.

Chapter 5, Managing Local and Global States in Next.js, introduces state management via React Context and Redux, teaching you how to handle local state (at the component level) and global state (application-wide).

Chapter 6, CSS and Built-In Styling Methods, introduces the basic styling methods built into Next.js, such as Styled JSX and CSS modules. It also shows how to enable the SASS preprocessor for local development and production builds.

Chapter 7, Using UI Frameworks, concludes the conversation around styling by introducing some modern UI frameworks, such as TailwindCSS, Chakra UI, and Headless UI.

Chapter 8, Using a Custom Server, explores the reasons why we might (and might not!) need a custom server for our Next.js applications. It also shows how to integrate Next.js with Express.js and Fastify, two of the most popular web frameworks for Node.js.

Chapter 9, Testing Next.js, introduces some unit and end-to-end testing best practices by adopting Cypress and react-testing-library.

Chapter 10, Working with SEO and Managing Performance, dives into SEO and performance enhancements by introducing useful tips and tricks for improving any Next.js application.

Chapter 11, Different Deployment Platforms, shows how to choose the right platform to host a Next.js app, depending on its features and many other aspects.

Chapter 12, Managing Authentication and User Session, describes how to manage user authentication securely by choosing the right authentication provider. It also shows how to integrate Auth0, a popular identity management platform, with any Next.js app.

Chapter 13, Building an E-Commerce Website with Next.js and GraphCMS, dives into creating a real-world Next.js e-commerce platform with Next.js, Chakra UI, and GraphCMS.

Chapter 14, Example Projects and Next Steps for Learning More, concludes the book by giving some valuable tips on how to proceed with learning the framework and provides some example projects to implement to acquire even more confidence with Next.js.

To get the most out of this book

To get the most out of this book, you can follow along by writing all the code examples displayed in the following chapters. If you find yourself stuck with an error, you can download all the working code examples from the book's GitHub repository.

Software/hardware covered in the book	Operating system requirements
Next.js	Windows, macOS, or Linux
Node.js (including npm and yarn)	Windows, macOS, or Linux
Docker For *Chapter 11, Different Deployment Platforms*	Windows, macOS, or Linux

If you are using the digital version of this book, we advise you to type the code yourself or access the code from the book's GitHub repository (a link is available in the next section). Doing so will help you avoid any potential errors related to the copying and pasting of code.

Download the example code files

You can download the example code files for this book from GitHub at `https://github.com/PacktPublishing/Real-World-Next.js`. If there's an update to the code, it will be updated in the GitHub repository.

We also have other code bundles from our rich catalog of books and videos available at `https://github.com/PacktPublishing/`. Check them out!

Download the color images

We also provide a PDF file that has color images of the screenshots and diagrams used in this book. You can download it here:

`https://static.packt-cdn.com/downloads/9781801073493_ColorImages.pdf`.

Conventions used

There are a number of text conventions used throughout this book.

`Code in text`: Indicates code words in text, database table names, folder names, filenames, file extensions, pathnames, dummy URLs, user input, and Twitter handles. Here is an example: "We're going to use Next.js' built-in `getServerSideProps` function to dynamically get the `[name]` variable from the URL and greet the user."

A block of code is set as follows:

```
export async function getServerSideProps({ params }) {
  const { name } = params;

  return {
    props: {
      name
    }
  }
}

function Greet(props) {
  return (
    <h1> Hello, {props.name}! </h1>
  )
}

export default Greet;
```

When we wish to draw your attention to a particular part of a code block, the relevant lines or items are set in bold:

```
<Link href='/blog/2021-01-01/happy-new-year'>
  Read post
</Link>
<Link href='/blog/2021-03-05/match-update'>
  Read post
</Link>
<Link href='/blog/2021-04-23/i-love-nextjs'>
  Read post
</Link>
```

Any command-line input or output is written as follows:

```
echo "Hello, world!" >> ./public/index.txt
```

Bold: Indicates a new term, an important word, or words that you see onscreen. For instance, words in menus or dialog boxes appear in **bold**. Here is an example: "In fact, if we open the Google Chrome developer tools and go to **Network**, we can select the HTTP request for the endpoint above and see the authorization token in plain text under the **Request Headers** section."

> **Tips or Important Notes**
> Appear like this.

Get in touch

Feedback from our readers is always welcome.

General feedback: If you have questions about any aspect of this book, email us at customercare@packtpub.com and mention the book title in the subject of your message.

Errata: Although we have taken every care to ensure the accuracy of our content, mistakes do happen. If you have found a mistake in this book, we would be grateful if you would report this to us. Please visit www.packtpub.com/support/errata and fill in the form.

Piracy: If you come across any illegal copies of our works in any form on the internet, we would be grateful if you would provide us with the location address or website name. Please contact us at copyright@packt.com with a link to the material.

If you are interested in becoming an author: If there is a topic that you have expertise in and you are interested in either writing or contributing to a book, please visit authors.packtpub.com.

Share Your Thoughts

Once you've read *Real-World Next.js*, we'd love to hear your thoughts! Scan the QR code below to go straight to the Amazon review page for this book and share your feedback.

https://packt.link/r/180107349X

Your review is important to us and the tech community and will help us make sure we're delivering excellent quality content.

Part 1: Introduction to Next.js

In this part, we will cover the basics of Next.js, starting with what differentiates it from other frameworks, its unique features, and how to bootstrap a new project from scratch.

This section comprises the following chapters:

- *Chapter 1, A Brief Introduction to Next.js*
- *Chapter 2, Exploring Different Rendering Strategies*
- *Chapter 3, Next.js Basics and Built-In Components*

1
A Brief Introduction to Next.js

Next.js is an open source JavaScript web framework for React that ships with a rich set of features out of the box, such as server-side rendering, static site generation, and incremental static regeneration. These are just some of the many built-in components and plugins that make Next.js a framework ready for both enterprise-level applications and small websites.

This book aims to show you the full potential of this framework while building real-world applications and use cases, such as e-commerce websites and blogging platforms. You will learn the basics of Next.js, how to choose between different rendering strategies and deployment methodologies, and different tips and approaches for making your web application both scalable and maintainable.

In this chapter, we will cover the following topics:

- Introduction to the Next.js framework
- Comparing Next.js with other popular alternatives
- Differences between Next.js and client-side React
- Anatomy of a default Next.js project
- How to develop Next.js applications using TypeScript
- How to customize both Babel and webpack configurations

Technical requirements

To get started with Next.js, you need to install a couple of dependencies on your machine.

First of all, you need to install **Node.js** and **npm**. Please refer to this blog post if you need a detailed guide for installing them: `https://www.nodejsdesignpatterns.com/blog/5-ways-to-install-node-js`.

If you don't want to install Node.js on your local machine, some online platforms will let you follow the code examples in this book using an online IDE for free, such as `https://codesandbox.io` and `https://repl.it`.

Once you have both Node.js and npm installed (or you're using an online environment), you'll only need to follow the instructions displayed in each section of this book for installing the required project-specific dependencies using npm.

You can find complete code examples on GitHub under the following repository: `https://github.com/PacktPublishing/Real-World-Next.js`. Feel free to fork, clone, and edit this repository for any experimentation with Next.js.

Introducing Next.js

Web development has changed a lot over the last few years. Before the advent of modern JavaScript frameworks, creating dynamic web applications was complex, and it required many different libraries and configurations to make them work as expected.

Angular, React, Vue, and all the other frameworks have enabled the web to evolve very quickly, and brought with them some very innovative ideas to frontend web development.

React, in particular, was created by *Jordan Walke* at Facebook and was heavily influenced by the *XHP Hack Library*. XHP allowed Facebook's PHP and Hack developers to create reusable components for the frontend of their applications. The JavaScript library became open source in 2013 and forever changed how we build websites, web apps, native apps (with **React Native** later on), and even VR experiences (with **React VR**). As a result, React has quickly become one of the most loved and popular JavaScript libraries, with millions of websites using it in production for many different purposes.

There was just one problem: by default, React runs on the **client side** (meaning that it runs on the web browser), so a web application written entirely with that library could negatively affect **Search Engine Optimization** (**SEO**) and initial load performance, as it takes some time to be correctly rendered on screen. In fact, to display the complete web app, the browser had to download the entire application bundle, parse its content, then execute it and render the result in the browser, which could take up to a few seconds (with very large applications).

Many companies and developers started investigating how to pre-render the application on the server, letting the browser display the rendered React app as plain HTML, making it interactive as soon as the JavaScript bundle has been transferred to the client.

Then, **Vercel** came up with Next.js, which has turned out to be a game-changer.

Since its first release, the framework has provided many innovative features out of the box, such as automatic code-splitting, server-side rendering, file-based routing systems, route pre-fetching, and so on. Next.js showed how easy it should be to write universal web applications by allowing developers to write reusable code for both client and server sides and making very complex tasks (such as code-splitting and server-side rendering) effortless to implement.

Today, Next.js provides tons of new features out of the box, such as the following:

- Static site generation

- Incremental static generation

- Native TypeScript support

- Automatic polyfills

- Image optimization

- Support for internationalization

- Performance analytics

All this, along with many other great features that we'll look at in depth later on in this book.

Today, Next.js is used in production by top-level companies such as Netflix, Twitch, TikTok, Hulu, Nike, Uber, Elastic, and many others. If you're interested, you can read the complete list at `https://nextjs.org/showcase`.

Next.js showed how versatile React could be for building many different applications at any scale, and it's not surprising to see it in use by both big companies and small start-ups. By the way, it is not the only framework that lets you render JavaScript on the server side, as we'll see in the next section.

Comparing Next.js to other alternatives

As you may be wondering, Next.js is not the only player in the server-side rendered JavaScript world. However, alternatives might be considered depending on the final purpose of a project.

Gatsby

One popular alternative is Gatsby. You may want to consider this framework if you seek to build static websites. Unlike Next.js, Gatsby only supports static site generation and does it incredibly well. Every page is pre-rendered at build time and can be served on any **Content Delivery Network (CDN)** as a static asset, allowing the performance to be incredibly competitive compared to dynamically server-side rendered alternatives. The biggest downside of using Gatsby over Next.js is that you'll lose the ability of dynamic server-side rendering, which is an important feature for building more dynamically data-driven and complex websites.

Razzle

Less popular than Next.js, Razzle is a tool for creating server-side rendered JavaScript applications. It aims to maintain the ease of use of `create-react-app` while abstracting all the complex configurations needed for rendering the application both on the server and client sides. The most significant advantage of using Razzle instead of Next.js (or the following alternatives) is that it is framework agnostic. You can choose your favorite frontend framework (or language), such as React, Vue, Angular, Elm, or Reason-React… it's your choice.

Nuxt.js

If you have experience with Vue, then Nuxt.js can be a valid Next.js competitor. They both offer support for server-side rendering, static site generation, progressive web app management, and so on, with no significant differences regarding performance, SEO, or development speed. While Nuxt.js and Next.js serve the same purpose, Nuxt.js needs more configuration, which is sometimes not a bad thing. In your Nuxt.js configuration file, you can define layouts, global plugins and components, routes, and so on, while with Next.js, you need to do it *the React way*. Apart from that, they share many functionalities, but the most significant difference is the library underneath. That said, if you already have a Vue component library, you could consider Nuxt.js for server-side rendering it.

Angular Universal

Of course, Angular has also made its move to the JavaScript server-side rendering scene, and it proposes Angular Universal as an official way for server-side rendering Angular applications. It supports both static site generation and server-side rendering and, unlike Nuxt.js and Next.js, it was developed by one of the biggest companies out there: Google. So if you are into Angular development and already have some components written with that library, Angular Universal can be a natural alternative to Nuxt.js, Next.js, and other similar frameworks.

So, why Next.js?

We've now seen some popular alternatives to Next.js, and their strengths and weaknesses.

The main reason why I'd suggest using Next.js instead of any other framework is because of its incredible feature set. With Next.js, you get everything you need right out of the box, and I'm not only referring to components, configurations, and deployment options, although they're probably the most complete I've ever seen.

In addition, Next.js has an incredibly welcoming and active community ready to support you at every step you take in building your application. I would consider this as a huge bonus point, because as soon as you have a problem with your code base, you'll be able to get help from the massive community across many different platforms, including StackOverflow and GitHub, where the Vercel team is also often involved in discussions and support requests.

Now that you know how Next.js competes with other similar frameworks, let's see the main differences between a default client-side React app and a fully-featured server-side environment for rendering your JavaScript code base dynamically for each request, and statically at build time.

Moving from React to Next.js

If you already have some experience with React, you'll find it incredibly easy to build your first Next.js website. Its philosophy is very close to React and provides a *convention-over-configuration* approach for most of its settings, so if you want to take advantage of a specific Next.js feature, you'll easily find the official way for doing it without any need for complex configurations. An example? In a single Next.js app, you can specify which pages shall be server-side rendered and which shall be statically generated at build time without the need to write any configuration files or anything like that. You just have to export a specific function from your page and let Next.js do its magic (we'll see that in *Chapter 2, Exploring Different Rendering Strategies*).

The most significant difference between React and Next.js is that while React is just a JavaScript library, Next.js is a framework for building rich and complete user experiences both on the client and server sides, adding tons of incredibly useful features. Every server-side rendered or statically generated page will run on Node.js, so you'll lose access to some browser-specific global objects, such as `fetch`, `window`, and `document`, as well as some HTML elements such as `canvas`. You will always need to keep that in mind when you're writing your Next.js pages, even if the framework provides its own way for dealing with components that *must* use such global variables and HTML elements, as we'll see in *Chapter 2, Exploring Different Rendering Strategies*.

On the other hand, there might be times when you want to use Node.js specific libraries or APIs, such as `fs` or `child_process`, and Next.js allows you to use them by running your server-side code on each request or at build time (depending on how you choose to render your pages) before sending the data to the client.

But even if you want to create a client-side rendered app, Next.js can be a great alternative to the well-known `create-react-app`. Next.js, in fact, can be used as a framework for writing progressive and offline-first web apps with ease, taking advantage of its incredible built-in components and optimizations. So let's get started with Next.js.

Getting started with Next.js

Now that we have some basic knowledge about Next.js use cases and the differences between client-side React and other frameworks, it's time to look at the code. We'll start by creating a new Next.js app and customizing its default webpack and Babel configurations. We'll also see how to use TypeScript as the primary language for developing Next.js apps.

Default project structure

Getting started with Next.js is incredibly easy. The only system requirement is to have both Node.js and npm installed on your machine (or development environment). The Vercel team created and published a straightforward but powerful tool called `create-next-app` for generating the boilerplate code for a basic Next.js app. You can use it by typing the following command in the terminal:

```
npx create-next-app <app-name>
```

It will install all the required dependencies and create a couple of default pages. At this point, you can just run `npm run dev`, and a development server will start on port `3000`, showing a landing page.

Next.js will initialize your project using the Yarn package manager if installed on your machine. You can override this option by passing a flag to tell `create-next-app` to use npm instead:

```
npx create-next-app <app-name> --use-npm
```

You can also ask `create-next-app` to initialize a new Next.js project by downloading the boilerplate code from the Next.js GitHub repository. In fact, inside the Next.js repository, there's an `examples` folder containing tons of great examples about how to use Next.js with different technologies.

Let's say that you want to do some experiments with using Next.js on Docker – you can just pass the `--example` flag to the boilerplate code generator:

```
npx create-next-app <app-name> --example with-docker
```

`create-next-app` will download the code from `https://github.com/vercel/next.js/tree/canary/examples/with-docker` and will install the required dependencies for you. At this point, you only have to edit the downloaded files, customize them, and you're ready to go.

You can find other great examples at `https://github.com/vercel/next.js/tree/canary/examples`. If you're already familiar with Next.js, feel free to explore how Next.js can integrate with different services and toolkits (we'll see some of them in more detail later on in this book).

Now, let's go back to a default `create-next-app` installation for a moment. Let's open the terminal and generate a new Next.js app together:

```
npx create-next-app my-first-next-app --use-npm
```

After a few seconds, the boilerplate generation will succeed, and you'll find a new folder called `my-first-next-app` with the following structure:

```
- README.md
- next.config.js
- node_modules/
- package-lock.json
- package.json
- pages/
  - _app.js
  - api/
    - hello.js
  - index.js
- public/
  - favicon.ico
  - vercel.svg
- styles/
  - Home.module.css
  - globals.css
```

If you're coming from React, you may be used to **react-router** or similar libraries for managing client-side navigation. Next.js makes navigation even easier by using the pages/ folder. In fact, every JavaScript file inside the pages/ directory will be a public page, so if you try to duplicate the index.js page and rename it about.js, you'll be able to go to http://localhost:3000/about and see an exact copy of your home page. We'll look in detail how Next.js handles client-side and server-side routes in the next chapter; for now, let's just think of the pages/ directory as a container for your public pages.

The public/ folder contains all the public and static assets used in your website. For example, you can put your images, compiled CSS stylesheets, compiled JavaScript files, fonts, and so on there.

By default, you will also see a styles/ directory; while this is very useful for organizing your application stylesheets, it is not strictly required for a Next.js project. The only mandatory and reserved directories are public/ and pages/, so make sure not to delete or use them for different purposes.

That said, you're free to add more directories and files to the project root, as it won't negatively interfere with the Next.js build or development process. If you want to organize your components under a components/ directory and your utilities under a utilities/ directory, feel free to add those folders inside your project.

If you're not into boilerplate generators, you can bootstrap a new Next.js application by just adding all the required dependencies (as previously listed) and the basic folder structure that we just saw to your existing React application, and it'll just work with no other configuration required.

TypeScript integration

The Next.js source code is written in TypeScript and natively provides high-quality **type** definitions to make your developer experience even better. Configuring TypeScript as the default language for your Next.js app is very easy; you just have to create a TypeScript configuration file (tsconfig.json) inside the root of your project. If you try to run npm run dev, you'll see the following output:

```
It looks like you're trying to use TypeScript but do not have
the required package(s) installed.
Please install typescript and @types/react by running:
      npm install --save typescript @types/react
      If you are not trying to use TypeScript, please remove
      the tsconfig.json file from your package root (and any
      TypeScript files in your pages directory).
```

As you can see, Next.js has correctly detected that you're trying to use TypeScript and asks you to install all the required dependencies for using it as the primary language for your project. So now you just have to convert your JavaScript files to TypeScript, and you're ready to go.

You may notice that even if you created an empty `tsconfig.json` file, after installing the required dependencies and rerunning the project, Next.js fills it with its default configurations. Of course, you can always customize the TypeScript options inside that file, but keep in mind that Next.js uses Babel to handle TypeScript files (via the `@babel/plugin-transform-typescript`), and it has some caveats, including the following:

- The `@babel/plugin-transform-typescript` plugin does not support `const enum`, often used in TypeScript. To support it, make sure to add `babel-plugin-const-enum` to the Babel configuration (we'll see how in the *Custom Babel and webpack configuration* section).

- Neither `export` = nor `import` = are supported because they cannot be compiled to valid ECMAScript code. You should either install `babel-plugin-replace-ts-export-assignment`, or convert your imports and exports to valid ECMAScript directives, such as `import x, {y} from 'some-package'` and `export default x`.

There are other caveats, too; I'd suggest you read them before going further with using TypeScript as the main language for developing your Next.js app: `https://babeljs.io/docs/en/babel-plugin-transform-typescript#caveats`.

Also, some compiler options might be a bit different from the default TypeScript ones; once again, I'd suggest you read the official Babel documentation, which will always be up to date: `https://babeljs.io/docs/en/babel-plugin-transform-typescript#typescript-compiler-options`.

Next.js also creates a `next-env.d.ts` file inside the root of your project; feel free to edit it if you need, but make sure not to delete it.

Custom Babel and webpack configuration

As already mentioned in the *TypeScript Integration* section, we can customize **Babel** and **webpack** configurations.

There might be many reasons we would like to customize our Babel configuration. If you're not very familiar with it, let me quickly explain what I'm talking about. Babel is a JavaScript transcompiler mainly used for transforming modern JavaScript code into a backward-compatible script, which will run without problem on any browser.

If you're writing a web app that *must* support older browsers such as **Internet Explorer (IE)** 10 or Internet Explorer 11, Babel will help you a lot. It allows you to use modern ES6/ESNext features and will transform them into IE-compatible code at build time, letting you maintain a beautiful developer experience with very few compromises.

Also, the JavaScript language (standardized under the ECMAScript specification) is quickly evolving. So while some fantastic features have already been announced, you'll have to wait for years before being able to use them in both browsers and Node.js environments. That's because after the ECMA committee has accepted these features, the companies developing web browsers and communities working on the Node.js project will have to plan a roadmap for adding support for these enhancements. Babel solves this problem by transpiling modern code into a compatible script for today's environments.

For example, you may be familiar with this code:

```
export default function() {
    console.log("Hello, World!");
};
```

But if you try to run it in Node.js, it will throw a syntax error because the JavaScript engine won't recognize the `export default` keywords.

Babel will transform the preceding code into this equivalent ECMAScript code, at least until Node.js gets support for the `export default` syntax:

```
"use strict";
Object.defineProperty(exports, "__esModule", {
    value: true
});
exports.default = _default;
function _default() {
    console.log("Hello, World!");
};
```

This makes it possible to run this code on Node.js with no problems.

You can customize your default Next.js Babel configuration by simply creating a new file called `.babelrc` inside the root of your project. You will notice that if you leave it empty, the Next.js build/development process will throw an error, so make sure to add at least the following code:

```
{
    "presets": ["next/babel"]
}
```

This is the Babel preset created by the Vercel team specifically for building and developing Next.js applications. Let's say that we're building an application, and we want to use an experimental ECMAScript feature such as the pipeline operator; if you're not familiar with it, it basically allows you to re-write this code as follows:

```
console.log(Math.random() * 10);
// written using the pipeline operator becomes:
Math.random()
    |> x => x * 10
    |> console.log
```

This operator has not been officially accepted yet by **TC39** (the technical committee behind the ECMAScript specification), but you can start using it today, thanks to Babel.

To provide support for this operator in your Next.js app, all you need to do is install the Babel plugin using npm:

```
npm install --save-dev @babel/plugin-proposal-pipeline-operator
@babel/core
```

Then update your custom `.babelrc` file as follows:

```
{
    "presets": ["next/babel"],
    "plugins": [
      [
        "@babel/plugin-proposal-pipeline-operator",
        { "proposal": "fsharp" }
      ]
    ]
}
```

You can now restart your development server and use this experimental feature.

If you're interested in using TypeScript as the main development language for your Next.js app, you can just follow the same procedure for adding all the TypeScript-specific plugins to your Babel configuration. There are chances that during your Next.js development experience, you may also want to customize the default webpack configuration.

While Babel only takes modern code as input and produces backward-compatible scripts as output, webpack creates the bundles containing all the compiled code for a specific library, page, or feature. For instance, if you create a page containing three components from three different libraries, webpack will merge everything into a single bundle to be shipped to the client. To put it simply, we can think of webpack as an infrastructure for orchestrating different compilation, bundle, and minification tasks for every web asset (JavaScript files, CSS, SVG, and so on).

If you want to use CSS preprocessors such as **SASS** or **LESS** to create your app styles, you will need to customize the default webpack configuration to parse **SASS/LESS** files and produce plain CSS as output. The same, of course, occurs for JavaScript code using Babel as a transpiler.

We talk more in detail about CSS preprocessors in the following chapters, but for now, we just need to keep in mind that Next.js provides an easy way for customizing the default webpack configuration.

As we saw earlier, Next.js provides a *convention-over-configuration* approach, so you don't need to customize most of its settings for building a real-world application; you just have to follow some code conventions.

But if you really need to build something custom, you'll be able to edit the default settings via the next.config.js file most of the time. You can create this file inside the root of your project. It should export an object by default, where its properties will override the default Next.js configurations:

```
module.exports = {
    // custom settings here
};
```

You can customize the default webpack configuration by creating a new property inside this object called webpack. Let's suppose that we want to add a new imaginary webpack loader called my-custom-loader; we can proceed as follows:

```
module.exports = {
    webpack: (config, options) => {
        config.module.rules.push({
```

```
      test: /\.js/,
      use: [
        options.defaultLoaders.babel,
        // This is just an example
        //don't try to run this as it won't work
        {
          loader: "my-custom-loader", // Set your loader
          options: loaderOptions, // Set your loader
          options
        },
      ],
    });
    return config;
  },
};
```

So, as you can see, we're writing a proper webpack configuration that will later be merged with Next.js' default settings. This will allow us to extend, override, or even delete any setting from the default configuration, as although deleting default settings is generally never a good idea, there might be cases where you need it (if you're brave enough!).

Summary

In this chapter, you have seen the main differences between default and client-side React apps and Next.js, and how Next.js compares with other well-known alternatives. You've also learned how to customize a default Next.js project by editing the Babel and webpack configurations, as well as adding TypeScript as an alternative to JavaScript for developing your applications.

In the next chapter, we will take a closer look at three different rendering strategies: client-side rendering, server-side rendering, and static site generation.

2
Exploring Different Rendering Strategies

When talking about rendering strategies, we refer to how we serve a web page (or a web application) to a web browser. There are frameworks, such as Gatsby (as seen in the previous chapter), that are incredibly good at serving statically generated pages. Other frameworks will make it easy to create server-side rendered pages.

But Next.js brings those concepts to a whole new level, letting you decide which page should be rendered at build time and which should be served dynamically at runtime, regenerating the entire page for each request making certain parts of your applications incredibly dynamic. The framework also allows you to decide which components should exclusively be rendered on the client side, making your development experience extremely satisfying.

In this chapter, we'll have a closer look at:

- How to dynamically render a page for each request using server-side rendering

- Different ways to render certain components on the client side only

- Generating static pages at build time

- How to regenerate static pages in production using incremental static regeneration

Technical requirements

To run the code examples in this chapter, make sure you have Node.js and npm installed on your machine. As an alternative, you can use an online IDE such as `https://repl.it` or `https://codesandbox.io`.

You can find the code for this chapter in the GitHub repository: `https://github.com/PacktPublishing/Real-World-Next.js`.

Server-side rendering (SSR)

Even though **server-side rendering** (**SSR**) sounds like a new term in the developer's vocabulary, it is actually the most common way for serving web pages. If you think of languages such as PHP, Ruby, or Python, they all render the HTML on the server before sending it to the browser, which will make the markup dynamic once all the JavaScript contents have been loaded.

Well, Next.js does the same thing by dynamically rendering an HTML page on the server for each request, then sending it to the web browser. The framework will also inject its own scripts to make the server-side rendered pages dynamic in a process called **hydration**.

Imagine you're building a blog and you want to display all the articles written by a specific author on a single page. This can be a great use case for SSR: a user wants to access this page, so the server renders it and sends the resulting HTML to the client. At this point, the browser will download all the scripts requested by the page and hydrate the DOM, making it interactive without any kind of page refresh or glitch (you can read more about React hydration at `https://reactjs.org/docs/react-dom.html#hydrate`). From this point, thanks to React hydration, the web app can also become a **single-page application** (**SPA**), taking all the advantages of both **client-side rendering** (**CSR**) (as we'll see in the next section) and SSR.

Talking about the advantages of adopting a specific rendering strategy, SSR provides multiple benefits over the standard React CSR:

- **More secure web apps**: Rendering a page on the server side means that activities such as managing cookies, calling private APIs, and data validation happen on the server, so we will never expose private data to the client.

- **More compatible websites**: The website will be available even if the user has disabled JavaScript or uses an older browser.

- **Enhanced search engine optimization**: Since the client will receive the HTML content as soon as the server renders and sends it, the search engine spiders (bots that crawl the web pages) will not need to wait for the page to be rendered on the client side. This will improve your web app's SEO score.

Despite those great advantages, there are times where SSR might not be the best solution for your website. In fact, with SSR, you will need to deploy your web application to a server that will re-render a page as soon as it's required. As we'll see later, with both CSR and **static site generation** (**SSG**), you can deploy static HTML files to any cloud provider, such as Vercel or Netlify, for free (or at a meager cost); if you're already deploying your web app using a custom server, you have to remember that an SSR app will always lead to a more significant server workload and maintenance costs.

Another thing to keep in mind when you want to server-side render your pages is that you're adding some latency to each request; your pages might need to call some external API or data source, and they'll call it for every page render. Navigating between server-side rendered pages will always be a bit slower than navigating between client-side rendered or statically served pages.

Of course, Next.js provides some great features for improving navigation performances, as we'll see in *Chapter 3, Next.js Basics and Built-In Components*.

Another thing to consider is that by default, a Next.js page is statically generated at build time. If we want to make it more dynamic by calling an external API, a database, or other data sources, we will need to export a particular function from our page:

```
function IndexPage() {
   return <div>This is the index page.</div>;
}


export default IndexPage;
```

As you can see, the page only prints the **This is the index page.** text inside a `div`. It doesn't need to call external APIs or any other data source to work, and its content will always be the same for each request. But now, let's pretend that we want to greet the user on every request; we will need to call a REST API on the server to get some specific user information and pass the result to the client using the Next.js flow. We will do that by using the reserved `getServerSideProps` function:

```
export async function getServerSideProps() {
   const userRequest =
     await fetch('https://example.com/api/user');
```

```
    const userData = await userRequest.json();

  return {
    props: {
      user: userData
    }
  };
}

function IndexPage(props) {
  return <div>Welcome, {props.user.name}!</div>;
}

export default IndexPage;
```

In the preceding example, we used the Next.js reserved `getServerSideProps` function for making a REST API call on the server side for each request. Let's break it down into small steps so that we can better understand what we're doing:

1. We start by exporting an async function called `getServerSideProps`. During the build phase, Next.js will look for every page exporting this function and make them dynamically server-side rendered for each request. All the code written within this function scope will always be executed on the server side.

2. Inside the `getServerSideProps` function, we return an object containing a property called `props`. This is required because Next.js will inject those props inside our `page` component, making them available both on the client and server side. In case you're wondering, we don't need to polyfill the fetch API when we use it on the server side, as Next.js already does that for us.

3. We then refactor the `IndexPage` function, which now accepts a `props` parameter containing all the props passed from the `getServerSideProps` function.

And that's all! After we ship this code, Next.js will always dynamically render our `IndexPage` on the server, calling an external API and showing different results as soon as we make changes in our data source.

As seen at the beginning of this section, SSR provides some significant advantages but has some caveats. If you want to use any component that relies on browser-specific APIs, you will need to render it on the browser explicitly because, by default, Next.js renders the entire page content on the server, which does not expose certain APIs, such as `window` or `document`. So here comes the concept of CSR.

Client-side rendering (CSR)

As seen in the previous chapter, a standard React app is rendered once the JavaScript bundle has been transferred from the server to the client.

If you're familiar with **create-react-app** (**CRA**), you may have noticed that right before the web app renders, the whole web page is entirely white. That's because the server only serves a very basic HTML markup, which contains all the required scripts and styles to make our web app dynamic. Let's take a closer look at that HTML generated by CRA:

```html
<!DOCTYPE html>
<html lang="en">
  <head>
    <meta charset="utf-8" />
    <link rel="icon" href="%PUBLIC_URL%/favicon.ico" />
    <meta
      name="viewport"
      content="width=device-width, initial-scale=1"
    />
    <meta name="theme-color" content="#000000" />
    <meta
      name="description"
      content="Web site created using create-react-app"
    />
    <link rel="apple-touch-icon"
      href="%PUBLIC_URL%/logo192.png" />
    <link rel="manifest" href="%PUBLIC_URL%/manifest.json" />
    <title>React App</title>
  </head>
  <body>
    <noscript>
      You need to enable JavaScript to run this app.
    </noscript>
    <div id="root"></div>
  </body>
</html>
```

As you can see, we can only find one `div` inside the `body` tag: `<div id="root"></div>`.

During the build phase, `create-react-app` will inject the compiled JavaScript and CSS files into this HTML page and use the `root` div as a target container for rendering the whole application.

That means that once we publish this page to any hosting provider (Vercel, Netlify, Google Cloud, AWS, and so on), the first time we call the desired URL, our browser will first render the preceding HTML. Then, following the `script` and `link` tags contained in the preceding markup (injected by CRA at build time), the browser will render the whole application, making it available for any sort of interaction.

The main advantages of CSR are:

- **It makes your app feel like a native app**: Downloading the whole JavaScript bundle means that you already have every page of your web app downloaded in your browser. If you want to navigate to a different page, it will swap the page content instead of downloading new content from the server. You don't need to refresh the page to update its content.

- **Page transitions made easy**: Client-side navigation allows us to switch from one page to another without reloading the browser window. This comes in handy when you want to show some cool transitions between pages with ease because you don't have any reload that might interrupt your animations.

- **Lazy loading and performances**: With CSR, the browser will only render the minimum HTML markup required for the web app to work. If you have a modal that appears once the user clicks on a button, its HTML markup is not present on the HTML page. It will be created dynamically by React once the button click event occurs.

- **Less server-side workload**: Given that the whole rendering phase is delegated to the browser, the server only needs to send a very basic HTML page to the client. You then don't need a very powerful server; indeed, there are cases where you can host your web app on **serverless** environments, such as AWS Lambda, Firebase, and so on.

But all those benefits come at a cost. As we've previously seen, the server only sends an empty HTML page. If the user's internet connection is slow, the downloading of JavaScript and CSS files will take some seconds to complete, leaving the user waiting with an empty screen for several moments.

This will also affect your web app SEO score; the search engine spiders will reach your page and will find it empty. Google bots, for instance, will wait for the JavaScript bundle to be transferred but will assign a low-performance score to your website because of their waiting time.

By default, Next.js renders all the React components inside a given page on the server side (as seen in the previous section) or at build time. In the first chapter, under the Moving from React to *Next.js* section, we saw that the Node.js runtime doesn't expose some browser-specific APIs, such as `window` or `document`, or HTML elements, such as `canvas`, so if you try to render any component that needs access to those APIs, the rendering process will crash.

There are many different ways to avoid those kinds of problems with Next.js, demanding the rendering of specific components to the browser.

Using the React.useEffect hook

If you're coming from a React version before 16.8.0, you may be used to the `componentDidMount` method of the `React.Component` class. With more modern versions of React, which emphasize the usage of **function components**, you can achieve the same results using the `React.useEffect` hook. It will let you perform side effects (such as data fetching and manual DOM changes) inside your function components, and it will do it after the component has been mounted. That means that with Next.js, the `useEffect` callback will run on the browser after React hydration, letting you perform certain actions only on the client side.

For example, let's pretend that we want to display a code snippet on a web page using the Highlight.js library, making it easy to highlight and make code more readable. We could just create a component called `Highlight`, which would look as follows:

```
import Head from 'next/head';
import hljs from 'highlight.js';
import javascript from 'highlight.js/lib/languages/javascript';

function Highlight({ code }) {
    hljs.registerLanguage('javascript', javascript);
    hljs.initHighlighting();

    return (
      <>
        <Head>
          <link rel='stylesheet' href='/highlight.css' />
        </Head>
        <pre>
          <code className='js'>{code}</code>
```

```
        </pre>
      </>
    );
  }
```

```
export default Highlight;
```

While this piece of code would perfectly run on a client-side React app, it will crash during the rendering or build phase on Next.js because Highlight.js needs the document global variable, which does not exist in Node.js, as it's exposed by browsers only.

You can easily fix this by wrapping all the hljs calls in the useEffect hook:

```
import { useEffect } from 'react';
import Head from 'next/head';
import hljs from 'highlight.js';
import javascript from
  'highlight.js/lib/languages/javascript';

function Highlight({ code }) {

  useEffect(() => {
    hljs.registerLanguage('javascript', javascript);
    hljs.initHighlighting();
  }, []);

  return (
    <>
      <Head>
        <link rel='stylesheet' href='/highlight.css' />
      </Head>
      <pre>
        <code className='js'>{code}</code>
      </pre>
```

```
      </>
    );
  }
```

```
export default Highlight;
```

That way, Next.js will render the HTML markup returned by our component, inject the Highlight.js script into our page, and, once the component is mounted on the browser, it will call the library functions on the client side.

You can also use that exact approach for rendering a component exclusively on the client side by using both React.useEffect and React.useState together:

```
import {useEffect, useState} from 'react';
import Highlight from '../components/Highlight';

function UseEffectPage() {
  const [isClient, setIsClient] = useState(false);

  useEffect(() => {
    setIsClient(true);
  }, []);

  return (
    <div>
      {isClient &&
        (<Highlight
          code={"console.log('Hello, world!')"}
          language='js'
        />)
      }
    </div>
  );
}
```

```
export default UseEffectPage;
```

That way, the Highlight component will be rendered on the browser exclusively.

Using the process.browser variable

Another way of avoiding the server-side process crashing when using browser-specific APIs is to conditionally execute scripts and components depending on the `process.browser` global variable. Indeed, Next.js appends this incredibly useful property to Node.js' `process` object. It is a Boolean value set to `true` when the code runs on the client side and `false` when running on the server. Let's see how it works:

```
function IndexPage() {
  const side = process.browser ? 'client' : 'server';

  return <div>You're currently on the {side}-side.</div>;
}

export default IndexPage;
```

If you try to run the preceding example, you will notice that for a brief moment, the browser will show the following text: **You're currently running on the server-side**; it will be replaced by the **You're currently running on the client-side** text as soon as React hydration occurs.

Using dynamic component loading

As we saw in the first chapter, Next.js extends React functionalities by adding some great built-in components and utility functions. One of these is called `dynamic`, and it's one of the most interesting modules provided by the framework.

Remember the Highlight.js component that we built to understand how to render a component on the browser using the `React.useEffect` hook? Here is another way to render it using the Next.js `dynamic` function:

```
import dynamic from 'next/dynamic';
const Highlight = dynamic(
  () => import('../components/Highlight'),
  { ssr: false }
);
import styles from '../styles/Home.module.css';

function DynamicPage() {
  return (
    <div className={styles.main}>
```

```
        <Highlight
          code={"console.log('Hello, world!')"}
          language='js'
        />
      </div>
    );
  }

export default DynamicPage;
```

With the preceding code, we're importing our `Highlight` component via **dynamic imports**, specifying that we want it to be executed on the client only thanks to the `ssr: false` option. That way, Next.js won't try to render that component on the server and we'll have to wait for React hydration to make it available on the browser.

CSR can be a fantastic alternative to SSR for building very dynamic web pages. If you're working on a page that doesn't need to be indexed by search engines, it could make sense to first load your application's JavaScript, and then, from the client side, fetch any necessary data from the server; this would lighten the server-side workload since this approach does not involve SSR and your application could scale better.

So, here's a question – if we need to build a dynamic page and SEO is not really important (admin pages, private profile pages, and so on), why don't we just send a static page to the client and load all the data once the page has been transferred to the browser? We'll explore this possibility in the next section.

Static site generation

So far, we've seen two different ways of rendering our web apps: on the client side and server side. Next.js gives us a third option called **static site generation** (**SSG**).

With SSG, we will be able to pre-render some specific pages (or even the whole website if necessary) at build time; that means that when we're building our web app, there might be some pages that won't change their content very often, so it makes sense for us to serve them as static assets. Next.js will render these pages during the build phase and will always serve that specific HTML that, just like SSR, will become interactive thanks to the React hydration process.

SSG brings a lot of advantages when compared to both CSR and SSR:

- **Easy to scale**: Static pages are just HTML files that can be served and cached easily by any **content delivery network** (from now on, **CDN**). But even if you want to serve them using your own web server, it will result in a very low workload, given that no hard computations are needed for serving a static asset.

- **Outstanding performances**: As said before, the HTML is pre-rendered at build time, so both the client and server can bypass the runtime rendering phase for each request. The web server will send the static file and the browser will just display it, as easy as that. No data fetching is required on the server side; everything we need is already pre-rendered inside the static HTML markup, and that reduces the potential latency for each request.

- **More secure requests**: We don't need to send any sensitive data to the web server for rendering the page, and that makes life a bit harder for malicious users. No access to APIs, databases, or other private information is required because every piece of information needed is already part of the pre-rendered page.

SSG is probably one of the best solutions for building performant and highly scalable frontend applications. The biggest concern about this rendering technique is that once the page has been built, the content will remain the same until the next deployment.

For instance, let's pretend that we're writing a blog post and we misspell a word in the title. Using other static site generators, such as Gatsby or Jekyll, we would need to rebuild the whole website to change just a word in a blog post title because we would need to repeat the data fetching and rendering phase at build time. Remember what we said at the beginning of this section: statically generated pages are created at build time and served as static assets for each request.

While this is true for other static site generators, Next.js provides a unique approach for solving this problem: **incremental static regeneration** (**ISR**). Thanks to ISR, we can specify at the page level how long Next.js should wait before re-rendering a static page updating its content.

For instance, let's say that we want to build a page showing some dynamic content, but the data fetching phase, for some reason, takes too long to succeed. This would lead to bad performance, giving our users a terrible user experience. A combination of SSG and ISR would solve this problem by taking a hybrid approach between SSR and SSG.

Let's pretend we've built a very complex dashboard that can handle a lot of data... but the REST API request for this data is taking up to a few seconds to succeed. In that case, we are lucky because that data won't change a lot during this time, so we can **cache** it for up to 10 minutes (600 seconds) using SSG and ISR:

```
import fetch from 'isomorphic-unfetch';
import Dashboard from './components/Dashboard';

export async function getStaticProps() {
  const userReq = await fetch('/api/user');
  const userData = await userReq.json();

  const dashboardReq = await fetch('/api/dashboard');
  const dashboardData = await dashboardReq.json();

  return {
    props: {
      user: userData,
      data: dashboardData,
    },
    revalidate: 600 // time in seconds (10 minutes)
  };
}

function IndexPage(props) {
  return (
    <div>
      <Dashboard
        user={props.user}
        data={props.data}
      />
    </div>
  );
}

export default IndexPage;
```

We're now using a function called `getStaticProps`, which looks similar to the `getServerSideProps` one that we saw in the previous section. As you may have guessed, `getStaticProps` is used at build time by Next.js for getting the data and rendering the page, and it won't be called again until the next build. As said before, while this can be incredibly powerful, it comes with a cost: if we want to update the page content, we have to rebuild the entire website.

To avoid the whole website rebuild, Next.js recently introduced an option called `revalidate`, which can be set inside the returning object of our `getStaticProps` function. It indicates after how many seconds we should rebuild the page once a new request arrives.

In the preceding code, we've set our `revalidate` option to `600` seconds, so Next.js will behave as follows:

1. Next.js fills the page with the results of `getStaticProps` at build time, statically generating the page during the build process.
2. In the first 10 minutes, every user will access the exact same static page.
3. After 10 minutes, if a new request occurs, Next.js will server-side render that page, re-execute the `getStaticProps` function, save and cache the newly rendered page as a static asset, overriding the previous one created at build time.
4. Every new request, within the next 10 minutes, will be served with that new statically generated page.

Remember that the ISR process is lazy, so if no requests occur after 10 minutes, Next.js won't rebuild its pages.

In case you're wondering, at the moment there's no way of forcing ISR revalidation via the API; once your website has been deployed, you'll have to wait the length of the expiration time set in the `revalidate` option for the page to be rebuilt.

Static-site generation is a great way to create fast and secure web pages, but sometimes we might want to have more dynamic content. Thanks to Next.js, we can always decide which page should be rendered at build time (SSG) or request time (SSR). We can take the best of both approaches by using SSG + ISR, making our pages a "hybrid" between SSR and SSG, and that's a game-changer for modern web development.

Summary

In this chapter, we've seen three different rendering strategies and why Next.js brings them to a whole new level with its hybrid rendering approach. We've also seen the benefits of these strategies, when we want to use them, and how they can affect the user experience or the server workload. We will always keep an eye on these rendering methodologies during the following chapters, adding more and more examples and use cases for each of them. They are the core concepts behind the choice of using Next.js as a framework.

In the next chapter, we're going to have a closer look at some of the most useful built-in Next.js components, its routing system, and how to manage metadata dynamically for improving both SEO and user experience.

3
Next.js Basics and Built-In Components

Next.js is not only about server-side rendering. It provides some incredibly useful built-in components and functions that we can use to create performant, dynamic, and modern websites.

In this chapter, we're going to take a look at some concepts at the core of Next.js, such as routing systems, client-side navigation, serving optimized images, handling metadata, and more. These notions will be very beneficial once we move on to building some real-world applications with this framework.

We will also take a closer look at the `_app.js` and `_document.js` pages, which will allow us to customize our web app behavior in several ways.

In this chapter, we will cover the following topics:

- How the routing system works, both on the client and server sides
- How to optimize navigation between pages
- How Next.js serves static assets
- How to optimize image serving via automatic image optimization and the new `Image` component

- How to dynamically handle HTML metadata from any component
- What are the _app.js and _document.js files and how can they be customized?

Technical requirements

To run the code examples in this chapter, you need to have both Node.js and npm installed on your local machine.

If you prefer, you can use an online IDE such as https://repl.it or https://codesandbox.io; they both support Next.js, and you don't need to install any dependency on your computer.

You can find the code for this chapter on the GitHub repository: https://github.com/PacktPublishing/Real-World-Next.js.

Routing system

If you're coming from client-side React, you might be familiar with libraries such as *React Router*, *Reach Router*, or *Wouter*. They allow you to create client-side routes only, meaning that all the pages will be created and rendered on the client side; no server-side rendering is involved.

Next.js uses a different approach: filesystem-based pages and routes. As seen in *Chapter 2, Exploring Different Rendering Strategies*, a default Next.js project ships with a pages/ directory. Every file inside that folder represents a new page/route for your application.

Therefore, when talking about a page, we refer to a React component exported from any of the .js, .jsx, .ts, or .tsx files inside the pages/ folder.

To make things a bit clearer, let's say that we want to create a simple website with just two pages; the first one will be the home page, while the second one will be a simple contact page. To do that, we will only need to create two new files inside our pages/ folder: index.js and contacts.js. Both files will need to export a function returning some JSX content; it will be rendered on the server side and sent to the browser as standard HTML.

As we've just seen, a page must return valid JSX code, so let's make a very simple and concise index.js page:

```
function Homepage() {
  return (
    <div> This is the homepage </div>
```

```
  )
};
export default Homepage;
```

If we run `yarn dev` or `npm run dev` in our terminal, then move to `http://localhost:3000` in our browser, we will only see the **This is the homepage** message appear on the screen. We've just made our first page!

We can do the same with our contact page:

```
function ContactPage() {
  return (
    <div>
      <ul>
        <li> Email: myemail@example.com</li>
        <li> Twitter: @myusername </li>
        <li> Instagram: myusername </li>
      </ul>
    </div>
  )
};
export default ContactPage;
```

Given that we've called our contact page `contacts.js`, we can navigate to `http://localhost:3000/contacts` and see the contacts list displayed on the browser. If we want to move that page to `http://localhost:3000/contact-us`, we can just rename our `contacts.js` file to `contact-us.js`, and Next.js will automatically rebuild the page using the new route name for us.

Now, let's try to make things a bit harder. We're building a blog, so we want to create a route for each post. We also want to create a `/posts` page that will show every post present on the website.

To do that, we will use a dynamic route as follows:

```
pages/
  - index.js
  - contact-us.js
  - posts/
      - index.js
      - [slug].js
```

We haven't mentioned yet that we can create nested routes using folders inside our pages/ directory. If we want to make a /posts route, we can create a new index.js file inside the pages/posts/ folder, export a function containing some JSX code, and visit http://localhost:3000/posts.

We then want to create a dynamic route for every blog post so that we don't have to manually create a new page every time we want to publish an article on our website. To do that, we can create a new file inside the pages/posts/ folder, pages/posts/ [slug].js, where [slug] identifies a route variable that can contain any value, depending on what the user types in the browser's address bar. In that case, we're creating a route containing a variable called slug, which can vary for every blog post. We can export a simple function returning some JSX code from that file and then browse to http://localhost:3000/posts/my-firstpost, http://localhost:3000/ posts/foo-bar-baz, or any other http://localhost:3000/posts/* route. Whatever route you browse to, it will always render the same JSX code.

We can also nest multiple dynamic routes inside the pages/ folder; let's say that we want our post page structure to be as follows: /posts/[date]/[slug]. We can just add a new folder called [date] inside our pages/ directory and move the slug.js file inside it:

```
pages/
  - index.js
  - contact-us.js
  - posts/
      - index.js
      - [date]/
          - [slug].js
```

We can now visit http://localhost:3000/posts/2021-01-01/my-first-post and see the JSX content we've created previously. Once again, both the [date] and [slug] variables can represent whatever you want, so feel free to experiment by calling different routes on the browser.

Until now, we have always used route variables to render the same page, but these variables are mainly meant for creating highly dynamic pages with different content depending on the route variables we're using. Let's see how to render different content depending on the variables in the next sections.

Using route variables inside our pages

Route variables are incredibly useful for creating very dynamic page content.

Let's take an easy example: a greetings page. Inside the project used in the previous section, let's create the following file: `pages/greet/[name].js`. We're going to use Next.js' built-in `getServerSideProps` function to dynamically get the `[name]` variable from the URL and greet the user:

```
export async function getServerSideProps({ params }) {
  const { name } = params;
  return {
    props: {
      name
    }
  }
}
function Greet(props) {
  return (
    <h1> Hello, {props.name}! </h1>
  )
}
export default Greet;
```

Now, open your favorite browser and go to `http://localhost:3000/greet/Mitch`; you should see a "**Hello, Mitch!**" message appear on the screen. Remember that we're using a `name` variable, so feel free to try with some different names!

> **Important Note**
>
> When using both the `getServerSideProps` and `getStaticProps` functions, remember that they *must* return an object. Also, if you want to pass any prop from one of those two functions to your page, make sure to pass them inside the returning object's `props` property.

Being able to get data from the URL is fundamental for many reasons. In the previous code example, we made a simple greetings page, but we could have used the `[name]` variable for other purposes, such as getting that user data from a database to show their profile. We will take a closer look at data fetching in *Chapter 4, Organizing the Code Base and Fetching Data in Next.js.*

There are times when you need to fetch route variables from your components rather than your pages. Next.js makes this effortless thanks to a React hook that we'll see in the next section.

Using route variables inside components

In the previous section, we have learned how to use route variables inside our pages. Next.js does not allow us to use both `getServerSideProps` and `getStaticProps` functions outside of our pages, so how are we supposed to use them inside other components?

Next.js makes this effortless thanks to the `useRouter` hook; we can import it from the `next/router` file:

```
import { useRouter } from 'next/router';
```

It works just like any other React hook (a function that lets you interact with the React state and life cycle in function components), and we can instantiate it inside any component. Let's refactor the previous greetings page as follows:

```
import { useRouter } from 'next/router';
function Greet() {
   const { query } = useRouter();
   return <h1>Hello {query.name}!</h1>;
}
export default Greet;
```

As you can see, we are extracting the `query` parameter from the `useRouter` hook. It contains both our route variables (in this case, it only contains the `name` variable) and the parsed query string parameters.

We can observe how Next.js passes both route variables and query strings via the `useRouter` hook by trying to append any query parameter to our URL and log the `query` variable inside our component:

```
import { useRouter } from 'next/router';
function Greet() {
   const { query } = useRouter();
   console.log(query);
   return <h1>Hello {query.name}!</h1>;
}
export default Greet;
```

If we now try to call the following URL, `http://localhost:3000/greet/Mitch?learning_nextjs=true`, we will see the following object logged inside our terminal:

```
{learning_nextjs: "true", name: "Mitch"}
```

> **Important Note**
> Next.js does not throw any error if you try to append a query parameter
> with the same key as your routing variable. You can easily try that by
> calling the following URL: `http://localhost:3000/greet/Mitch?name=Christine`. You will notice that Next.js will give
> precedence to your route variable, such that you will see **Hello, Mitch!**
> displayed on the page.

Client-side navigation

As we have already seen so far, Next.js is not only about rendering React on the server. It provides several ways to optimize your website's performance, and one of these optimizations is how it handles client-side navigation.

In fact, it supports the HTML standard `<a>` tags for linking pages, but it also provides a more optimized way for navigating between different routes: the `Link` component.

We can import it as a standard React component and use it for linking different pages or sections of our website. Let's look at an easy example:

```
import Link from 'next/link';
function Navbar() {
  return (
    <div>
      <Link href='/about'>Home</Link>
      <Link href='/about'>About</Link>
      <Link href='/about'>Contacts</Link>
    </div>
  );
}
export default Navbar;
```

By default, Next.js will preload every single `Link` found on the viewport, meaning that once we click on one of the links, the browser will already have all the data needed to render the page.

You can disable this feature by passing the `preload={false}` prop to the `Link` component:

```
import Link from 'next/link';
function Navbar() {
  return (
    <div>
      <Link href='/about' preload={false}>Home</Link>
      <Link href='/about' preload={false}>About</Link>
      <Link href='/about' preload={false}>Contacts</Link>
    </div>
  );
}
export default Navbar;
```

Starting with Next.js 10, we're also able to link pages with dynamic route variables with ease.

Let's say that we want to link the following page: `/blog/[date]/[slug].js`. With previous versions of Next.js, we needed to add two different props:

```
<Link href='/blog/[date]/[slug]'
  as='/blog/2021-01-01/happy-new-year'>
  Read post
</Link>
```

The `href` prop tells Next.js which page we want to render, and the `as` prop will tell how we want to display it in the browser's address bar.

Thanks to the enhancements introduced in Next.js 10, we no longer need to use the `as` prop as the `href` prop is enough for setting both the page we want to render and the URL displayed in the browser's address bar. For instance, we can now write our links as follows:

```
<Link href='/blog/2021-01-01/happy-new-year'> Read post </Link>
<Link href='/blog/2021-03-05/match-update'> Read post </Link>
<Link href='/blog/2021-04-23/i-love-nextjs'> Read post </Link>
```

> **Important Note**
>
> Although the legacy method for linking dynamic pages using the `Link` component is still working in Next.js >10, the framework's newest version makes it way easier. If you have some experience with previous Next.js versions or you're willing to upgrade to version >10, keep that new feature in mind as it will simplify the development of components, including dynamic links.

If we are building complex URLs, we can also pass an object to the `href` prop:

```
<Link
  href={{
    pathname: '/blog/[date]/[slug]'
    query: {
      date: '2020-01-01',
      slug: 'happy-new-year',
      foo: 'bar'
    }
  }}
/>
  Read post
</Link>
```

Once the user clicks that link, Next.js will redirect the browser to the following URL: `http://localhost:3000/blog/2020-01-01/happy-new-year?foo=bar`.

Using the router.push method

There is another way to move between your Next.js website pages: by using the `useRouter` hook.

Let's pretend that we want to give access to a given page only to logged-in users, and we already have a `useAuth` hook for that. We can use the `useRouter` hook to dynamically redirect a user if, in this case, they're not logged in:

```
import { useEffect } from 'react';
import { useRouter } from 'next/router';
import PrivateComponent from '../components/Private';
import useAuth from '../hooks/auth';

function MyPage() {
```

```
    const router = useRouter();
    const { loggedIn } = useAuth();

    useEffect(() => {
      if (!loggedIn) {
        router.push('/login')
      }
    }, [loggedIn]);

    return loggedIn
      ? <PrivateComponent />
      : null;
}

export default MyPage;
```

As you can see, we're using the useEffect hook to run the code on the client side only.
In that case, if the user isn't logged in, we use the router.push method to redirect them
to the login page.

Just like with the Link component, we can create more complex page routes by passing
an object to the push method:

```
router.push({
  pathname: '/blog/[date]/[slug]',
  query: {
    date: '2021-01-01',
    slug: 'happy-new-year',
    foo: 'bar'
  }
});
```

Once the router.push function has been called, the browser will be redirected to
http://localhost:3000/blog/2020-01-01/happy-new-year?foo=bar.

> **Important Note**
>
> Next.js won't be able to prefetch all the linked pages as it does with the `Link` component.
>
> Using the `router.push` method is handy when you need to redirect a user on the client side after a certain action occurs, but it's not recommended to be used as a default way for handling client-side navigation.

So far, we've seen how Next.js handles navigation through static and dynamic routes and how to force redirection and navigation on both the client and server sides programmatically.

In the next section, we're going to look at how Next.js helps us to serve static assets and optimize images on the fly for improved performance and SEO scores.

Serving static assets

Using the term **static asset**, we refer to all of those non-dynamic files, such as images, fonts, icons, compiled CSS, and JS files.

The easiest way to serve those assets is by using the default `/public` folder provided by Next.js. In fact, every file inside this folder will be considered and served as a static asset. We can prove that by creating a new file called `index.txt` and putting it inside the `/public` folder:

```
echo "Hello, world!" >> ./public/index.txt
```

If we now try to launch the server, when we go to `http://localhost:3000/index.txt`, we will see the text **Hello, world!** displayed in the browser.

In *Chapter 4, Organizing the Code Base and Fetching Data in Next.js*, we will take a closer look at organizing the public folder for serving common CSS and JS files, images, icons, and all the other types of static files.

Serving static assets is relatively easy. However, a specific type of file can critically affect your website performance (and SEO): the image file.

Most of the time, serving non-optimized images will worsen your user experience, as they may take some time to load, and once they do, they'll move part of the layout after the rendering, which can cause many problems in terms of UX. When this occurs, we're talking about **Cumulative Layout Shift (CLS)**. Here is a simple representation of how CLS works:

Figure 3.1 – Representation of how CLS works

In the first browser tab, the image has not been loaded yet, so the two text areas look quite close to each other. After the image loads, it shifts the second text area down. If the user were reading the second text area, they would easily miss the mark.

> **Important Note**
> If you want to learn more about CLS, I'd recommend the following article:
> `https://web.dev/cls`.

Of course, Next.js makes it easy to avoid CLS, and it does so with a new built-in `Image` component. We will take a look at this in the next section.

Next.js' automatic image optimization

Starting with Next.js 10, the framework introduced a new helpful `Image` component and automatic image optimization.

Before Next.js introduced these two new features, we had to optimize every image using an external tool and then write down a complex `srcset` property for every HTML `<img>` tag to set responsive images for different screen sizes.

Indeed, automatic image optimization will take care of serving your images using modern formats (such as **WebP**) to all those browsers that support it. But it will also be able to fall back on older image formats, such as *png* or *jpg*, in case the browser you're using doesn't support it. It also resizes your images to avoid serving heavy pictures to the client as it would negatively affect the asset's download speed.

One great thing to keep in mind is that automatic image optimization works on-demand, as it optimizes, resizes, and renders the image only when the browser has requested it. This is important as it will work with any external data source (any CMS or image service, such as Unsplash or Pexels), and it won't slow down the build phase.

We can try this feature on our local machine in a few minutes to see in person how it works. Let's say that we want to serve the following image:

Figure 3.2 – Picture by Łukasz Rawa on Unsplash (https://unsplash.com/@lukasz_rawa)

Using standard HTML tags, we could just do the following:

```
<img
  src='https://images.unsplash.com/photo-1605460375648-
  278bcbd579a6'
  alt='A beautiful English Setter'
/>
```

However, we may also want to use the srcset property for responsive images, so we'll actually need to optimize the picture for different screen resolutions, which involves some extra steps for serving our assets.

Next.js makes it very easy by just configuring the `next.config.js` file and using the `Image` component. We just said that we want to serve images coming from Unsplash, so let's add that service hostname to our `next.config.js` file, under the `images` property:

```
module.exports = {
  images: {
    domains: ['images.unsplash.com']
  }
};
```

That way, every time we use an image coming from that hostname inside an `Image` component, Next.js will automatically optimize it for us.

Now, let's try to import that image inside a page:

```
import Image from 'next/image';

function IndexPage() {
  return (
    <div>
      <Image
        src='https://images.unsplash.com/photo-
          1605460375648-278bcbd579a6'
        width={500}
        height={200}
        alt='A beautiful English Setter'
      />
    </div>
  );
}
export default IndexPage;
```

Opening the browser, you will notice that the image is stretched to fit both the `width` and `height` props specified in your `Image` component.

Figure 3.3 – Representation of the image component we just created

We can crop our image to fit the desired dimensions using the optional `layout` prop. It accepts four different values: `fixed`, `intrinsic`, `responsive`, and `fill`. Let's look at these in more detail:

- `fixed` works just like the `img` HTML tag. If we change the viewport size, it will keep the same size, meaning that it won't provide a responsive image for smaller (or bigger) screens.

- `responsive` works in the opposite way to `fixed`; as we resize our viewport, it will serve differently optimized images for our screen size.

- `intrinsic` is halfway between `fixed` and `responsive`; it will serve different image sizes as we resize down our viewport, but it will leave the largest image untouched on bigger screens.

- `fill` will stretch the image according to its parent element's width and height; however, we can't use `fill` alongside the `width` and `height` props. You can use `fill` *or* `width` and `height`).

So now, if we want to fix our English Setter image to display it properly on our screen, we can refactor our `Image` component as follows:

```
import Image from 'next/image';

function IndexPage() {
  return (
```

```
  <div>
    <div
      style={{ width: 500, height: 200, position:
      'relative' }}
    >
      <Image
        src='https://images.unsplash.com/photo-
          1605460375648-278bcbd579a6'
        layout='fill'
        objectFit='cover'
        alt='A beautiful English Setter'
      />
    </div>
  </div>
  );
}
export default IndexPage;
```

As you can see, we wrapped the `Image` component with a fixed size `div` and the CSS `position` property set to `relative`. We also removed both the `width` and `height` props from our `Image` component, as it will stretch following its parent `div` sizes.

We also added the `objectFit` prop set to `cover` so that it will crop the image according to its parent `div` size, and that's the final result.

Figure 3.4 – Representation of the image component with the layout prop set to "fill"

If we now try to inspect the resulting HTML on the browser, we will see that the `Image` component generated many different image sizes, which will be served using the `srcset` property of a standard `img` HTML tag:

```
<div style="...">
<img alt="A beautiful English Setter"src="/_next/
image?url=https%3A%2F%2Fimages.unsplash.com%2Fphoto-
1605460375648-278bcbd579a6&w=3840&q=75" decoding="async"
sizes="100vw" srcset="/_next/image?url=https%3A%2F%2Fimages.
unsplash.com%2Fphoto-1605460375648-278bcbd579a6&w=640&q=75
640w, /_next/image?url=https%3A%2F%2Fimages.unsplash.
com%2Fphoto-1605460375648-278bcbd579a6&w=750&q=75 750w, /_
next/image?url=https%3A%2F%2Fimages.unsplash.com%2Fphoto-
1605460375648-278bcbd579a6&w=828&q=75 828w, /_next/
image?url=https%3A%2F%2Fimages.unsplash.com%2Fphoto-
1605460375648-278bcbd579a6&w=1080&q=75 1080w, /_next/
image?url=https%3A%2F%2Fimages.unsplash.com%2Fphoto-
1605460375648-278bcbd579a6&w=1200&q=75 1200w, /_next/
image?url=https%3A%2F%2Fimages.unsplash.com%2Fphoto-
1605460375648-278bcbd579a6&w=1920&q=75 1920w, /_next/
image?url=https%3A%2F%2Fimages.unsplash.com%2Fphoto-
1605460375648-278bcbd579a6&w=2048&q=75 2048w, /_next/
image?url=https%3A%2F%2Fimages.unsplash.com%2Fphoto-
1605460375648-278bcbd579a6&w=3840&q=75 3840w" style="..."
</div>
```

One last thing worth mentioning is that if we inspect the image format on Google Chrome or Firefox, we will see that it has been served as `WebP`, even if the original image served from Unsplash was a `jpeg`. If we now try to render the same page on iOS with Safari, Next.js will serve the original `jpeg` format, as (at the time of writing) that iOS browser does not yet support the `WebP` format.

As said at the beginning of this section, Next.js runs automatic image optimization on-demand, meaning that if a given image is never requested, it will never be optimized.

The whole optimization phase occurs on the server where Next.js is running. If you're running a web app containing tons of images, it could affect your server performance. In the next section, we'll see how to delegate the optimization phase to external services.

Running automatic image optimization on external services

By default, automatic image optimization runs on the same server as Next.js. Of course, if you're running your website on a small server with low resources, this could potentially affect its performance. For that reason, Next.js allows you to run automatic image optimization on external services by setting the `loader` option inside your `next.config.js` file:

```
module.exports = {
  images: {
    loader: 'akamai',
    domains: ['images.unsplash.com']
  }
};
```

If you're deploying your web app to Vercel, you don't actually need to set up any loader in your `next.config.js` file as Vercel will take care of optimizing and serving the image files for you. Otherwise, you can use the following external services:

- Akamai: `https://www.akamai.com`

- Imgix: `https://www.imgix.com`

- Cloudinary: `https://cloudinary.com`

If you don't want to use any of these services, or you want to use your custom image optimization server, you can use the `loader` prop directly inside your component:

```
import Image from 'next/image'
const loader = ({src, width, quality}) => {
  return `https://example.com/${src}?w=${width}&q=${quality
    || 75}`
}
function CustomImage() {
  return (
    <Image
      loader={loader}
      src="/myimage.png"
      alt="My image alt text"
      width={350}
```

```
        height={540}
    />
  )
}
```

This way, you'll be able to serve images coming from any external service and this allows you to take advantage of custom image optimization servers or free, open source projects such as *Imgproxy* (`https://github.com/imgproxy/imgproxy`) or *Thumbor* (`https://github.com/thumbor/thumbor`).

> **Important Note**
> When you're using custom loaders, keep in mind that every service has its own APIs for resizing and serving images. For instance, to serve an image from *Imgproxy*, you would need to call it with the following URL: `https://imgproxy.example.com/<auth-key>/fill/500/500/sm/0/plain/https://example.com/images/myImage.jpg`. With *Thumbor*, you'd need to call it with a different URL schema: `https://thumbor.example.com/500x500/smart/example.com/images/myImage.jpg`.
>
> Before creating a custom loader, read the documentation of your image optimization server.

Correctly serving images has become more and more complex during the last years, but it is worth spending some time fine-tuning that process as it can affect our user experience in many critical ways. Thankfully, Next.js makes it quite effortless thanks to its built-in components and optimizations.

However, we should also think of web scrapers, bots, and web spiders when we're building a web app! I'm referring to web technologies that will look at our web page's metadata for taking actions such as indexing, linking, and evaluation. We'll see how to handle metadata in the next section.

Handling metadata

Correctly handling metadata is a crucial part of modern web development. To keep it simple, let's think about when we share a link on Facebook or Twitter. If we share the React website (`https://reactjs.org`) on Facebook, we will see the following card appear inside our post:

Figure 3.5 – Open Graph data of `https://reactjs.org`

To know which data should be displayed inside the card, Facebook uses a protocol called **Open Graph** (`https://ogp.me`). In order to give that information to any social network or website, we need to add some metadata to our pages.

So far, we haven't yet talked about how to set open graph data, HTML titles, or HTML meta tags dynamically. While a website could technically work even without that data, search engines would penalize your pages, as they would miss important information. The user experience could also be negatively affected as these meta tags would help the browser create an optimized experience for our users.

Once again, Next.js provides a great way of solving these problems: the built-in `Head` component. Indeed, this component allows us to update the `<head>` section of our HTML page from any component, meaning that we can dynamically change, add, or delete any metadata, link, or script at runtime depending on our user's navigation.

We can start with one of the most common dynamic parts of our metadata: the HTML `<title>` tag. Let's set up a new Next.js project and then create two new pages.

The first page we will create is `index.js`:

```
import Head from 'next/head';
import Link from 'next/link';
function IndexPage() {
```

```
  return (
    <>
      <Head>
        <title> Welcome to my Next.js website </title>
      </Head>
      <div>
        <Link href='/about' passHref>
          <a>About us</a>
        </Link>
      </div>
    </>
  );
}
export default IndexPage;
```

The second page is about.js:

```
import Head from 'next/head';
import Link from 'next/link';
function AboutPage() {
  return (
    <>
      <Head>
        <title> About this website </title>
      </Head>
      <div>
        <Link href='/'passHref>
          <a>Back to home</a>
        </Link>
      </div>
    </>
  );
}
export default AboutPage;
```

Running the server, you will be able to navigate between those two pages and see that the <title> content changes depending on the route you're visiting.

Now, let's make things a bit more complex. We want to create a new component that only displays a button. Once we click on it, our page title will change depending on the page we're currently on; we can always roll back to the original title by clicking on the button again.

Let's create a new folder, components/, in your project root and a new file, components/Widget.js, inside it:

```
import { useState } from 'react;
import Head from 'next/head';
function Widget({pageName}) {
  const [active, setActive] = useState(false);
  if (active) {
    return (
      <>
        <Head>
          <title> You're browsing the {pageName} page
          </title>
        </Head>
        <div>
          <button onClick={() =>setActive(false)}>
            Restore original title
          </button>
          Take a look at the title!
        </div>
      </>
    );
  }
  return (
    <>
      <button onClick={() =>setActive(true)}>
        Change page title
      </button>
    </>
  );
}
export default Widget;
```

Great! Now let's edit both our index.js and about.js pages to include that component.

We'll start by opening the index.js file and importing the Widget component and then we're going to render it inside a new <div>:

```
import Head from 'next/head';
import Link from 'next/link';
import Widget from '../components/Widget';
function IndexPage() {
  return (
    <>
      <Head>
        <title> Welcome to my Next.js website </title>
      </Head>
      <div>
        <Link href='/about' passHref>
          <a>About us</a>
        </Link>
      </div>
      <div>
        <Widget pageName='index' />
      </div>
    </>
  );
}
export default IndexPage;
```

Let's do the same thing with the about.js page:

```
import Head from 'next/head';
import Link from 'next/link';
import Widget from '../components/Widget';

function AboutPage() {
  return (
    <>
      <Head>
```

```
            <title> About this website </title>
        </Head>
        <div>
            <Link href='/'passHref>
                <a>Back to home</a>
            </Link>
        </div>
        <div>
            <Widget pageName='about' />
        </div>
    </>
  );
}
export default AboutPage;
```

After this title is refactored, every time we click on **Change page title**, Next.js will update the HTML `<title>` element.

> **Important Note**
>
> If multiple components are trying to update the same meta tag, Next.js occasionally will duplicate the same tag but with different content. For instance, if we have two components editing the `<title>` tag, we could end up having two distinct `<title>` tags inside our `<head>`. We can avoid that by adding the `key` prop to our HTML tags:
>
> `<title key='htmlTitle'>some content</title>`. This way, Next.js will look for every HTML tag with that specific key and update it instead of adding a new one.

So far, we've seen how to handle metadata inside our pages and components, but there are cases where you want to use the same meta tags on different components. In those cases, you may not want to rewrite all the metadata from scratch for each component, so here comes the concept of grouping metadata by creating a whole component just for handling that kind of HTML tag. We'll take a closer look at this approach in the next section.

Grouping common meta tags

At this point, we may want to add many other meta tags to our website to improve its SEO performance. The problem is that we could easily end up creating huge page components containing basically the same tags. For that reason, it is common practice to create one or more components (depending on your needs) to handle most of the common head meta tags.

Let's say that we want to add a blog section to our website. We may want to add support for open graph data, Twitter cards, and other metadata for our blog posts, so we could easily group all this common data inside a PostHead component.

Let's create a new file, components/PostHead.js, and add the following script:

```javascript
import Head from 'next/head';

function PostMeta(props) {
  return (
    <Head>
      <title> {props.title} </title>
      <meta name="description" content={props.subtitle} />

      {/* open-graph meta */}
      <meta property="og:title" content={props.title} />
      <meta property="og:description"
       content={props.subtitle} />
      <meta property="og:image" content={props.image} />

      {/* twitter card meta */}
      <meta name="twitter:card" content="summary" />
      <meta name="twitter:title" content={props.title} />
      <meta name="twitter:description"
       content={props.description} />
      <meta name="twitter:image" content={props.image} />
    </Head>
  );
}
export default PostMeta;
```

Now, let's create a mock for our posts. We will create a new folder called `data` and a file called `posts.js` inside it:

```javascript
export default [
  {
    id: 'qWD3Pzce',
    slug: 'dog-of-the-day-the-english-setter',
    title: 'Dog of the day: the English Setter',
    subtitle:     'The English Setter dog breed was named
      for these dogs\' practice of "setting", or crouching
      low, when they found birds so hunters could throw
      their nets over them',
    image: 'https://images.unsplash.com/photo-
      1605460375648-278bcbd579a6'
  },
  {
    id: 'yI6BK404',
    slug: 'about-rottweiler',
    title: 'About Rottweiler',
    subtitle:
      "The Rottweiler is a breed of domestic dog, regarded
        as medium-to-large or large. The dogs were known in
        German as Rottweiler Metzgerhund, meaning Rottweil
        butchers' dogs, because their main use was to herd
        livestock and pull carts laden with butchered meat
        to market",
    image: 'https://images.unsplash.com/photo-
      1567752881298-894bb81f9379'
  },
  {
    id: 'VFOyZVyH',
    slug: 'running-free-with-collies',
    title: 'Running free with Collies',
    subtitle:
      'Collies form a distinctive type of herding dogs,
        including many related landraces and standardized
        breeds. The type originated in Scotland and Northern
```

```
            England. Collies are medium-sized, fairly lightly-
            built dogs, with pointed snouts. Many types have a
            distinctive white color over the shoulders',
        image: 'https://images.unsplash.com/photo-
          1517662613602-4b8e02886677'
    }
];
```

Great! Now we only need to create a `[slug]` page to display our posts. The full route will be `/blog/[slug]`, so let's create a new file called `[slug].js` inside `pages/blog/` and add the following content:

```
import PostHead from '../../components/PostHead';
import posts from '../../data/posts';
export function getServerSideProps({ params }) {
  const { slug } = params;
  const post = posts.find((p) => p.slug === slug);
  return {
    props: {
      post
    }
  };
}
function Post({ post }) {
  return (
    <div>
      <PostHead {...post} />
        <h1>{post.title}</h1>
        <p>{post.subtitle}</p>
    </div>
  );
}
export default Post;
```

If we now go to `http://localhost:3000/blog/dog-of-the-day-the-english-setter` and inspect the resulting HTML, we will see the following tags:

```
<head>

   ...

   <title> Dog of the day: the English Setter </title>
   <meta name="description" content="The English Setter dog
     breed was named for these dogs' practice of "setting",
     or crouching low, when they found birds so hunters could
     throw their nets over them">
   <meta property="og:title" content="Dog of the day: the
     English Setter">
   <meta property="og:description" content="The English
     Setter dog breed was named for these dogs' practice of
     "setting", or crouching low, when they found birds so
     hunters could throw their nets over them">
   <meta property="og:image" content=
     "https://images.unsplash.com/photo-1605460375648-
     278bcbd579a6">
   <meta name="twitter:card" content="summary">
   <meta name="twitter:title" content="Dog of the day: the
     English Setter">
   <meta name="twitter:description">
   <meta name="twitter:image" content=
     "https://images.unsplash.com/photo-1605460375648-
     278bcbd579a6">

   ...

</head>
```

Now, try to browse other blog posts and see how the HTML content changes for each one of them.

This approach is not mandatory, but it allows you to logically separate head-related components from other components, leading to a more organized code base.

But what if we need the same meta tags (or, at least, some common basic data) on every page? We don't actually need to rewrite every single tag or import a common component on each page. We'll see in the next section how to avoid that by customizing our _app.js file.

Customizing _app.js and _document.js pages

There are certain cases where you need to take control over page initialization, so that every time we render a page, Next.js will need to run certain operations before sending the resulting HTML to the client. To do that, the framework allows us to create two new files, called _app.js and _document.js, inside our pages/ directory.

The _app.js page

By default, Next.js ships with the following pages/_app.js file:

```
import '../styles/globals.css'

function MyApp({ Component, pageProps }) {
  return <Component {...pageProps} />
}


export default MyApp
```

As you can see, the function is just returning the Next.js page component (the Component prop) and its props (pageProps).

But now, let's say that we want to share a navigation bar between all the pages without manually importing that component on each page. We can start by creating the navbar inside components/Navbar.js:

```
import Link from 'next/link';
function Navbar() {
  return (
    <div
      style={{
        display: 'flex',
        flexDirection: 'row',
        justifyContent: 'space-between',
        marginBottom: 25
      }}
    >
      <div>My Website</div>
      <div>
        <Link href="/">Home </Link>
```

```
            <Link href="/about">About </Link>
            <Link href="/contacts">Contacts </Link>
        </div>
    </div>
  );
}
export default Navbar;
```

That is a really simple navigation bar with just three links that will allow us to navigate our website.

Now, we need to import it inside our _app.js page as follows:

```
import Navbar from '../components/Navbar';
function MyApp({ Component, pageProps }) {
  return (
    <>
        <Navbar />
        <Component {...pageProps} />
    </>
  );
}
export default MyApp;
```

If we now create two more pages (about.js and contacts.js), we will see that the navbar component will be rendered on any page.

Now, let's make it a bit more complex by adding support for both dark and light themes. We'll do that by creating a React context and wrapping the <Component /> component inside our _app.js file.

Let's start by creating a context in components/themeContext.js:

```
import { createContext } from 'react';
const ThemeContext = createContext({
  theme: 'light',
  toggleTheme: () => null
});
export default ThemeContext;
```

Now let's go back to our _app.js file and create the theme state, inline CSS styles, and wrap the page component in a context provider:

```
import { useState } from 'react';
import ThemeContext from '../components/themeContext';
import Navbar from '../components/Navbar';
const themes = {
  dark: {
    background: 'black',
    color: 'white'
  },
  light: {
    background: 'white',
    color: 'black'
  }
};

function MyApp({ Component, pageProps }) {
  const [theme, setTheme] = useState('light');
  const toggleTheme = () => {
    setTheme(theme === 'dark' ? 'light' : 'dark');
  };

  return (
    <ThemeContext.Provider value={{ theme, toggleTheme }}>
      <div
        style={{
          width: '100%',
          minHeight: '100vh',
          ...themes[theme]
        }}
      >
        <Navbar />
        <Component {...pageProps} />
      </div>
    </ThemeContext.Provider>
  );
```

```
}
export default MyApp;
```

Last but not least, we need to add a button for toggling dark/light themes. We're going to add it to our navigation bar, so let's open the `components/Navbar.js` file and add the following code:

```
import { useContext } from 'react';
import Link from 'next/link';
import themeContext from '../components/themeContext';

function Navbar() {
  const { toggleTheme, theme } = useContext(themeContext);
  const newThemeName = theme === 'dark' ? 'light' : 'dark';

  return (
    <div
      style={{
        display: 'flex',
        flexDirection: 'row',
        justifyContent: 'space-between',
        marginBottom: 25
      }}
    >
      <div>My Website</div>
      <div>
        <Link href="/">Home </Link>
        <Link href="/about">About </Link>
        <Link href="/contacts">Contacts </Link>
        <button onClick={toggleTheme}>
          Set {newThemeName} theme
        </button>
      </div>
    </div>
  );
}
export default Navbar;
```

If you try to toggle the dark theme, and then navigate between all the website pages using the navigation bar, you will see that Next.js keeps the theme state consistent between every route.

One important thing to remember when customizing the _app.js page is that it is not meant for running data fetching using getServerSideProps or getStaticProps, as other pages do. Its main use cases are maintaining state between pages during navigation (dark/light themes, items in a cart, and so on), adding global styles, handling page layouts, or adding additional data to the page props.

If, for some reason, you absolutely need to fetch data on the server side every time you want to render a page, you can still use the built-in getInitialProps function, but it has a cost. You'll lose automatic static optimization in dynamic pages, as Next.js will need to perform server-side rendering for every single page.

If that cost is acceptable for your web app, you can easily use that built-in method as follows:

```
import App from 'next/app'
function MyApp({ Component, pageProps }) {
  return <Component {...pageProps} />
};
MyApp.getInitialProps = async (appContext) => {
  const appProps = await App.getInitialProps(appContext);
  const additionalProps = await fetch(...)
  return {
    ...appProps,
    ...additionalProps
  }
};
export default MyApp;
```

While a custom _app.js file allows us to customize the way we render page components, there might be cases where it cannot help; for example, when we need to customize HTML tags such as <html> or <body>. We will learn how to do that right in the next section.

The _document.js page

When we're writing Next.js page components, we don't need to define fundamental HTML tags, such as `<head>`, `<html>`, or `<body>`. We've already seen how to customize the `<head>` tag using the `Head` component, but we will need a change of approach for both `<html>` and `<body>`tags.

In order to render those two essential tags, Next.js uses a built-in class called `Document`, and it allows us to extend it by creating a new file called `_document.js` inside our `pages/` directory, just like we do for our `_app.js` file:

```js
import Document, {
    Html,
    Head,
    Main,
    NextScript
} from 'next/document';

class MyDocument extends Document {
  static async getInitialProps(ctx) {
    const initialProps =
      await Document.getInitialProps(ctx);
    return { ...initialProps };
  }

  render() {
    return (
      <Html>
        <Head />
        <body>
          <Main />
          <NextScript />
        </body>
      </Html>
    );
  }
}
export default MyDocument;
```

Let's break down the `_document.js` page we've just created. First, we start by importing the `Document` class, which we're going to extend to add our custom scripts. We then import four mandatory components in order for our Next.js application to work:

- `Html`: The `<html>` tag for our Next.js application. We can pass any standard HTML property (such as `lang`) to it as a prop.

- `Head`: We can use this component for all the tags common to all the application pages. This is *not* the `Head` component we've seen in the previous chapter. They behave similarly, but we should use it only for code that is common to all the website pages.

- `Main`: This will be the place where Next.js renders our page components. The browser won't initialize every component outside `<Main>`, so if we need to share common components between our pages, we should place them inside the `_app.js` file.

- `NextScript`: If you've tried to inspect an HTML page generated by Next.js, you may have noticed that it adds some custom JavaScript scripts to your markup. Inside those scripts, we can find all the code required to run client-side logic, React hydration, and so on.

Removing any of the preceding four components will break our Next.js application, so make sure to import them before editing your `_document.js` page.

Just like `_app.js`, `_document.js` does not support server-side data fetching methods such as `getServerSideProps` and `getStaticProps`. We still get access to the `getInitialProps` method, but we should avoid putting data fetching functions inside it as this would disable automatic site optimization, forcing the server to server-side render the page on each request.

Summary

In this chapter, we've covered many important concepts that make Next.js a great framework to work with. We now know how to serve images correctly and with minimum effort, navigate between pages by pre-fetching the destination page, dynamically create and delete custom metadata, and create dynamic routes to make the user experience even more dynamic. We've also taken a look at customizing the `_app.js` and `_document.js` files, which will allow us to keep our user interface consistent between all the application pages with minimum effort.

So far, we've always avoided calling external REST APIs, as it introduces an extra layer of complexity for our application. We will cover this topic in the next chapter, understanding how to integrate *REST* and *GraphQL* APIs on both the client and server sides.

Part 2: Hands-On Next.js

In this part, we will start writing some small Next.js apps, focusing on each chapter's main topic. We will see how to make correct decisions when adopting UI frameworks, styling methods, testing strategies, and more.

This section comprises the following chapters:

- *Chapter 4, Organizing the Code Base and Fetching Data in Next.js*
- *Chapter 5, Managing Local and Global States in Next.js*
- *Chapter 6, CSS and Built-In Styling Methods*
- *Chapter 7, Using UI Frameworks*
- *Chapter 8, Using a Custom Server*
- *Chapter 9, Testing Next.js*
- *Chapter 10, Working with SEO and Managing Performance*
- *Chapter 11, Different Deployment Platforms*

4

Organizing the Code Base and Fetching Data in Next.js

Next.js initially became popular thanks to its ability to make it easy to render React pages on the server instead of the client only. However, to render specific components, we often need some data coming from external sources such as APIs and databases.

In this chapter, we will first see how to organize our folder structure, as this will be the determinant for keeping the Next.js dataflow neat when managing the application state (as we will see in *Chapter 5*, *Managing Local and Global States in Next.js*), and then we will see how to integrate external REST and GraphQL APIs, both on client and server-side.

As our application grows, its complexity will inevitably increase, and we need to be prepared for this since the bootstrapping phase of the project. As soon as we implement new features, we will need to add new components, utilities, styles, and pages. For that reason, we will take a closer look at organizing our components on the basis of the atomic design principles, utility functions, styles, and how to make your code base ready for handling the application state quickly and neatly.

We will cover the following topics in detail:

- Organizing our components using the atomic design principle
- Organizing our utility functions
- Organizing static assets neatly
- An introduction to organizing styling files
- What `lib` files are and how to organize them
- Consuming REST APIs on the server side only
- Consuming REST APIs on the client side only
- Setting Apollo to consume GraphQL APIs both on client and server

By the end of this chapter, you will know how to organize your code base by following the atomic design principles for your components and how to split up different utility files logically. You will also learn how to consume REST and GraphQL APIs.

Technical requirements

To run the code examples in this chapter, you need to have both Node.js and npm installed on your local machine. If you prefer, you can use an online IDE such as `https://repl.it` or `https://codesandbox.io`, as they both support Next.js and you don't need to install any dependency on your computer.

You can find the code base for this chapter on GitHub: `https://github.com/PacktPublishing/Real-World-Next.js`.

Organizing the folder structure

Organizing your new project's folder structure neatly and clearly is incredibly important in terms of keeping your code base scalable and maintainable.

As we've already seen, Next.js forces you to place some files and folders in particular locations of your code base (think of `_app.js` and `_documents.js` files, the `pages/` and `public/` directories, and so on), but it also provides a way to customize their placement inside your project repository.

We've already seen that, but let's do a quick recap on a default Next.js folder structure:

```
next-js-app
  - node_modules/
  - package.json
  - pages/
  - public/
  - styles/
```

Reading from top to bottom, when we create a new Next.js app using `create-next-app`, we get the following folders:

- `node_modules/`: The default folder for Node.js project dependencies
- `pages/`: The directory where we place our pages and build the routing system for our web app
- `public/`: The directory where we place files to be served as static assets (compiled CSS and JavaScript files, images, and icons)
- `styles/`: The directory where we place our styling modules, regardless of their format (CSS, SASS, LESS)

From here, we can start customizing our repository structure to make it easier to navigate through. The first thing to know is that Next.js allows us to move our `pages/` directory inside an `src/` folder. We can also move all the other directories (except for the `public/` one and `node_modules`, of course) inside `src/`, making our root directory a bit tidier.

> **Important Note**
>
> Remember that if you have both `pages/` and `src/pages/` directories in your project, Next.js will ignore `src/pages/`, as the root level `pages/` directory takes precedence.

We will now take a look at some popular conventions for organizing the whole code base, starting with React components, in the next section.

Organizing the components

Now, let's see an example of a real-world folder structure, including some styling assets (*Chapter 6, CSS and Built-In Styling Methods*) and test files (*Chapter 9, Testing Next.js*).

As for now, we will only discuss a folder structure that can help us write and find configuration files, components, tests, and styles with ease. We will dig into the previously quoted technologies in their respective chapters.

We have different ways of setting up our folder structure. We can start by separating components into three different categories and then putting styles and tests in the same folder for each component.

To do that, create a new `components/` folder inside our root directory. Then, by moving inside it, create the following folders:

```
mkdir components && cd components
mkdir atoms
mkdir molecules
mkdir organisms
mkdir templates
```

As you may have noticed, we're following the *atomic design principle*, where we want to divide our components into different levels so as to organize our code base better. This is just a popular convention, and you're free to follow any other approach for organizing your code.

We will divide our components into four categories:

- `atoms`: These are the most basic components that we will ever write in our code base. Sometimes, they act as a wrapper for standard HTML elements such as `button`, `input`, and `p`, but we can also add animations, color palettes, and so on, to this category of components.

- `molecules`: These are a small group of atoms combined to create slightly more complex structures with a minimum of utility. The input atom and the label atom together can be a straightforward example of what a molecule is.

- `organisms`: Molecules and atoms combine to create complex structures, such as a registration form, a footer, and a carousel.

- `templates`: We can think of templates as the skeleton of our pages. Here, we decide where to put organisms, atoms, and molecules together to create the final page that the user will browse.

If you're interested in learning more about atomic design, here's a good article explaining it in detail: `https://bradfrost.com/blog/post/atomic-web-design`.

Now, let's pretend that we want to create a `Button` component. When we create a new component, we often need at least three different files: the component itself, its style, and a test file. We can create those files by moving inside `components/atoms/` and then creating a new folder called `Button/`. Once we create this folder, we can move on to creating the components' files:

```
cd components/atoms/Button
touch index.js
touch button.test.js
touch button.styled.js # or style.module.css
```

Organizing our components that way will help us a lot when we need to search, update, or fix a given component. Let's say that we spot a bug in production that involves our `Button` component. We can easily find the component inside our code base, find its test and styling files, and fix them.

Of course, following the atomic design principle is not a must, but I'd personally recommend it as it helps keep the project structure tidy and easy to maintain over time.

Organizing utilities

There are specific files that don't export any component; they're just modular scripts used for many different purposes. We're talking here about the utility scripts.

Let's pretend that we have several components whose purpose is to check whether a particular hour of the day has passed to display certain information. It wouldn't make any sense to write the same function inside every component. We can therefore write a generic utility function and then import it inside every component that needs that kind of feature.

We can put all of our utility functions inside a `utility/` folder and then divide our utilities into different files according to their purpose. For example, let's say that we need four utility functions: the first one will make computations based on the current time, the second will execute certain operations on `localStorage`, the third will work with **JWT (JSON Web Token)**, and the last one will help us to write better logs for our applications.

We can proceed by creating four different files inside the `utilities/` directory:

```
cd utilities/
touch time.js
touch localStorage.js
touch jwt.js
touch logs.js
```

Now that we've created our files, we can proceed by creating their respective test files:

```
touch time.test.js
touch localStorage.test.js
touch jwt.test.js
touch logs.test.js
```

At this point, we have our utilities grouped by their scope, which makes it easy to remember from which file we need to import a specific function during the development process.

There might be other approaches for organizing utility files. You may want to create a folder for each utility file so that you can put tests, styles, and other stuff inside it, thereby making your code base even more organized. It's totally up to you!

Organizing static assets

As seen in the previous chapter, Next.js makes it easy to serve static files, as you only need to put them inside the `public/` folder, and the framework will do the rest.

From this point, we need to figure out which static files we need to serve from our Next.js application.

In a standard website, we may want to serve at least the following static assets:

- Images
- Compiled JavaScript files
- Compiled CSS files
- Icons (including favicon and web app icons)
- `manifest.json`, `robot.txt`, and other static files

Moving inside our `public/` folder, we can create a new directory called `assets/`:

```
cd public && mkdir assets
```

And inside that newly created directory, we will be creating a new folder for each type of static asset:

```
cd assets
mkdir js
mkdir css
mkdir icons
mkdir images
```

We will place our compiled vendor JavaScript files inside the `js/` directory and do the same with compiled vendor CSS files (inside the `css/` directory, of course). When starting our Next.js server, we will be able to reach those public files under `http://localhost:3000/assets/js/<any-js-file>` and `http://localhost:3000/assets/css/<any-css-file>`. We will also be able to reach every public image by calling the following URL, `http://localhost:3000/assets/image/<any-image-file>`, but I suggest that you serve those kinds of assets using the built-in `Image` component, as seen in the previous chapter.

The `icons/` directory will primarily be used to serve our *web app manifest* icons. The web app manifest is a JSON file that includes some useful information about the progressive web app that you're building, such as the app name and the icons to use when installing it on a mobile device. You can learn more about the web app manifest on `https://web.dev/add-manifest`.

We can easily create this manifest file by entering the `public/` folder and adding a new file called `manifest.json`:

```
cd public/ && touch manifest.json
```

At this point, we can fill the JSON file with some basic information. Let's take the following JSON as an example:

```
{
    "name": "My Next.js App",
    "short_name": "Next.js App",
    "description": "A test app made with next.js",
    "background_color": "#a600ff",
    "display": "standalone",
    "theme_color": "#a600ff",
    "icons": [
        {
```

```
        "src": "/assets/icons/icon-192.png",
        "type": "image/png",
        "sizes": "192x192"
      },
      {
        "src": "/assets/icons/icon-512.png",
        "type": "image/png",
        "sizes": "512x512"
      }
    ]
  }
```

We can include that file using an HTML meta tag, as seen in *Chapter 3, Next.js Basics and Built-In Components*:

```
<link rel="manifest" href="/manifest.json">
```

That way, users browsing your Next.js app from a mobile device will be able to install it on their smartphones or tablets.

Organizing styles

Style organization can really depend on the stack you want to use to style your Next.js application.

Starting from *CSSinJS* frameworks such as *Emotion, styled-components, JSS*, and similar ones, one common approach is to create a specific styling file for each component; that way, it will be easier for us to find a particular component style inside our code base when we need to make some changes.

However, even though separating styling files depending on their respective components can help us keep our code base organized, we may need to create some common styles or utility files, such as color palettes, themes, and media queries.

In that case, it can be useful to reuse the default `styles/` directory shipped with a default Next.js installation. We can put our common styles inside that folder and import them inside other styling files only when we need them.

That said, there isn't really a standard way to organize styling files. We will take a closer look at those files in both *Chapter 6, CSS and Built-In Styling Methods*, and *Chapter 7, Using UI Frameworks*.

Lib files

When talking about lib files, we refer to scripts that explicitly wrap third-party libraries as lib files. While the utility scripts are very generic and can be used by many different components and libraries, the lib files are specific for a certain library. To make the concept clearer, let's talk about GraphQL for a moment.

As we're going to see in *Data fetching*, the last section of this chapter, we will need to initialize a GraphQL client, save some GraphQL queries and mutations locally, and so on. To make those scripts more modular, we will store them inside a new folder called `graphql/`, which lies inside a `lib/` directory, at the root of our project.

If we try to visualize the folder structure for the preceding example, we will end up with the following schema:

```
next-js-app
  - lib/
    - graphql/
      - index.js
      - queries/
        - query1.js
        - query2.js
      - mutations/
        - mutation1.js
        - mutation2.js
```

Other lib scripts can include all those files connecting and making queries to Redis, RabbitMQ, and so on, or functions specific to any external library.

While an organized folder structure seems out of context when talking about the Next.js data flow, it can actually help us to manage the application state, as we will see in *Chapter 5, Managing Local and Global States in Next.js*

But talking about the application state, we want our components to be dynamic most of the time, meaning that they can render content and behave differently depending on the global application state or the data coming from external services. In fact, we need to call external APIs to retrieve our web app content dynamically in many cases. In the next section, we will see how to fetch data on the client and server sides, using both GraphQL and REST clients.

Data fetching

As seen in the previous chapters, Next.js allows us to fetch data on both the client and server sides. Server-side data fetching could happen in two different moments: at build time (using `getStaticProps` for static pages), and at runtime (using `getServerSideProps` for server-side rendered pages).

Data can come from several resources: databases, search engines, external APIs, filesystems, and many other sources. Even if it's technically possible for Next.js to access a database and query for specific data, I'd personally discourage that approach as Next.js should only care about the frontend of our application.

Let's take an example: we're building a blog, and we want to display an author page showing their name, job title, and biography. In that example, the data is stored in a MySQL database, and we could easily access it using any MySQL client for Node.js.

Even though accessing that data from Next.js can be relatively easy, it would make our app less secure. A malicious user could potentially find a way to exploit our data using an unknown framework vulnerability, injecting malicious code, and using other techniques to steal our data.

For that reason, I strongly suggest delegating database connections and queries to external systems (in other words, CMSes such as *WordPress*, *Strapi*, and *Contentful*) or backend frameworks (in other words, *Spring*, *Laravel*, and *Ruby on Rails*), which will make sure that the data is coming from a trusted source, will sanitize the user input detecting potentially malicious code, and will establish a secure connection between your Next.js application and their APIs.

In the following sections, we will see how to integrate *REST* and *GraphQL* APIs from both the client side and the server side.

Fetching data on the server side

As we've seen so far, Next.js allows us to fetch data on the server side by using its built-in `getStaticProps` and `getServerSideProps` functions.

Given that Node.js doesn't support JavaScript `fetch` APIs like browsers do, we have two options for making HTTP requests on the server:

1. Using the Node.js' built-in `http` library: We can use this module without installing any external dependency, but even if its APIs are really simple and well made, it would require a bit of extra work when compared to third-party HTTP clients.

2. Using HTTP client libraries: There are several great HTTP clients for Next.js, making it really straightforward to make HTTP requests from the server. Popular libraries include *isomorphic-unfetch* (this renders the JavaScript `fetch` API available on Node.js), *Undici* (an official Node.js HTTP 1.1 client), and *Axios* (a very popular HTTP client that runs both on client and server with the same APIs).

In the next section, we will be using *Axios* to make REST requests, as it is probably one of the most frequently used HTTP clients for both client and server (with ~17,000,000 downloads per week on npm), and there's a high chance that you will be using it sooner or later.

Consuming REST APIs on the server side

When discussing the integration of REST APIs, we need to divide them into *public* and *private* APIs. The public ones are accessible by anyone without any kind of authorization, and the private ones always need to be authorized to return some data.

Also, the authorization method is not always the same (and different APIs might require different authorization methods), as it depends on who developed the APIs and the choices they made. For instance, if you want to consume any of the *Google* APIs, you would need to go into a process called *OAuth 2.0*, which is an industry standard for securing APIs under user authentication. You can read more about OAuth 2.0 in the official Google documentation: `https://developers.google.com/identity/protocols/oauth2`.

Other APIs, such as the *Pexels* APIs (`https://www.pexels.com/api/documentation`), allow you to consume their contents using an *API key*, which is basically an authorization token that you'll need to send within your request.

There may be other ways in which to authorize your requests, but Oauth 2.0, JWT, and API Key are the most common ways that you'll likely encounter while developing your Next.js applications.

If, after reading this section, you want to experiment with different APIs and authorization methods, here's an awesome GitHub repository containing a list of free REST APIs: `https://github.com/public-apis/public-apis`.

For now, we will be using a custom API explicitly made for this book: `https://api.realworldnextjs.com` (or, if you prefer: `https://api.rwnjs.com`). We can start by creating a new Next.js project:

```
npx create-next-app ssr-rest-api
```

After running the Next.js initialization script, we can add `axios` as a dependency, as we'll use it as an HTTP client for making REST requests:

```
cd ssr-rest-api
yarn add axios
```

At this point, we can easily edit the default Next.js index page. Here, we will list some users using a public API exposing just their usernames and personal IDs. After we click on one of the usernames, we will be redirected to a detail page to see more personal details for our users.

Let's start by creating the `pages/index.js` page layout:

```javascript
import { useEffect } from 'react';
import Link from 'next/link';

export async function getServerSideProps() {
    // Here we will make the REST request to our APIs
}

function HomePage({ users }) {
  return (
    <ul>
      {
        users.map((user) =>
          <li key={user.id}>
            <Link
              href={`/users/${user.username}`}
              passHref
            >
              <a> {user.username} </a>
            </Link>
          </li>
        )
      }
    </ul>
  )
```

```
}
```

```
export default HomePage;
```

If we try to run the preceding code, we will see an error, as we don't yet have our users'
data. We need to call a REST API from the built-in `getServerSideProps` and pass
the request result as a prop to the `HomePage` component:

```
import { useEffect } from 'react';
import Link from 'next/link';
import axios from 'axios';

export async function getServerSideProps() {
  const usersReq =
    await axios.get('https://api.rwnjs.com/04/users')
  return {
    props: {
      users: usersReq.data
    }
  }
}

function HomePage({ users }) {
  return (
    <ul>
      {
        users.map((user) =>
          <li key={user.id}>
            <Link
              href={`/users/${user.username}`}
              passHref
            >
              <a> {user.username} </a>
            </Link>
          </li>
        )
      }
```

```
        </ul>
    )
}

export default HomePage;
```

Now, run the server and then go to `http://localhost:3000`. We should see the following list of users to appear on the browser:

- mkastel0
- dskivington1
- ldugmore2
- fonion3
- amccarron4
- nlofts5
- tmistry6
- asilverman7
- mspadelli8
- bullyott9
- eplumera
- ecaspellb
- wbraleyc
- dgiggd
- gpepperralle

Figure 4.1 – API result rendered on the browser

If we now try to click on one of the listed users, we will be redirected to a 404 page, as we haven't created a single page user yet.

We can solve that problem by creating a new file, `pages/users/[username].js`, and calling another REST API to get the single user data.

To get the single user data, we can call the following URL, `https://api.rwnjs.com/04/users/[username]`, where `[username]` is a route variable representing the user we want to get the data of.

Let's move to the `pages/users/[username].js` file and add the following content, starting with the `getServerSideProps` function:

```
import Link from 'next/link';
import axios from 'axios';
```

```
export async function getServerSideProps(ctx) {
  const { username } = ctx.query;
  const userReq =
    await axios.get(
      `https://api.rwnjs.com/04/users/${username}`
    );

  return {
    props: {
      user: userReq.data
    }
  };
}
```

Now, inside the same file, let's add a `UserPage` function, which will be the page template for our /users/[username] route:

```
function UserPage({ user }) {
  return (
    <div>
      <div>
        <Link href="/" passHref>
          Back to home
        </Link>
      </div>
      <hr />
      <div style={{ display: 'flex' }}>
        <img
          src={user.profile_picture}
          alt={user.username}
          width={150}
          height={150}
        />
        <div>
          <div>
            <b>Username:</b> {user.username}
          </div>
```

```
        <div>
          <b>Full name:</b>
            {user.first_name} {user.last_name}
        </div>
        <div>
          <b>Email:</b> {user.email}
        </div>
        <div>
          <b>Company:</b> {user.company}
        </div>
        <div>
          <b>Job title:</b> {user.job_title}
        </div>
      </div>
    </div>
  );
}

export default UserPage;
```

But there's still a problem: if we try to render a single user page, we will get an error on the server side as we are not authorized to get the data from that API. Remember what we said at the beginning of this section? Not all APIs are public, which makes a lot of sense as there are times where we want to access very private information and companies and developers protect this information by restricting access to their APIs to authorized people only.

In that case, we need to pass a valid token as an HTTP authorization header while making the API request, such that the server will know that we are authorized to access this information:

```javascript
export async function getServerSideProps(ctx) {
  const { username } = ctx.query;
  const userReq = await axios.get(
    `https://api.rwnjs.com/04/users/${username}`,
    {
      headers: {
        authorization: process.env.API_TOKEN
      }
    }
  );

  return {
    props: {
      user: userReq.data
    }
  };
}
```

As you can see, `axios` makes it really easy to add an HTTP header to the request, as we only need to pass an object as the second argument of its `get` method, containing a property called `headers`, which is an object including all the HTTP headers we want to send to the server within our request.

You may be wondering what `process.env.API_TOKEN` stands for. While it is possible to pass a hardcoded string as a value for that header, it is bad practice for the following reasons:

1. When committing your code using Git or any other version control system, everyone having access to that repository will be able to read private information such as the authorization token (even outside collaborators). Consider this as a password that should be kept secret.

2.   Most of the time, API tokens change depending on the stage at which we're running our application: running our app locally, we may want to access APIs using a test token, and use a production one when deploying it. Using an environment variable will make it easier for us to use different tokens depending on the environment. The same is valid for API endpoints, but we will see that later on in this section.

3.   If an API token changes for any reason, you can easily edit it using a shared environment file for the whole app instead of changing the token value in every HTTP request.

So, instead of manually writing sensitive data inside our files, we can create a new file called .env inside our project's root and add all the information we need for our application to run.

> **Never Commit Your .env File**
>
> The .env file contains sensitive and private information and should never be committed using any version control software. Make sure to add .env to your .gitignore, .dockerignore, and other similar files before deploying or committing your code.

Now, let's create and edit the .env file by adding the following content:

```
API_TOKEN=realworldnextjs
API_ENDPOINT=https://api.rwnjs.com
```

Next.js has built-in support for .env and .env.local files, so you don't have to install external libraries to access those environment variables.

After we've edited the file, we can restart the Next.js server and click on any user listed on the home page, thereby accessing the user detail page, which should look like this:

Figure 4.2 – The user detail page

If we try to reach a page such as `http://localhost:3000/users/mitch`, we will get an error, as a user with `mitch` as their username does not exist, and the REST API will return a `404` status code. We can easily catch this error and return the Next.js default 404 page by just adding the following script to the `getServerSideProps` function:

```
export async function getServerSideProps(ctx) {

  const { username } = ctx.query;
  const userReq = await axios.get(
    `${process.env.API_ENDPOINT}/04/users/${username}`,
    {
      headers: {
        authorization: process.env.API_TOKEN
      }
    }
  );

  if (userReq.status === 404) {
    return {
      notFound: true
    };
  }

  return {
    props: {
      user: userReq.data
    }
  };
}
```

That way, Next.js will automatically redirect us to its default `404` page with no other configuration needed.

So, we've seen how Next.js allows us to fetch data exclusively on the server side by using its built-in `getServerSideProps` function. We could have used the `getStaticProps` function instead, meaning that the page would have been statically rendered at build time, as seen in *Chapter 2, Exploring Different Rendering Strategies*.

In the next section, we will see how to fetch data on the client side only.

Fetching data on the client side

Client-side data fetching is a crucial part of any dynamic web application. While server-side data fetching can be relatively secure (when done with caution), fetching data on the browser can add some extra complexities and vulnerabilities.

Making HTTP requests on the server hides the API endpoint, parameters, HTTP headers, and possibly the authorization tokens from the users. However, doing so from the browser can reveal that private information, making it easy for malicious users to perform a plethora of possible attacks that exploit your data.

When making HTTP requests on browsers, some specific rules are not optional:

1. *Make HTTP requests to trusted sources only*. You should always do some research about who is developing the APIs you're using and their security standards.

2. *Call HTTP APIs only when secured with an SSL certificate*. If a remote API is not secured under HTTPS, you're exposing yourself and your users to many attacks, such as man-in-the-middle, where a malicious user could sniff all the data passing from the client and the server using a simple proxy.

3. *Never connect to a remote database from the browser*. It may seem obvious, but it is technically possible for JavaScript to access remote databases. This exposes you and your users to high risk, as anyone could potentially exploit a vulnerability and gain access to your database.

In the next section, we will take a closer look at consuming REST APIs on the client side.

Consuming REST APIs on the client side

Similar to the server side, fetching data on the client side is relatively easy, and if you already have experience in React or any other JavaScript framework or library, you can re-use your current knowledge for making REST requests from the browser without any complications.

While the server-side data fetching phase in Next.js only occurs when declared inside its built-in `getServerSideProps` and `getStaticProps` functions, if we make a fetch request inside a given component, it will be executed on the client side by default.

We usually want our client-side requests to run in two cases:

*   Right after the component has mounted

*   After a particular event occurs

In both cases, Next.js doesn't force you to execute those requests differently than React, so you can basically make an HTTP request using the browser's built-in `fetch` API or an external library such as `axios`, just like we saw in the previous section. Let's try to recreate the same simple Next.js application from the previous section, but move all the API calls to the client side.

Create a new Next.js project and edit the `pages/index.js` file as follows:

```javascript
import { useEffect, useState } from 'react';
import Link from 'next/link';

function List({users}) {
  return (
    <ul>
      {
        users.map((user) =>
          <li key={user.id}>
            <Link
              href={`/users/${user.username}`}
              passHref
            >
              <a> {user.username} </a>
            </Link>
          </li>
        )
      }
    </ul>
  )
}

function Users() {

  const [loading, setLoading] = useState(true);
  const [data, setData] = useState(null);

  useEffect(async () => {

    const req =
```

```
    await fetch('https://api.rwnjs.com/04/users');
  const users = await req.json();

  setLoading(false);
  setData(users);

}, []);

return (
  <div>
    {loading &&<div>Loading users...</div>}
    {data &&<List users={data} />}
  </div>
)
}


export default Users;
```

Can you spot the differences between this component and its SSR counterpart?

- The HTML generated on the server side contains the Loading users... text, as it is the initial state of our HomePage component.

- We will be able to see a list of users only after React hydration occurs. We will need to wait for the component to mount on the client side and the HTTP request to be spawned using the browser's fetch API.

Now we need to implement the single user page as follows:

1. Let's create a new file, pages/users/[username].js, and start writing the getServerSideProps function, where we fetch the [username] variable from the route and the authorization token from the .env file:

```
import { useEffect, useState } from 'react'
import Link from 'next/link';

export async function getServerSideProps({ query }) {
  const { username } = query;

  return {
```

```
    props: {
      username,
      authorization: process.env.API_TOKEN
    }
  }
}
```

2. Now, inside the same file, let's create the UserPage component, where we'll execute the client-side data fetching function:

```
function UserPage({ username, authorization }) {

  const [loading, setLoading] = useState(true);
  const [data, setData] = useState(null);

  useEffect(async () => {

    const req = await fetch(
      `https://api.rwnjs.com/04/users/${username}`,
      { headers: { authorization } }
    );
    const reqData = await req.json();

    setLoading(false);
    setData(reqData);

  }, []);

  return (
    <div>
      <div>
        <Link href="/" passHref>
          Back to home
        </Link>
      </div>
      <hr />
      {loading && <div>Loading user data...</div>}
```

```
        {data && <UserData user={data} />}
    </div>
  );
}


export default UserPage;
```

As you may have noticed, once we set the data using the `setData` hook function, we render a `<UserData />` component.

3. Create that last component, always inside the same `pages/users/[username].js` component:

```
function UserData({ user }) {
  return (
    <div style={{ display: 'flex' }}>
      <img
        src={user.profile_picture}
        alt={user.username}
        width={150}
        height={150}
      />
      <div>
        <div>
          <b>Username:</b> {user.username}
        </div>
        <div>
          <b>Full name:</b>
            {user.first_name} {user.last_name}
        </div>
        <div>
          <b>Email:</b> {user.email}
        </div>
        <div>
```

```
          <b>Company:</b> {user.company}
        </div>
        <div>
          <b>Job title:</b> {user.job_title}
        </div>
      </div>
    </div>
  )
}
```

As you can see, we're using the same approach as we did for the home page, making an HTTP request as soon as the component mounts on the client side. We're also passing the `API_TOKEN` from the server to the client using `getServerSideProps` so that we can use it for making an authorized request. However, if you try to run the preceding code, you will see at least two problems.

The first one is related to **CORS**.

CORS (which stands for **Cross-Origin Resource Sharing**) is a security mechanism implemented by browsers that aims to control the requests made from domains different from those of the API domain. In our `HomePage` component, we've been able to call the `https://api.rwnjs.com/04/users` API from a different domain (localhost, a replit.co domain, CodeSandbox domain, and so on) as the server allowed any domain to access its resources for that specific route.

In that case, however, the browser makes some restrictions on the `https://api.rwnjs.com/04/users/[username]` endpoint, and we're not able to call this API directly from the client as we get blocked by CORS policy. CORS can be tricky sometimes, and I encourage you to read more about it on the Mozilla Developer Network page dedicated to this security policy: `https://developer.mozilla.org/en-US/docs/Web/HTTP/CORS`.

The second problem relates to exposing the authorization token to the client. In fact, if we open the Google Chrome developer tools and go to **Network**, we can select the HTTP request for the endpoint and see the authorization token in plain text in the **Request Headers** section:

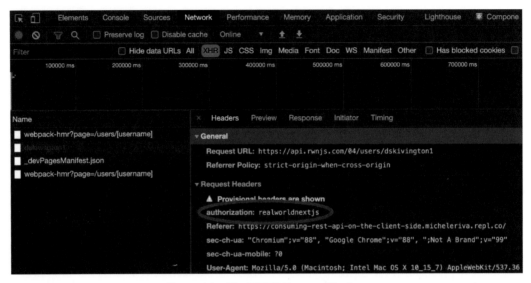

Figure 4.3 – The HTTP Request Headers

So, what's wrong with that?

Imagine that you're paying for a service exposing live weather updates via an API and pretend that it costs $1 for every 100 requests.

A malicious user who wants to use that same service without paying could easily find your private authorization token in the request header and use it to power their weather web app. That way, if the malicious user makes 1,000 requests, you'll be paying $10 without actually using their services.

We can quickly solve both problems thanks to the Next.js API pages, which allows us to quickly create a REST API, making the HTTP request for use on the server side and returning the result to the client.

Let's create a new folder inside pages/ called api/ and a new file, pages/api/ singleUser.js:

```
import axios from 'axios';

export default async function handler(req, res) {
  const username = req.query.username;
```

```
const API_ENDPOINT = process.env.API_ENDPOINT;
const API_TOKEN = process.env.API_TOKEN;

const userReq = await axios.get(
  `${API_ENDPOINT}/04/users/${username}`,
  { headers: { authorization: API_TOKEN } }
);

res
  .status(200)
  .json(userReq.data);
}
```

As you can see, in this case, we're exposing a simple function taking two arguments:

- req: An instance of Node.js' http.IncomingMessage (https://nodejs.
  org/api/http.html#http_class_http_incomingmessage) merged
  with some pre-built middlewares such as req.cookies, req.query, and
  req.body.

- res: An instance of Node.js' http.serverResponse (https://nodejs.
  org/api/http.html#http_class_http_serverresponse), merged with
  some pre-built middleware such as res.status(code) for setting the HTTP
  status code, res.json(json) for returning a valid JSON, res.send(body)
  for sending an HTTP response containing a string, an object, or a Buffer,
  and res.redirect([status,] path) for redirecting to a specific page with
  a given (and optional) status code.

Every file inside the pages/api/ directory will be considered by Next.js as an API route.

Now we can refactor our UserPage component by changing the API endpoint to the
newly created one:

```
function UserPage({ username }) {

  const [loading, setLoading] = useState(true);
  const [data, setData] = useState(null);

  useEffect(async () => {
    const req = await fetch(
```

```
      `/api/singleUser?username=${username}`,
    );
    const data = await req.json();

    setLoading(false);
    setData(data);
  }, []);

  return (
    <div>
      <div>
        <Link href="/" passHref>
          Back to home
        </Link>
      </div>
      <hr />
      {loading && <div>Loading user data...</div>}
      {data && <UserData user={data} />}
    </div>
  );
}
```

If we now try to run our website, we will see that both our problems are solved!

But there's still something we need to pay attention to. We've hidden the API token by writing a kind of *proxy* for the single user API, but a malicious user would still be able to use the /api/singleUser route to access private data with ease.

To solve that specific problem, we can act in a variety of different ways:

- Render the component list exclusively on the server, just like in the previous section: That way, a malicious user won't call a private API or steal a secret API token. However, there are cases where you cannot run those kinds of API calls on the server only; if you need to make a REST request after the user clicks on a button, you're forced to make it on the client side.

- Use an authentication method to let authenticated users only access a specific API (JWT, API key, and so on).

- Use a backend framework such as **Ruby on Rails**, **Spring**, **Laravel**, **Nest.js**, and **Strapi**: They all provide different ways of securing your API calls from the client, making it way more comfortable for us to create secure Next.js applications.

In *Chapter 13*, *Building an E-commerce Website with Next.js and GraphCMS*, we will see how to use Next.js as a frontend for different CMSes and e-commerce platforms, and we'll also cover user authentication and secure API calls. For now, in this chapter, we will only focus on how to make HTTP requests from both the server and client.

In the next section, we will see how to adopt GraphQL as a REST alternative for fetching data in Next.js.

Consuming GraphQL APIs

GraphQL has been a game-changer in the API world, and it is increasing its popularity thanks to its ease of use, modularity, and flexibility.

For those who are not very familiar with GraphQL, it is basically a query language for APIs first invented by *Facebook* back in 2012. It improves many key aspects of data fetching and manipulation compared to other web service architectures such as REST or SOAP. In fact, it allows you to avoid data over-fetching (you can simply query the data fields you need), get multiple resources within a single request, obtain a strongly and statically typed interface for your data, avoid API versioning, and so on.

In this section, we will be using Apollo Client (`https://www.apollographql.com/docs/react`), a very popular GraphQL client with built-in support for both React and Next.js for building a very simple online signbook.

Let's start by creating a new project:

```
npx create-next-app signbook
```

Now, let's add a couple of dependencies:

```
yarn add @apollo/client graphql isomorphic-unfetch
```

We will need now to create an Apollo client for our Next.js application. We will do that by creating a new file inside `lib/apollo/index.js` and then writing the following function:

```
import { useMemo } from 'react';
import {
  ApolloClient,
  HttpLink,
```

```
    InMemoryCache
} from '@apollo/client';


let uri = 'https://rwnjssignbook.herokuapp.com/v1/graphql';
let apolloClient;


function createApolloClient() {
  return new ApolloClient({
    ssrMode: typeof window === 'undefined',
    link: new HttpLink({ uri }),
    cache: new InMemoryCache(),
  });
}
```

As you can assume, by setting ssrMode: typeof window === "undefined", we will use the same Apollo instance for both client and server. Also, ApolloClient uses the browser fetch API to make HTTP requests, so we'll need to import a polyfill to make it work on the server side; in that case, we'll be using isomorphic-unfetch.

If you try to run https://api.realworldnextjs.com/04/signbook/graphql on a browser, it will redirect you to a public *GraphCMS* GraphQL editor. In fact, we will be using that headless CMS as the data source for the application we're currently writing.

Inside the same lib/apollo/index.js file, let's add a new function to initialize the Apollo client:

```
export function initApollo(initialState = null) {

  const client = apolloClient || createApolloClient();

  if (initialState) {
    client.cache.restore({
      ...client.extract(),
      ...initialState
    });
  }

  if (typeof window === "undefined") {
    return client;
```

```
    }

    if (!apolloClient) {
      apolloClient = client;
    }

    return client;
}
```

This function will allow us to avoid recreating a new Apollo client for each page. In fact, we will store a client instance on the server (inside the previously written `apolloClient` variable), where we can pass an initial state as an argument. If we pass that parameter to the `initApollo` function, it will be merged with the local cache to restore a full representation of the state once we move to another page.

To achieve that, we will first need to add another `import` statement to the `lib/apollo/index.js` file. Given that re-initializing the Apollo client with a complex initial state can be an expensive task in terms of performance, we will use the React `useMemo` hook to speed up the process:

```
import { useMemo } from "react";
```

And then, we will `export` one last function:

```
export function useApollo(initialState) {
  return useMemo(
    () => initApollo(initialState),
    [initialState]
  );
}
```

Moving to our `pages/` directory, we can now create a new `_app.js` file, as seen in *Chapter 3, Next.js Basics and Built-In Components*. Here, we will wrap the whole app using the official Apollo context provider:

```
import { ApolloProvider } from "@apollo/client";
import { useApollo } from "../lib/apollo";

export default function App({ Component, pageProps }) {
  const apolloClient =
```

```
    useApollo(pageProps.initialApolloState);

  return (
    <ApolloProvider client={apolloClient}>
      <Component {...pageProps} />
    </ApolloProvider>
  );
}
```

We can finally start to write our queries!

We will organize our queries inside a new folder called `lib/apollo/queries/`.

Let's start by creating a new file, `lib/apollo/queries/getLatestSigns.js`, exposing the following GraphQL query:

```
import { gql } from "@apollo/client";

const GET_LATEST_SIGNS = gql`
  query GetLatestSigns($limit: Int! = 10, $skip: Int! = 0){
    sign(
      offset: $skip,
      limit: $limit,
      order_by: { created_at: desc }
    ) {
      uuid
      created_at
      content
      nickname
      country
    }
  }
`;

export default GET_LATEST_SIGNS;
```

We can now `import` this query inside our `pages/index.js` file and try to make our first GraphQL request using Apollo and Next.js:

```
import { useQuery } from "@apollo/client";
import GET_LATEST_SIGNS from
   '../lib/apollo/queries/getLatestSigns'

function HomePage() {
  const { loading, data } = useQuery(GET_LATEST_SIGNS, {
    fetchPolicy: 'no-cache',
  });

  return <div></div>
}

export default HomePage
```

As you can see, the Apollo client is incredibly easy to use. Thanks to the `useQuery` hook, we will have access to three different states:

- `loading`: As the name suggests, it only returns `true` or `false` when a request is fulfilled or is still pending.
- `error`: If the request fails for any reason, we will be able to catch the error and send a nice message to the user.
- `data`: Contains the data we asked for with our query.

Now, let's move back to our home page page for a moment. For simplicity, we will just add a remote *TailwindCSS* dependency for styling our demo app. In *Chapter 6, CSS and Built-In Styling Methods*, and *Chapter 7, Using UI Frameworks*, we will see how to optimize and integrate UI frameworks, but for now, we will keep things simple as we want to focus just on the data-fetching part of our application.

Open the `pages/index.js` file and edit it as follows:

```
import Head from "next/head";
import { ApolloProvider } from "@apollo/client";
import { useApollo } from "../lib/apollo";

export default function App({ Component, pageProps }) {
```

```
    const apolloClient =
        useApollo(pageProps.initialApolloState || {});

  return (
    <ApolloProvider client={apolloClient}>
      <Head>
        <link href="https://unpkg.com/tailwindcss@^2/dist/
          tailwind.min.css"
         rel="stylesheet"
        />
      </Head>
      <Component {...pageProps} />
    </ApolloProvider>
  );
}
```

Now, we can create a new file, components/Loading.js. We will render it while we're fetching the signs from GraphCMS:

```
function Loading() {
  return (
    <div
      className="min-h-screen w-screen flex justify-center
        items-center">
      Loading signs from Hasura...
    </div>
  );
}

export default Loading;
```

Once we have successfully fetched the desired data, we need to display it on the home page. To do that, we will create a new component inside the components/Sign.js file with the following content:

```
function Sign({ content, nickname, country }) {
  return (
    <div className="max-w-7xl rounded-md border-2 border-
```

```
      purple-800 shadow-xl bg-purple-50 p-7 mb-10">
        <p className="text-gray-700"> {content} </p>
        <hr className="mt-3 mb-3 border-t-0 border-b-2
          border-purple-800" />
        <div>
          <div className="text-purple-900">
            Written by <b>{nickname}</b>
            {country && <span> from {country}</span>}
          </div>
        </div>
      </div>
    );
}
```

```
export default Sign;
```

Now, let's integrate those two new components inside our home page:

```
import { useQuery } from "@apollo/client";
import GET_LATEST_SIGNS from
  '../lib/apollo/queries/getLatestSigns'
import Sign from '../components/Sign'
import Loading from '../components/Loading'

function HomePage() {
  const { loading, error, data } =
    useQuery(GET_LATEST_SIGNS, {
      fetchPolicy: 'no-cache',
    });



  if (loading) {
    return <Loading />;
  }

  return (
    <div className="flex justify-center items-center flex-
```

```
          col mt-20">
          <h1 className="text-3xl mb-5">Real-World Next.js
            signbook</h1>
          <Link href="/new-sign">
            <button className="mb-8 border-2 border-purple-800
              text-purple-900 p-2 rounded-lg text-gray-50
                m-auto  mt-4">
              Add new sign
            </button>
          </Link>
          <div>
            {data.sign.map((sign) => (
              <Sign key={sign.uuid} {...sign} />
            ))}
          </div>
        </div>
      );
    }
```

```
export default HomePage
```

If we now try to browse the home page, we will see a list of signs!

We could also create a simple route for adding a new sign by creating a new page under pages/new-sign.js. Let's start by adding the required imports for that page:

```
import { useState } from "react";
import Link from "next/link";
import { useRouter } from "next/router";
import { useMutation } from "@apollo/client";
import ADD_SIGN from "../lib/apollo/queries/addSign";
```

As you can see, we're importing a bunch of functions from different libraries. We will use the useState React hook to keep track of the changes in our form for submitting the sign, Next.js' useRouter hook for redirecting the user to the home page once they have created a new sign, and Apollo's useMutation hook for creating a new sign on GraphCMS. We also import a new GraphQL mutation called ADD_SIGN, and we will see this in detail after we have created this page.

Moving on, we create the page structure:

```
function NewSign() {
  const router = useRouter();
  const [formState, setFormState] = useState({});
  const [addSign] = useMutation(ADD_SIGN, {
    onCompleted() {
      router.push("/");
    }
  });

  const handleInput = ({ e, name }) => {
    setFormState({
      ...formState,
      [name]: e.target.value
    });
  };
}

export default NewSign;
```

Reading from top to bottom, we can see that we're using Apollo's `useMutation` hook to create a new sign. Once the sign has been created correctly, it will run the `onCompleted` callback, where we will redirect the user to the home page.

Moving to the next function declared inside the component body, we can clearly see that we'll use the `handleInput` function to dynamically set the form state using the React `useState` hook as soon as the user types something in any form input.

We now need to render the actual HTML containing a form with just three inputs: the user's `nickname`, a message to be written in the `signbook`, and (optionally) the `country` where the user is writing from:

```
return (
    <div className="flex justify-center items-center flex-
      col mt-20">
      <h1 className="text-3xl mb-10">Sign the Real-World
        Next.js signbook!</h1>
      <div className="max-w-7xl shadow-xl bg-purple-50 p-7
```

```
            mb-10 grid grid-rows-1 gap-4 rounded-md border-2
         border- purple-800">
    <div>
        <label htmlFor="nickname" className="text-purple-
            900 mb-2">
          Nickname
        </label>
        <input
          id="nickname"
          type="text"
          onChange={(e) => handleInput({ e, name:
            'nickname' })}
          placeholder="Your name"
          className="p-2 rounded-lg w-full"
        />
    </div>
    <div>
        <label htmlFor="content" className="text-purple-
            900 mb-2">
          Leave a message!
        </label>
        <textarea
          id="content"
          placeholder="Leave a message here!"
          onChange={(e) => handleInput({ e, name:
            'content' })}
          className="p-2 rounded-lg w-full"
        />
    </div>
    <div>
        <label htmlFor="country" className="text-purple-
            900 mb-2">
          If you want, write your country name and its
            emoji flag
        </label>
        <input
```

```
            id="country"
            type="text"
            onChange={(e) => handleInput({ e, name:
              'country' })}
            placeholder="Country"
            className="p-2 rounded-lg w-full"
          />

          <button
            className="bg-purple-600 p-4 rounded-lg text-
              gray-50 m-auto mt-4"
            onClick={() => addSign({ variables: formState })}>
            Submit
          </button>
        </div>
      </div>
      <Link href="/" passHref>
        <a className="mt-5 underline"> Back to the
          homepage</a>
      </Link>
    </div>
  );
)
```

Let's take a closer look at how we create a mutation by clicking the submit button:

```
onClick={() => addSign({ variables: formState})}
```

As you can see, we're taking the entire state stored inside the `formState` variable coming from the `useState` hook and passing it as a value for the `variables` property used by the `addSign` function:

```
const [addSign] = useMutation(ADD_SIGN, {
  onCompleted() {
    router.push("/");
  }
});
```

The `addSign` function represents the mutation that will add a new sign to GraphCMS, and we can add dynamic data by passing an object matching the mutation variables written inside the `lib/apollo/queries/addSign.js` file:

```javascript
import { gql } from "@apollo/client";

const ADD_SIGN = gql`
  mutation InsertNewSign(
    $nickname: String!,
    $content: String!,
    $country: String
  ) {
    insert_sign(objects: {
        nickname: $nickname,
        country: $country,
        content: $content
    }) {
      returning {
        uuid
      }
    }
  }
`;

export default ADD_SIGN;
```

The `ADD_SIGN` mutation, in fact, takes three argument variables: `$nickname`, `$content`, and `$country`. Using form field names that reflect the naming of the mutation variables, we can simply pass the whole form state as a value to our mutation.

You can now try to create a new sign. After submitting the form, you will be automatically redirected to the home page and you will see your sign at the top of the page.

Summary

In this chapter, we've taken a look at two crucial topics when talking about Next.js: the project structure organization and the different ways of fetching data. Even if these two topics seem unrelated, being able to logically separate components and utilities, and fetching data in different ways, are essential skills that will allow you to better understand the next chapter, *Chapter 5, Managing Local and Global States in Next.js*. As we've seen in this chapter, the complexity of any application can only grow over time as we add more features, bug fixes, and suchlike. Having a well-organized folder structure and a clear data flow can help us keep track of our application's state.

We've also taken a look at how to fetch data using GraphQL. This is an exciting topic as, in the next chapter, we will see how to use Apollo Client as a state manager other than a GraphQL client.

5
Managing Local and Global States in Next.js

State management is one of the central parts of any React application, Next.js apps included. When talking about state, we refer to those dynamic pieces of information that allow us to create highly interactive **user interfaces** (**UIs**), making our customers' experience as beautiful and enjoyable as possible.

Thinking about modern websites, we can spot state changes in many parts of the UI: switching from light to dark theme means that we're changing the UI theme state, filling an e-commerce form with our shipping information means that we're changing that form state, even clicking on a simple button can potentially change a local state, as it can lead our UI to react in many different ways, depending on how the developers decided to manage that state update.

Even though state management allows us to create beautiful interactions inside our applications, it comes with some extra complexities. Many developers have come up with very different solutions to manage them, allowing us to manage the application state in more straightforward and organized ways.

Talking about React specifically, since the first versions of the library, we had access to the class components, where the class kept a local state, allowing us to interact with it via the `setState` method. With more modern React versions (>16.8.0), that process has been simplified with the introduction of React Hooks, including the `useState` Hook.

The most significant difficulty in managing state in a React application is that the data flow should be unidirectional, meaning that we can pass a given state as a prop to a child component, but we cannot do the same with a parent element. That means that local state management can be effortless thanks to class components and Hooks, but global state management can become really convoluted.

In this chapter, we will take a look at two different approaches for managing the global application state. First, we will see how to use React Context APIs; then, we will rewrite the application using **Redux**, which will let us understand how to initialize an external library for state management both on the client and server side.

We will look in detail at the following topics:

- Local state management
- Managing the application state via the Context APIs
- Managing the application state via Redux

By the end of this chapter, you will learn the differences between local and global state management. You will also learn how to manage the global application state using the React built-in Context APIs or an external library such as Redux.

Technical requirements

To run the code examples in this chapter, you need to have both Node.js and npm installed on your local machine. If you prefer, you can use an online IDE such as `https://repl.it` or `https://codesandbox.io`, as they both support Next.js, and you don't need to install any dependency on your computer.

As with the other chapters, you can find the code base for this chapter on GitHub: `https://github.com/PacktPublishing/Real-World-Next.js`.

Local state management

When talking about local state management, we're referring to application state that is *component-scoped*. We can summarize that concept with an elementary `Counter` component:

```
import React, { useState } from "react";

function Counter({ initialCount = 0 }) {
  const [count, setCount] = useState(initialCount);

  return (
    <div>
      <b>Count is: {count}</b><br />
      <button onClick={() => setCount(count + 1)}>
        Increment +
      </button>
      <button onClick={() => setCount(count - 1)}>
        Decrement -
      </button>
    </div>
  )
}

export default Counter;
```

When we click on the `Increment` button, we will add 1 to the current `count` value. Vice-versa, we will subtract 1 to that value when we click on the `Decrement` button; nothing special!

But while it's easy for a parent component to pass an `initialCount` value as a prop for the `Counter` element, it can be way more challenging to do the opposite: passing the current `count` value to the parent component. There are many cases where we need to manage just the local state, and the React `useState` Hook can be an excellent way to do so. Those cases can include (but are not limited to) the following:

- **Atom components**: As seen in *Chapter 4, Organizing the Code Base and Fetching Data in Next.js*, atoms are the most essential React components we can encounter, and they're likely to manage little local states only. More complex states can be delegated to **molecules** or **organisms** in many cases.

- **Loading states**: When fetching external data on the client side, we always have a moment when we have neither some data nor an error, as we're still waiting for the HTTP request to complete. We can decide to handle that by setting a `loading` state to `true` until the fetch request is completed to display a nice loading spinner on the UI.

React Hooks such as `useState` and `useReducer` make local state management effortless, and most of the time, you don't need any external library to handle it.

Things can change once you need to maintain a global application state across all of your components. A typical example could be an e-commerce website, where once you add an item to the shopping cart, you may want to display the number of products you're buying with an icon inside your navigation bar.

We will talk about this specific example right in the next section.

Global state management

When talking about the global application state, we refer to a state shared between all the components for a given web application that is, therefore, reachable and modifiable by any component.

As seen in the previous section, the React data flow is unidirectional, meaning that components can pass data to their children components, but not to their parents (unlike Vue or Angular). That makes our components less error prone, easier to debug, and more efficient, but adds extra complexity: by default, there cannot be a global state.

Let's take a look at the following scenario:

Figure 5.1 – A link between product cards and items in the cart

In the web application shown in the preceding screenshot, we want to display many products and let our users put them in the shopping cart. The biggest problem here is that there's no link between the data shown in the navigation bar and the product cards, and it can be non-trivial to update the number of products in the cart as soon as the user clicks on the "add" button for a given product. And what if we want to keep this information on page change? It would be lost as soon as the single card components get unmounted with their local state.

Today, many libraries make it a bit easier to manage those situations: **Redux**, **Recoil**, and **MobX** are just some of the most popular solutions, but there are also other approaches. In fact, with React Hooks' introduction, we can use the *Context APIs* for managing the global application state without the need for external libraries. There's also a less popular approach that I'd like to take into consideration: using **Apollo Client** (and its **in-memory cache**). That would change the way we think of our state and gives us a formal query language for interacting with the global application data. If you're interested in that approach, I'd highly recommend reading the official Apollo GraphQL tutorial: `https://www.apollographql.com/docs/react/local-state/local-state-management`.

Starting from the next section, we will be building a very minimal storefront, just like the one we saw in the previous figure. Once the user adds one or more products to the shopping cart, we will update the count inside of the navigation bar. Once the user decides to proceed with the checkout, we will need to display the selected products on the checkout page.

Using the Context APIs

With **React v16.3.0**, released back in 2018, we finally got access to stable Context APIs. They give us a straightforward way to share data between all the components inside a given context without explicitly having to pass it via props from one component to another, even from children to a parent component. If you want to learn more about React Context, I highly recommend reading the official React documentation: `https://reactjs.org/docs/context.html`.

Starting with this section, we will always use the same boilerplate code for approaching global state management with different libraries. You can find this boilerplate code here: `https://github.com/PacktPublishing/Real-World-Next.js/tree/main/05-state-management-made-easy/boilerplate`.

We will also keep the same approach for storing the selected products in the global state for simplicity's sake; our state will be a JavaScript object. Each property is the ID of a product, and its value will represent the number of products that the user has selected. If you open the `data/items.js` file, you will find an array of objects representing our products. If a user selects four carrots and two onions, our state will look like this:

```
{
    "8321-k532": 4,
    "9126-b921": 2
}
```

That being said, let's start by creating the context for our shopping cart. We can do that by creating a new file: `components/context/cartContext.js`:

```
import { createContext } from 'react';

const ShoppingCartContext = createContext({
    items: {},
    setItems: () => null,
});

export default ShoppingCartContext;
```

Just like in a typical client-side rendered React app, we now want to wrap all the components that need to share the cart data under the same context. For instance, the `/components/Navbar.js` component needs to be mounted inside the same context as the `/components/ProductCard.js` component.

We should also consider that we want our global state to be persistent when changing the page, as we want to display the number of products selected by the user on the checkout page. That said, we can customize the `/pages/_app.js` page, as seen in *Chapter 3, Next.js Basics and Built-In Components*, to wrap the entire application under the same React context:

```
import { useState } from 'react';
import Head from 'next/head';
import CartContext from
    '../components/context/cartContext';
import Navbar from '../components/Navbar';
```

```
function MyApp({ Component, pageProps }) {
  const [items, setItems] = useState({});


  return (
    <>
      <Head>
        <link
href="https://unpkg.com/tailwindcss@^2/dist/tailwind.min.css"
          rel="stylesheet"
        />
      </Head>
      <CartContext.Provider value={{ items, setItems }}>
        <Navbar />
        <div className="w-9/12 m-auto pt-10">
          <Component {...pageProps} />
        </div>
      </CartContext.Provider>
    </>
  );
}


export default MyApp;
```

As you can see, we're wrapping both <Navbar /> and <Component {...
pageProps /> under the same context. That way, they gain access to the same global
state, creating a link between all the components rendered on every page and the
navigation bar.

Now let's take a quick look at the /pages/index.js page:

```
import ProductCard from '../components/ProductCard';
import products from '../data/items';


function Home() {
  return (
    <div className="grid grid-cols-4 gap-4">
      {products.map((product) => (
        <ProductCard key={product.id} {...product} />
```

```
      ))}
    </div>
  );
}


export default Home;
```

To make it simpler, we're importing all the products from a local JavaScript file, but of course, they could also come from a remote API. For each product, we render the `ProductCard` component, which will allow the users to add them to the shopping cart and then proceed to the checkout.

Let's take a look at the `ProductCard` component:

```
function ProductCard({ id, name, price, picture }) {
  return (
    <div className="bg-gray-200 p-6 rounded-md">
    <div className="relative 100% h-40 m-auto">
      <img src={picture} alt={name} className="object-cover" />
    </div>
    <div className="flex justify-between mt-4">
    <div className="font-bold text-1"> {name} </div>
    <div className="font-bold text-1 text-gray-500"> ${price}
      per kg </div>
    </div>
    <div className="flex justify-between mt-4 w-2/4 m-auto">
      <button
      className="pl-2 pr-2 bg-red-400 text-white rounded-md"
      disabled={false /* To be implemented */}
      onClick={() => {} /* To be implemented */}>

        -

      </button>
    <div>{/* To be implemented */}</div>
      <button
      className="pl-2 pr-2 bg-green-400 text-white rounded-md"
      onClick={()  => {} /* To be implemented */}>

        +

      </button>
```

```
    </div>
  </div>
    );
}
```

```
export default ProductCard;
```

As you can see, we are already building the UI for that component, but nothing happens when clicking on both the `increment` and `decrement` buttons. We now need to link that component to the `cartContext` context and then update the context state as soon as the user clicks on one of the two buttons:

```
import { useContext } from 'react';
import cartContext from '../components/context/cartContext';


function ProductCard({ id, name, price, picture }) {
const { setItems, items } = useContext(cartContext);


// ...
```

Using the `useContext` Hook, we're linking both `setItems` and `items` from the `_app.js` page to our `ProductCard` component. Every time we call `setItems` on that component, we will be updating the global `items` object, and that change will be propagated to all the components living under the same context and linked to the same global state. That also means that we don't need to keep a local state for each `ProductCard` component, as the information about the number of single products added to the shopping cart already exists in our context state. Therefore, if we want to know the number of products added to the shopping cart, we can proceed as follows:

```
import { useContext } from 'react';
import cartContext from '../components/context/cartContext';


function ProductCard({ id, name, price, picture })
   const { setItems, items } = useContext(cartContext);
   const productAmount = id in items ? items[id] : 0;


// ...
```

That way, every time the user clicks on the `increment` button for a given product, the global `items` state will change, the `ProductCard` component will be re-rendered, and the `productAmount` constant will end up having a new value.

Talking again about handling both `increment` and `decrement` actions, we need to control the user clicks on those buttons. We can write a generic `handleAmount` function taking a single argument that can be either `"increment"` or `"decrement"`. If the passed parameter is `"increment"`, we need to check if the current product already exists inside the global state (remember, an initial global state is an empty object). If it exists, we only need to increment its value by one; otherwise, we need to create a new property inside the `items` object where the key will be our product ID, and its value will be set to `1`.

If the parameter is `"decrement"`, we should check whether the current product already exists inside of the global `items` object. If that's the case, and the value is greater than `0`, we can just decrement it. In all other cases, we can just exit the function, as we cannot have a negative number as a value for an amount of our products:

```
import { useContext } from 'react';
import cartContext from '../components/context/cartContext';


function ProductCard({ id, name, price, picture }) {
  const { setItems, items } = useContext(cartContext);
  const productAmount = items?.[id] ?? 0;

  const handleAmount = (action) => {
    if (action === 'increment') {
      const newItemAmount = id in items ? items[id] + 1 : 1;
      setItems({ ...items, [id]: newItemAmount });
    }

    if (action === 'decrement') {
      if (items?.[id] > 0) {
        setItems({ ...items, [id]: items[id] - 1 });
      }
    }
  };

// ...
```

We now just need to update the `increment` and `decrement` buttons to trigger the `handleAmount` function on click:

```
<div className="flex justify-between mt-4 w-2/4 m-auto">
<button
   className="pl-2 pr-2 bg-red-400 text-white rounded-md"
   disabled={productAmount === 0}
   onClick={() => handleAmount('decrement')}>

   -
</button>
   <div>{productAmount}</div>
<button
   className="pl-2 pr-2 bg-green-400 text-white rounded-md"
   onClick={() => handleAmount('increment')}>

   +
</button>
</div>
```

If we now try to increment and decrement our products' amount, we will see the number inside of the `ProductCard` component changing after each button click! But looking at the navigation bar, the value will remain set to `0`, as we haven't linked the global items state to the `Navbar` component. Let's open the `/components/Navbar.js` file and type the following:

```
import { useContext } from 'react';
import Link from 'next/link';
import cartContext from '../components/context/cartContext';

function Navbar() {
   const { items } = useContext(cartContext);
   // ...
```

We don't need to update the global `items` state from our navigation bar, so, in that case, we don't need to declare the `setItems` function. In that component, we only want to display the total amount of products added to the shopping cart (for instance, if we add two carrots and one onion, we should see 3 as the total in our `Navbar`). We can do that quite easily:

```
import { useContext } from 'react';
import Link from 'next/link';
import cartContext from '../components/context/cartContext';

function Navbar() {
  const { items } = useContext(cartContext);
  const totalItemsAmount = Object.values(items)
    .reduce((x, y) => x + y, 0);

// ...
```

Now let's just display the `totalItemsAmount` variable inside of the resulting HTML:

```
// ...

<div className="font-bold underline">
  <Link href="/cart" passHref>
    <a>{totalItemsAmount} items in cart</a>
  </Link>
</div>

// ...
```

Great! We just missed one last thing: clicking on the `Navbar` link to the checkout page, we can't see any products displayed on the page. We can fix that by fixing the `/pages/cart.js` page:

```
import { useContext } from 'react';
import cartContext from '../components/context/cartContext';
import data from '../data/items';

function Cart() {
```

```
const { items } = useContext(cartContext);
// ...
```

As you can see, we're importing the context objects as usual and the complete product list. That's because we need to get the complete product info (inside the state, we only have the relationship between a product ID and product amount) for displaying the name of the product, the amount, and the total price for that product. We then need a way to get the whole product object given a product ID. We can write a getFullItem function (outside of our component) that only takes an ID and returns the entire product object:

```
import { useContext } from 'react';
import cartContext from '../components/context/cartContext';
import data from '../data/items';

function getFullItem(id) {
  const idx = data.findIndex((item) => item.id === id);
  return data[idx];
}

function Cart() {
  const { items } = useContext(cartContext);

// ...
```

Now that we have access to the complete product object, we can get the total price for all of our products inside of the shopping cart:

```
// ...

function Cart() {
  const { items } = useContext(cartContext);
  const total = Object.keys(items)
    .map((id) => getFullItem(id).price * items[id])
    .reduce((x, y) => x + y, 0);

// ...
```

We also want to display a list of products inside of the shopping cart in the format of *x2 Carrots ($7)*. We can easily create a new array called amounts and fill it with all the products we've added to the cart, plus the amount for every single product:

```
// ...

function Cart() {
  const { items } = useContext(cartContext);
  const total = Object.keys(items)
    .map((id) => getFullItem(id).price * items[id])
    .reduce((x, y) => x + y, 0);

  const amounts = Object.keys(items).map((id) => {
    const item = getFullItem(id);
    return { item, amount: items[id] };
  });

// ...
```

Now, we only need to update the returning template for that component:

```
// ...

<div>
<h1 className="text-xl font-bold"> Total: ${total} </h1>
<div>
  {amounts.map(({ item, amount }) => (
    <div key={item.id}>
      x{amount} {item.name} (${amount *
        item.price})
</div>
  ))}
</div>
</div>

// ...
```

And we're done! After booting the server, we can add as many products as we want to the shopping cart and see the total price going to the `/cart` page.

Using the context APIs in Next.js is not that difficult, as the concepts are the same for the vanilla React applications. In the next section, we will see how to achieve the same results using Redux as a global state manager.

Using Redux

In 2015, two years after the initial React public release, there weren't asmany frameworks and libraries as today for handling large-scale application states. The most advanced way for handling unidirectional data flow was Flux, which, as time has passed, has been superseded by more straightforward and modern libraries such as **Redux** and **MobX**.

Redux, in particular, had a significant impact on the React community and quickly became a de facto state manager for building large-scale applications in React.

In this section, we will be using plain Redux (without middlewares such as **redux-thunk** or **redux-saga**) for managing the storefront state instead of using the React Context APIs.

Let's start by cloning the boilerplate code from `https://github.com/ PacktPublishing/Real-World-Next.js/tree/main/05-managing- local-and-global-states-in-nextjs/boilerplate` (just like we did in the previous section).

At this point, we will need to install two new dependencies:

```
yarn add redux react-redux
```

We can also install the **Redux DevTools extension**, which allows us to inspect and debug the application state from our browser:

```
yarn add -D redux-devtools-extension
```

Now we can start coding our Next.js + Redux application.

First of all, we will need to initialize the global store, which is the part of our application containing the application state. We can do that by creating a new folder inside of the root of our project, calling it `redux/`. Here we can write a new `store.js` file containing the logic for initializing our store on both the client side and server side:

```
import { useMemo } from 'react';
import { createStore, applyMiddleware } from 'redux';
```

```
import { composeWithDevTools } from 'redux-devtools-extension';

let store;

const initialState = {};

// ...
```

As you can see, we start by instantiating a new variable, store, which (as you may have guessed) will be used later on for keeping the Redux store.

Then, we initialize the initialState for our Redux store. In that case, it will be an empty object, as we will add more properties depending on which product our users select on the storefront.

We now need to create our first and only reducer. In a real-world application, we would write many different reducers in many different files, making things more manageable in terms of maintainability for our project. In that case, we will write just one reducer (as it is the only one we need), and we will include that in the store.js file for simplicity's sake:

```
//...

const reducer = (state = initialState, action) => {
  const itemID = action.id;

  switch (action.type) {
    case 'INCREMENT':
      const newItemAmount = itemID in state ?
        state[itemID] + 1 : 1;
      return {
        ...state,
        [itemID]: newItemAmount,
      };
    case 'DECREMENT':
      if (state?.[itemID] > 0) {
        return {
          ...state,
          [itemID]: state[itemID] - 1,
```

```
        };
    }
    return state;
  default:
    return state;
  }
};
```

The reducer's logic is not that different from the one we wrote in the previous section inside the handleAmount function for our ProductCard component.

Now we need to initialize our store, and we can do that by creating two different functions. The first one will be a simple helper function called initStore, and it will make things easier later on:

```
// ...

function initStore(preloadedState = initialState) {
  return createStore(
    reducer,
    preloadedState,
    composeWithDevTools(applyMiddleware())
  );
}
```

The second function we need to create is the one we will use for properly initializing the store, and we're going to call it initializeStore:

```
// ...

export const initializeStore = (preloadedState) => {
  let _store = store ?? initStore(preloadedState);

  if (preloadedState && store) {
    _store = initStore({
      ...store.getState(),
      ...preloadedState,
    });
    store = undefined;
```

130 Managing Local and Global States in Next.js

```
    }

    //Return '_store' when initializing Redux on the server-side
    if (typeof window === 'undefined') return _store;
    if (!store) store = _store;

    return _store;
};
```

Now that we have our store set up, we can create one last function, a Hook we'll be using
in our components. We'll wrap it inside a `useMemo` function to take advantage of the
React built-in memoization system, which will cache complex initial states, avoiding the
system re-parsing it on every `useStore` function call:

```
// ...

export function useStore(initialState) {
  return useMemo(
    () => initializeStore(initialState), [initialState]
  );
}
```

Great! We're now ready to move on and attach Redux to our Next.js application.

Just as we did with the Context APIs in the previous section, we will need to edit our
`_app.js` file so that Redux will be globally available for every component living inside
of our Next.js app:

```
import Head from 'next/head';
import { Provider } from 'react-redux';
import { useStore } from '../redux/store';
import Navbar from '../components/Navbar';

function MyApp({ Component, pageProps }) {
  const store = useStore(pageProps.initialReduxState);
  return (
    <>
    <Head>
```

```
        <link href="https://unpkg.com/tailwindcss@^2/dist/tailwind.
          min.css" rel="stylesheet" />
    </Head>
      <Provider store={store}>
    <Navbar />
      <div className="w-9/12 m-auto pt-10">
        <Component {...pageProps} />
      </div>
      </Provider>
    </>
      );
    }
```

```
export default MyApp;
```

If you compare this _app.js file with the one we created in the previous section, you may notice some similarities. From this moment, the two implementations will look very similar, as Context APIs try to make global state management more accessible and easier for everyone, and the Redux influence in shaping those APIs is visible.

We now need to implement the increment/decrement logic for our ProductCard component using Redux. Let's start by opening the components/ProductCard.js file and add the following imports:

```
import { useDispatch, useSelector, shallowEqual } from 'react-
redux';
```

```
// ...
```

Now, let's create a Hook that will come in handy when we need to fetch all the products in our Redux store:

```
import { useDispatch, useSelector, shallowEqual } from 'react-
redux';
```

```
function useGlobalItems() {
  return useSelector((state) => state, shallowEqual);
}
```

```
// ...
```

Staying inside the same file, let's edit the `ProductCard` component by integrating the Redux Hooks we need:

```
// ...

function ProductCard({ id, name, price, picture }) {
  const dispatch = useDispatch();
  const items = useGlobalItems();
  const productAmount = items?.[id] ?? 0;

  return (

// ...
```

Finally, we need to trigger a dispatch when the user clicks on one of our component's buttons. Thanks to the `useDispatch` Hook we previously imported, that operation will be straightforward to implement. We just need to update the `onClick` callback for our HTML buttons inside the render function as follows:

```
// ...

<div className="flex justify-between mt-4 w-2/4 m-auto">
  <button
    className="pl-2 pr-2 bg-red-400 text-white rounded-md"
    disabled={productAmount === 0}
    onClick={() => dispatch({ type: 'DECREMENT', id })}>
    -
  </button>
<div>{productAmount}</div>
  <button
    className="pl-2 pr-2 bg-green-400 text-white rounded-md"
    onClick={() => dispatch({ type: 'INCREMENT', id })}>
    +
  </button>
</div>

// ...
```

Suppose you've installed the Redux DevTools extension for your browser. In that case, you can now start to increment or decrement a product and see the action as it is dispatched directly inside your debugging tools.

By the way, we still need to update the navigation bar when we add or remove a product from our cart. We can easily do that by editing the `components/NavBar.js` component just as we did for the `ProductCard` one:

```
import Link from 'next/link';
import { useSelector, shallowEqual } from 'react-redux';


function useGlobalItems() {
  return useSelector((state) => state, shallowEqual);
}


function Navbar() {
  const items = useGlobalItems();
  const totalItemsAmount = Object.keys(items)
    .map((key) => items[key])
    .reduce((x, y) => x + y, 0);


  return (
    <div className="w-full bg-purple-600 p-4 text-white">
    <div className="w-9/12 m-auto flex justify-between">
    <div className="font-bold">
      <Link href="/" passHref>
        <a> My e-commerce </a>
      </Link>
    </div>
    <div className="font-bold underline">
      <Link href="/cart" passHref>
        <a>{totalItemsAmount} items in cart</a>
      </Link>
    </div>
    </div>
    </div>
```

```
  );
}


export default Navbar;
```

We can now try to add and remove products from our storefront and see the state change reflected in the navigation bar.

One last thing before we can consider our e-commerce app complete: we need to update the /cart page so that we can see a summary of the shopping cart before moving to the checkout step. It will be incredibly easy, as we will combine what we learned from the previous section using the Context APIs and the knowledge of Redux Hooks we've just gained. Let's open the pages/Cart.js file and import the same Redux Hook we used for the other components:

```
import { useSelector, shallowEqual } from 'react-redux';
import data from '../data/items';


function useGlobalItems() {
   return useSelector((state) => state, shallowEqual);
}


// ...
```

At this point, we can just replicate the getFullItem function we created for the Context APIs in the previous section:

```
// ...


function getFullItem(id) {
   const idx = data.findIndex((item) => item.id === id);
   return data[idx];
}


// ...
```

The same happens for the `Cart` component. We will basically replicate what we did in the previous section, with a simple difference: the `items` object will come from the Redux store instead of a React context:

```
function Cart() {
  const items = useGlobalItems();
  const total = Object.keys(items)
    .map((id) => getFullItem(id).price * items[id])
    .reduce((x, y) => x + y, 0);

  const amounts = Object.keys(items).map((id) => {
    const item = getFullItem(id);
    return { item, amount: items[id] };
  });

  return (
    <div>
      <h1 className="text-xl font-bold"> Total: ${total}
      </h1>
      <div>
        {amounts.map(({ item, amount }) => (
          <div key={item.id}>
            x{amount} {item.name} (${amount * item.price})
      </div>
        ))}
      </div>
      </div>
  );
}

export default Cart;
```

If you now try to add a couple of products to your shopping cart, then move to the /cart page, you will see a summary of your expenses.

As you may have noticed, there aren't many differences between Context APIs and plain Redux (without using any middleware). By using Redux, by the way, you'll gain access to an incredibly vast ecosystem of plugins, middleware, and debugging tools that will make your developer experience way more effortless once you need to scale and handle very complex business logic inside of your web application.

Summary

In this chapter, we focused on state management using both React built-in APIs (the Context APIs and Hooks) and external libraries (Redux). There are many other tools and libraries for managing an application's global state (**MobX**, **Recoil**, **XState**, **Unistore**, to name just a few). You can use all of them inside your Next.js application by initializing them for both client-side and server-side usage, just like we did with Redux.

Also, you can use Apollo GraphQL and its in-memory cache for managing your application state, gaining access to a formal query language for mutating and querying your global data.

We can now create more complex and interactive web applications, managing different kinds of state with any library we want.

But once you have your data well organized and ready to use, you need to display it and render your application UI depending on your application state. In the next chapter, you will see how to style your web app by configuring and using different CSS and JavaScript libraries.

6
CSS and Built-In Styling Methods

What makes the difference between a great and a bad UI? Some people may answer "features!" and others may say "speed of interaction!" but I would personally define it as a good combination of a great design and ease of use. Your web application could potentially be the most powerful app in the world. Still, it would be difficult for your users to make it work as intended if the UI is not well designed and implemented. So here comes the concept of styling.

We all know what CSS is: *a basic set of rules telling the browser how to render HTML content graphically*. While this seems an easy task, the CSS ecosystem has evolved a lot during recent years, and so has all the tooling that helps developers build great user interfaces with modular, lightweight, and performant CSS rules.

In this chapter, we will look at several approaches to writing CSS rules. That will pave the way to *Chapter 7, Using UI Frameworks*, where we'll implement UIs using external UI frameworks and utilities to make the developer experience even smoother.

> **Attention**
>
> This chapter is not intended to teach you how to write CSS rules in any specific technology or language. Instead, we will look at the technologies Next.js integrates out of the box for writing modular, maintainable, and performant CSS styles. If any of the following technologies arouse your interest, I'd recommend reading the official documentation before moving any further into implementing a UI with them.

We will look in detail at the following topics:

- Styled JSX

- CSS modules

- How to integrate the SASS preprocessor

By the end of the chapter, you will have learned about the three different built-in styling methods, their differences, and how to configure them for your needs.

Technical requirements

To run the code examples in this chapter, you need to have both Node.js and npm installed on your local machine.

If you prefer, you can use an online IDE such as `https://repl.it` or `https://codesandbox.io`; they both support Next.js, and you don't need to install any dependency on your computer. As for the other chapters, you can find the code base for this chapter on GitHub: `https://github.com/PacktPublishing/Real-World-Next.js`.

Exploring and using Styled JSX

In this section, we will explore Styled JSX, a built-in styling mechanism provided by default by Next.js.

If you don't want to learn a new styling language such as **SASS** or **LESS** and want to integrate a bit of JavaScript into your CSS rules, you might be interested in **Styled JSX**. It's a **CSS-in-JS** library (meaning that we can use JavaScript to write CSS properties) created by Vercel, the company behind Next.js, that allows you to write CSS rules and classes that are scoped to a specific component.

Let me explain this concept with an easy example. Let's say that we have a `Button` component, and we want to style it using Styled JSX:

```
export default function Button(props) {
  return (
    <>
      <button className="button">{props.children}</button>
      <style jsx>{`
        .button {
          padding: 1em;
          border-radius: 1em;
          border: none;
          background: green;
          color: white;
        }
      `}</style>
    </>
  );
}
```

As you can see, we're using a very generic `button` class name, which is likely to cause some conflicts with other components using the same class name, right? The answer is no! Here's why Styled JSX is so powerful. Not only does it allow you to write highly dynamic CSS thanks to JavaScript, but it also makes sure that the rule you're declaring won't affect any component other than the one you're writing.

So, if we now want to create a new component called `FancyButton`, we can use the same class name and, thanks to Styled JSX, it won't override the `Button` components styles when both are rendered on page:

```
export default function FancyButton(props) {
  return (
    <>
      <button className="button">{props.children}</button>
      <style jsx>{`
        .button {
          padding: 2em;
          border-radius: 2em;
          background: purple;
```

```
            color: white;
            font-size: bold;
            border: pink solid 2px;
         }
      `}</style>
    </>
  );
}
```

The same happens with HTML selectors. If we're writing a `Highlight` component, we can simply use Styled JSX to style the whole component without even declaring a specific class:

```
export default function Highlight(props) {
  return (
    <>
      <span>{props.text}</span>
      <style jsx>{`
        span {
          background: yellow;
          font-weight: bold;
        }
      `}</style>
    </>
  );
}
```

In that case, the `<span>` style we wrote will be applied to the `Highlight` component only and won't affect any other `<span>` element inside of your pages.

If you want to create a CSS rule that will be applied to all components, you can just use the `global` prop, and Styled JSX will apply that rule to all the HTML elements matching your selector:

```
export default function Highlight(props) {
  return (
    <>
      <span>{props.text}</span>
      <style jsx global>{`
```

```
      span {
        background: yellow;
        font-weight: bold;
      }
    `}</style>
   </>
  )
}
```

In the previous example, we added the `global` prop to our style declaration, so now, every time we use a `<span>` element, it will inherit the styles we declared inside of our `Highlight` component. Of course, this can be risky, so make sure that's what you want.

If you're wondering how to get started using Styled JSX and why we haven't covered this package's installation yet... that's because Styled JSX is built into Next.js, so you can start using it right after initializing the project!

In the next section, we'll look at a more *classic* approach for writing CSS rules: CSS modules.

CSS modules

In the previous section, we saw a CSS-in-JS library, meaning that we had to write our CSS definitions in JavaScript, transforming those styling rules to plain CSS at runtime or compile time, depending on which library we choose and how we configure it.

While I personally like the CSS-in-JS approach, I eventually recognized that it has some significant drawbacks to consider when choosing the styling method for a new Next.js app.

Many CSS-in-JS libraries don't provide good IDE/code editor support, making things way harder for developers (no syntax highlighting, autocomplete, linting, and so on). Also, using CSS-in-JS forces you to adopt more and more dependencies, making your application bundle bigger and slower.

Talking about performance, here's another big drawback: even if we pre-generate CSS rules on the server side, we would need to re-generate them after React hydration on the client side. That adds a high runtime cost, making the web application slower and slower, and it will only worsen when we add more features to our app.

But here comes an excellent alternative to Styled-JSX: CSS modules. In the previous section, we talked about locally-scoped CSS rules and how Styled-JSX makes it easy to create CSS classes with the same names but different purposes (avoiding naming collisions). CSS modules bring the same concept to the table by writing plain CSS classes, then importing them to your React components without any runtime cost.

Let's look at an elementary example: a simple landing page with a blue background and welcome text. Let's start by creating a new Next.js app, then creating the `pages/index.js` file as follows:

```
import styles from '../styles/Home.module.css';

export default function Home() {
  return (
    <div className={styles.homepage}>
      <h1> Welcome to the CSS Modules example </h1>
    </div>
  );
}
```

As you can see, we're importing our CSS classes from a plain CSS file ending with `.module.css`. Even though `Home.module.css` is a CSS file, CSS modules transform its content into a JavaScript object, where every key is a class name. Let's look at the `Home.module.css` file in detail:

```
.homepage {
  display: flex;
  justify-content: center;
  align-items: center;
  width: 100%;
  min-height: 100vh;
  background-color: #2196f3;
}


.title {
  color: #f5f5f5;
}
```

And after running it, here's the result:

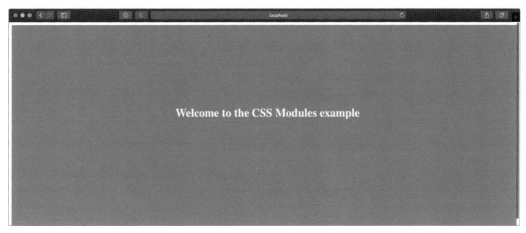

Figure 6.1 – Home page styled with CSS modules

As mentioned before, those classes are component-scoped. If you inspect the generated HTML page, your landing page will contain a `div` with a class that looks like this:

```
<div class="Home_homepage__14e3j">
  <h1 class="Home_title__3DjR7">
    Welcome to the CSS Modules example
  </h1>
</div>
```

As you can see, CSS modules generated unique class names for our rules. Even if we now create new classes using the same generic `title` and `homepage` names in other CSS files, there won't be any naming collision thanks to that strategy.

But there might be cases where we want our rules to be global. For instance, if we try to render the home page we just created, we will notice that the font family is still the default one. There's also the default `body` margin, and we might want to override those default settings. We can quickly solve that problem by creating a new `styles/globals.css` file with the following content:

```
html,
body {
  padding: 0;
  margin: 0;
  font-family: sans-serif;
}
```

We can then import it into our pages/_app.js file:

```
import '../styles/globals.css';

function MyApp({ Component, pageProps }) {
  return <Component {...pageProps} />;
}

export default MyApp;
```

If we try to render the home page now, we will see that the default body margin has disappeared, and the font now is a sans-serif one:

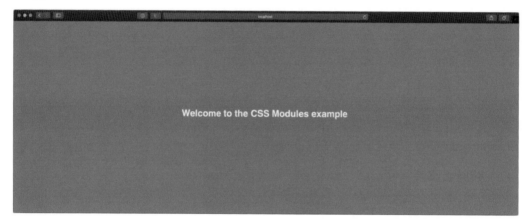

Figure 6.2 – Home page styled with global CSS module styles

We can also use the :global keyword to create globally available CSS rules, for example:

```
.button :global {
  padding: 5px;
  background-color: blue;
  color: white;
  border: none;
  border-radius: 5px;
}
```

There's also another excellent CSS module feature that I'd like you to consider when testing out that styling method: **selector composition**.

In fact, you can create a very generic rule and then override some of its properties by using the `composes` property:

```css
.button-default {
  padding: 5px;
  border: none;
  border-radius: 5px;
  background-color: grey;
  color: black;
}

.button-success {
  composes: button-default;
  background-color: green;
  color: white;
}

.button-danger {
  composes: button-default;
  background-color: red;
  color: white;
}
```

The main idea of CSS modules is to provide a straightforward way to write modular CSS classes with zero runtime costs in every language. Thanks to **PostCSS modules** (`https://github.com/madyankin/postcss-modules`), you can use CSS modules in basically every language (PHP, Ruby, Java, and so on) and templating engine (Pug, Mustache, EJS, and so on).

We've only scratched the surface of CSS modules and why they are an excellent solution for writing modular, lightweight, classes with zero runtime cost. If you want to learn more about CSS module specifications, you can look at the official repository: `https://github.com/css-modules/css-modules`.

Just like Styled JSX, CSS modules are available out of the box in every Next.js installation, so once you bootstrap your project, you can get started using them immediately. Still, you might need to tweak the default configuration to add, remove, or edit some features, and Next.js makes this step easy too.

In fact, Next.js compiles CSS modules using **PostCSS**, a popular tool for compiling CSS at build time.

By default, it is configured by Next.js to include the following features:

- *Autoprefixer*: It adds vendor prefixes to your CSS rules using values from **Can I Use** (`https://caniuse.com`). For instance, if you're writing a rule for the `::placeholder` selector, it will compile it to make it compatible with all the browsers where the selector is slightly different, such as `:-ms-input-placeholder`, `::-moz-placeholder`, and so on. You can learn more about that feature at `https://github.com/postcss/autoprefixer`.

- *Cross-browser flexbox bug fixes*: PostCSS follows a community-curated list of flexbox issues (which can be found at `https://github.com/philipwalton/flexbugs`) and adds some workarounds for making it work correctly on every browser.

- *IE11 compatibility*: PostCSS compiles new CSS features, making them available on older browsers such as IE11. Still, there's an exception: CSS variables are not compiled, as it is not safe to do so. If you really need to support older browsers and still want to use them, you can jump to the next section (*Integrating SASS with Next.js*) and use SASS/SCSS variables.

We can edit the PostCSS default configuration by creating a `postcss.config.json` file inside of our project root, then adding the default Next.js configuration:

```
{
  "plugins": [
    "postcss-flexbugs-fixes",
    [
      "postcss-preset-env",
      {
        "autoprefixer": {
          "flexbox": "no-2009"
        },
        "stage": 3,
        "features": {
          "custom-properties": false
        }
      }
    ]
```

```
        ]
    }
```

From this point, we can edit the configuration as we prefer, adding, removing, or changing any property.

In the next section, we will see how to integrate another popular CSS preprocessor: **Sass**.

Integrating SASS with Next.js

SASS is probably one of the most loved and used CSS preprocessors out there, and Next.js did an excellent job making it possible to integrate it with ease. In fact, just like CSS modules and Styled JSX, SASS is supported out of the box; we just need to install the `sass` npm package inside of our Next.js project, and we're ready to go:

```
yarn add sass
```

At this point, you can start using CSS modules with SASS and SCSS syntax, just like we did in the previous section.

Let's look at a simple example. If we open the `pages/index.js` file from the previous section, we can just change the CSS import to look as follows:

```
import styles from '../styles/Home.module.scss';

export default function Home() {
  return (
    <div className={styles.homepage}>
      <h1> Welcome to the CSS Modules example </h1>
    </div>
  );
}
```

Now we need to rename our `styles/Home.module.css` file to `styles/Home.module.scss` and we're ready to edit that file using the Sass (or SCSS) specific syntax.

Thanks to SASS and SCSS syntax, we can take advantage of a large set of features that makes our code even more modular and easy to maintain.

> **Pay Attention to the Names!**
>
> SASS and SCSS are two different syntaxes for the same CSS preprocessor. However, they both provide enhanced ways for writing CSS styles such as `for` variables, loops, mixins, and many other features.
>
> While the names may look similar, and the final purpose remains the same, the main difference is that SCSS (Sassy CSS) extends the CSS syntax by adding those features available in every `.scss` file. Any standard `.css` file can be renamed as `.scss` without any problem, as the CSS syntax is valid in `.scss` files.
>
> SASS is an older syntax that is not compatible with standard CSS. It doesn't use curly brackets or semicolons; it just uses indentation and new lines to separate properties and nested selectors.
>
> Both of those syntaxes need to be transpiled into vanilla CSS in order to be used on regular web browsers.

Let's take the CSS module `compose` property as an example. We've previously seen how to create new CSS classes extending an existing one:

```css
.button-default {
    padding: 5px;
    border: none;
    border-radius: 5px;
    background-color: grey;
    color: black;
}

.button-success {
    composes: button-default;
    background-color: green;
    color: white;
}

.button-danger {
    composes: button-default;
    background-color: red;
    color: white;
}
```

With SCSS, we can choose between many different approaches, such as using the `@extend` keyword (which works just like the `compose` keyword from CSS modules):

```scss
.button-default {
  padding: 5px;
  border: none;
  border-radius: 5px;
  background-color: grey;
  color: black;
}

.button-success {
  @extend .button-default;
  background-color: green;
  color: white;
}

.button-danger {
  @extend .button-default;
  background-color: red;
  color: white;
}
```

Alternatively, we can change our class names a bit and take advantage of the **selector nesting** feature:

```scss
.button {
  padding: 5px;
  border: none;
  border-radius: 5px;
  background-color: grey;
  color: black;

  &.success {
    background-color: green;
    color: white;
  }
```

```
    &.danger {
        background-color: red;
        color: white;
    }
}
```

SCSS ships with a large set of features, such as loops, mixins, functions, and more, allowing any developer to write complex UIs with ease.

Even though Next.js integrates it natively, you may still need to enable or disable some specific feature or edit the default SASS configuration.

You can easily do that by editing the `next.config.js` configuration file:

```
module.exports = {
    sassOptions: {
        outputStyle: 'compressed'
        // ...add any SASS configuration here
    },
}
```

If you're interested in learning more about SASS and SCSS, I'd highly recommend looking at the official documentation at `https://sass-lang.com`.

Summary

The CSS ecosystem has evolved a lot in recent years, and the Next.js team keeps the framework up to date with the most modern, performant, and modular solutions for writing CSS styles.

In this chapter, we've looked at three different built-in solutions, and of course, any one of them has some trade-offs compared with the others.

Styled JSX, for instance, is definitely one of the easiest ways of writing CSS rules. You can interoperate with JavaScript, dynamically change some CSS rules and properties depending on the user actions, and so on, but it also has some significant drawbacks. Like most CSS-in-JS libraries, Styled JSX first renders on the server side but re-renders the whole generated CSS on the client right after React hydration occurs. That adds some runtime cost to your application, making your application less performant and more challenging to scale. Also, it makes it impossible for the browser to cache your CSS rules, as they get regenerated on every request for server-side and client-side rendered pages.

SASS and SCSS syntaxes are well integrated into Next.js, and they give you tons of great features for writing complex UIs with zero runtime cost. In fact, Next.js will compile all the `.scss` and `.sass` files to plain CSS at build time, making it possible for the browser to cache all your styling rules. However, we should consider that we can't see the production-optimized plain CSS output until the final build phase. Unlike CSS modules, where what we write is really close to what we get in the final production bundle, the vast set of features provided by SASS could potentially produce a huge final CSS file, and it's not always easy to predict the compiler output while writing deeply nested rules, loops, and so on.

Ultimately, CSS modules and PostCSS seems to be an excellent option for writing modern CSS styles. The produced output is more easily predictable, and PostCSS automatically polyfills modern CSS features for older browsers (down to IE11).

In the next chapter, will see how to integrate external UI libraries, making it even easier to write style and feature-rich components and UIs.

7
Using UI Frameworks

In the previous chapter, we saw how Next.js can improve our productivity by giving us many valid alternatives for writing CSS without the need to install and configure many different external packages.

Still, there are cases where we may want to use pre-built UI libraries to take advantage of their components, themes, and built-in features so that we don't have to build them from scratch and to take advantage of a vast community that can help us when any problem occurs.

In this chapter, we will discover some modern UI libraries and learn how to integrate them properly in any Next.js application. We will look at the following in detail:

- What UI libraries are and why we might need them
- How to integrate **Chakra UI**
- How to integrate **TailwindCSS**
- How to use **Headless UI** components

By the end of the chapter, you will be able to integrate any UI library by following the tips and principles that we'll see in the following sections.

Technical requirements

To run the code examples in this chapter, you need to have both Node.js and npm installed on your local machine.

If you prefer, you can use an online IDE such as `https://repl.it` or `https://codesandbox.io`; they both support Next.js, and you don't need to install any dependency on your computer. As for the other chapters, you can find the code base for this chapter on GitHub: `https://github.com/PacktPublishing/Real-World-Next.js`.

An introduction to UI libraries

UI libraries, frameworks, and utilities are not essential. We could build any user interface (despite its complexity) from scratch using vanilla JavaScript, HTML, and CSS. Still, we would often find ourselves using the same patterns, accessibility rules, optimizations, and utility functions on every user interface we build. So here comes the concept of a UI library.

The idea is to abstract our most common use cases, reuse most of the code on different user interfaces, improve our productivity, and use well-known, tested, and **themeable** UI components.

With "themeable," we refer to those libraries and components that allow us to customize the color scheme, spacing, and the whole design language of a given framework.

We could take the popular *Bootstrap* library as an example. It allows us to override its default variables (such as colors, fonts, mixins, and so on) to customize the default theme. Thanks to that feature, we could potentially use Bootstrap on dozens of different UIs, with each UI having a very different look and feel.

While Bootstrap is still a good, tested, and well-known library, we will concentrate on more modern alternatives in the following sections. Each option will take a different approach, allowing you to understand what to look for when choosing a UI library.

Integrating Chakra UI in Next.js

Chakra UI is an open source component library used for building modular, accessible, and good-looking user interfaces.

Its main strengths are the following:

- *Accessibility*: Chakra UI allows us to use pre-built components (such as buttons, modals, inputs, and many more) created by the Chakra UI team with extra attention to accessibility.

- *Themeable*: The library ships with a default theme, where (for instance) buttons have a particular default background color, border radius, padding, and so on. We can always customize the default theme using Chakra UI built-in functions for editing every style of the library components.

- *Light and dark mode*: They're both supported out of the box and can rely on the user's system settings. If users set their computer to use dark mode by default, Chakra UI will load the dark theme as soon as it loads.

- *Composability*: We can create more and more components starting from the Chakra UI ones. The library will give us the building blocks for creating custom components with ease.

- *TypeScript support*: Chakra UI is written in TypeScript and provides first-class types for a beautiful developer experience.

To see how to integrate Chakra UI into a Next.js application, we will be building a simple company employee directory using static Markdown documents as pages.

So, let's start by creating a new Next.js project:

```
npx create-next-app employee-directory-with-chakra-ui
```

We now need to install Chakra UI and its dependencies:

```
yarn add @chakra-ui/react @emotion/react@^11 @emotion/
styled@^11 framer-motion@^4 @chakra-ui/icons
```

We're now ready to integrate Chakra UI with Next.js. To do that, let's open the pages/_ app.js file and wrap the default <Component /> component in the Chakra provider:

```
import { ChakraProvider } from '@chakra-ui/react';

function MyApp({ Component, pageProps }) {
  return (
```

```
    <ChakraProvider>
      <Component {...pageProps} />
    </ChakraProvider>
  );
}
```

```
export default MyApp;
```

Using ChakraProvider, we can also pass a theme prop containing an object representing the themes overrides. In fact, we can overwrite the default Chakra UI theme by using our custom colors, fonts, spacing, and so on, by using the built-in extendTheme function:

```
import { ChakraProvider, extendTheme } from '@chakra-
  ui/react';

const customTheme = extendTheme({
  colors: {
    brand: {
      100: '#ffebee',
      200: '#e57373',
      300: '#f44336',
      400: '#e53935',
    },
  },
});

function MyApp({ Component, pageProps }) {
  return (
    <ChakraProvider theme={customTheme}>
      <Component {...pageProps} />
    </ChakraProvider>
  );
}

export default MyApp;
```

We can now open the pages/index.js file and add some Chakra UI components using our custom colors:

```
import { VStack, Button } from '@chakra-ui/react';

export default function Home() {
  return (
    <VStack padding="10">
      <Button backgroundColor="brand.100"> brand.100
      </Button>
      <Button backgroundColor="brand.200"> brand.200
      </Button>
      <Button backgroundColor="brand.300"> brand.300
      </Button>
      <Button backgroundColor="brand.400"> brand.400
      </Button>
    </VStack>
  );
}
```

Opening the page in a web browser, we will see the following result:

Figure 7.1 – Chakra UI buttons with custom theme colors

You can feel free to add your custom styles to that Chakra UI installation before moving any further with the chapter so that the result will reflect your taste!

If you want to learn more about custom property names, I suggest you read the official guide before proceeding: https://chakra-ui.com/docs/theming/customize-theme.

One thing we've already talked about but haven't seen yet is the built-in dark/light mode support provided by Chakra UI.

The library uses the light mode by default, but we can modify this behavior by opening the pages/_document.js file and adding the following content:

```
import { ColorModeScript } from '@chakra-ui/react';
import NextDocument, {
    Html,
    Head,
    Main,
    NextScript
} from 'next/document';
import { extendTheme } from '@chakra-ui/react';

const config = {
  useSystemColorMode: true,
};

const theme = extendTheme({ config });

export default class Document extends NextDocument {
  render() {
    return (
      <Html lang="en">
        <Head />
        <body>
          <ColorModeScript
            initialColorMode={theme.config.initialColorMode}
          />
          <Main />
          <NextScript />
        </body>
      </Html>
    );
  }
}
```

The `ColorModeScript` component will inject a script allowing our application to run in light/dark mode depending on the user's preference. Given the preceding configuration, we will adopt the user system's preference for rendering the components. For example, suppose the user has set their operating system to run in dark mode. In that case, our website will render the components in dark mode by default, and vice versa, it will render the components in light mode if the user sets their operating system to that preference.

We can test that the script is working correctly by opening the `pages/index.js` file and replacing its content as follows:

```
import {
    VStack,
    Button,
    Text,
    useColorMode
} from '@chakra-ui/react';

export default function Home() {
  const { colorMode, toggleColorMode } = useColorMode();

  return (
    <VStack padding="10">
      <Text fontSize="4xl" fontWeight="bold" as="h1">
        Chakra UI
      </Text>
      <Text fontSize="2xl" fontWeight="semibold" as="h2">
        Rendering in {colorMode} mode
      </Text>
      <Button
        aria-label="UI Theme"
        onClick={toggleColorMode}
      >
        Toggle {colorMode === 'light' ? 'dark' : 'light'}
          mode
      </Button>
    </VStack>
  );
}
```

Thanks to Chakra UI's useColorMode hook, we always know what color mode is being used and can render specific components (or changing colors) depending on that value. Also, Chakra UI will remember the user's decision, so if they set the color mode to dark, they will find the same color mode applied to the web page once they come back to the website.

If we now open our website's home page, we will be able to change its color mode. The result should look like this:

Figure 7.2 – Chakra UI color mode

Now that we have taken our first steps with Chakra UI and Next.js, we're finally ready to start developing an employee directory.

The website will be pretty simple: it will only have a home page listing all the employees of a fictional company that we'll call *ACME Corporation* and a single page for every single user.

On every page, we will have a button for switching from dark to light mode and vice versa.

Building an employee directory with Chakra UI and Next.js

We can reuse the project we already set up in the introduction section for Chakra UI and Next.js to build our employee directory. Still, we will need to make some minor changes to the code we have already written.

If you have any doubts, you can see the complete website example on GitHub: https://github.com/PacktPublishing/Real-World-Next.js/tree/main/07-using-ui-frameworks/with-chakra-ui.

First of all, we will need the employee data. You can find a complete employee list (generated with fake data) at this URL: `https://github.com/PacktPublishing/Real-World-Next.js/blob/main/07-using-ui-frameworks/with-chakra-ui/data/users.js`. If you prefer, you can write custom employee data by creating an array of objects, where each object must have the following properties:

- `id`
- `username`
- `first_name`
- `last_name`
- `description`
- `job_title`
- `avatar`
- `cover_image`

Now create a new directory called `/data` and a JavaScript file called `users.js`, where we'll place our employee data:

```
export default [
  {
    id: 'QW3xhqQmTI4',
    username: 'elegrice5',
    first_name: 'Edi',
    last_name: 'Le Grice',
    description: 'Aenean lectus. Pellentesque eget
      nunc...',
    job_title: 'Marketing Assistant',
    avatar:
      'https://robohash.org/elegrice5.jpg?size=350x350',
    Cover_image:
      'https://picsum.photos/seed/elegrice5/1920/1080',
  },
  // ...other employee's data
];
```

We can leave the `pages/_document.js` file untouched from the introduction section. This way, we will have access to the dark/light theme switch for our website.

Going to the pages/_app.js page, we can modify its content by including a new
TopBar component (which we will create in just a moment) and removing the custom
theme, as we don't need it for the moment:

```
import { ChakraProvider, Box } from '@chakra-ui/react';
import TopBar from '../components/TopBar';

function MyApp({ Component, pageProps }) {
  return (
    <ChakraProvider>
      <TopBar />
      <Box maxWidth="container.xl" margin="auto">
        <Component {...pageProps} />
      </Box>
    </ChakraProvider>
  );
}

export default MyApp;
```

As you can see in the previous code block, we've wrapped our <Component />
component in a Chakra UI Box component.

By default, <Box> acts as an empty <div>, and like any other Chakra UI component, it
accepts any CSS directive as a prop. In this case, we're using margin="auto" (which
translates to margin: auto) and maxWidth="container.xl", which translates to
max-width: var(--chakra-sizes-container-xl).

Let's create a new file, /components/TopBar/index.js, and create the
TopBar component:

```
import { Box, Button, useColorMode } from '@chakra-ui/react';
import { MoonIcon, SunIcon } from '@chakra-ui/icons';

function TopBar() {
  const { colorMode, toggleColorMode } = useColorMode();
```

```
const ColorModeIcon = colorMode === 'light' ? SunIcon :
  MoonIcon;

return (
  <Box width="100%" padding="1"
    backgroundColor="whatsapp.500">
    <Box maxWidth="container.xl" margin="auto">
      <Button
        aria-label="UI Theme"
        leftIcon={<ColorModeIcon />}
        onClick={toggleColorMode}
        size="xs"
        marginRight="2"
        borderRadius="sm">
        Toggle theme
      </Button>
    </Box>
  </Box>
);
}

export default TopBar;
```

This component is not different from the one we already created in the previous section; every time the user clicks on the button, it will toggle dark/light mode using the Chakra UI built-in `toggleColorMode` function.

We can now create one more component inside a new `components/UserCard/index.js` file:

```
import Link from 'next/link';
import {
  Box, Text, Avatar, Center, VStack, useColorModeValue
  } from '@chakra-ui/react';

function UserCard(props) {
  return (
    <Link href={`/user/${props.username}`} passHref>
```

```
            <a>
                <VStack
                    spacing="4"
                    borderRadius="md"
                    boxShadow="xl"
                    padding="5"
                    backgroundColor={
                        useColorModeValue('gray.50', 'gray.700')
                    }>
                    <Center>
                        <Avatar size="lg" src={props.avatar} />
                    </Center>
                    <Center>
                        <Box textAlign="center">
                            <Text fontWeight="bold" fontSize="xl">
                                {props.first_name} {props.last_name}
                            </Text>
                            <Text fontSize="xs"> {props.job_title}</Text>
                        </Box>
                    </Center>
                </VStack>
            </a>
        </Link>
    );
}


export default UserCard;
```

As you can see, we're wrapping the whole component inside a Next.js `<Link>` component, passing the `href` value to an `<a>` child element.

We're then using the vertical stack (`VStack`) component, which uses *flexbox* under the hood, to help us to arrange the child elements vertically.

Depending on the selected color theme, we may want different background colors for our user card. We can achieve that by using the Chakra UI built-in `useColorModeValue`:

```
backgroundColor={useColorModeValue('gray.50', 'gray.700')}>
```

The first value (`'gray.50'`) will be applied by Chakra UI when the user selects the light theme. When the dark theme is selected, the UI library will use the second value (`'gray.700'`) instead.

If we now pass the right props to our `<UserCard>` component, we will see something like this:

Figure 7.3 – The UserCard component

We're finally ready to render the employee list on our home page! Let's head to our `pages/index.js` file, import the employee list, and display them using the newly created `UserCard` component:

```
import { Box, Grid, Text, GridItem } from '@chakra-ui/react';
import UserCard from '../components/UserCard';
import users from '../data/users';

export default function Home() {
  return (
    <Box>
      <Text
        fontSize="xxx-large"
        fontWeight="extrabold"
        textAlign="center"
        marginTop="9">
        ACME Corporation Employees
      </Text>
      <Grid
        gridTemplateColumns={
          ['1fr', 'repeat(2, 1fr)', 'repeat(3, 1fr)']
        }
        gridGap="10"
```

```
        padding="10">
        {users.map((user) => (
            <GridItem key={user.id}>
                <UserCard {...user} />
            </GridItem>
        ))}
        </Grid>
    </Box>
  );
}
```

On this page, we can spot another nice Chakra UI feature: responsive props. We're using the `<Grid>` component to build a grid template for our users' cards:

```
gridTemplateColumns={
    ['1fr', 'repeat(2, 1fr)', 'repeat(3, 1fr)']
}
```

Every Chakra UI prop can accept an array of values as input. In the preceding example, the UI library will render `'1fr'` on mobile screens, `'repeat(2, 1fr)'` on medium screens (for example, a tablet), and `'repeat(3, 1fr)'` on larger screens (desktop).

We can finally run the development server and see the result:

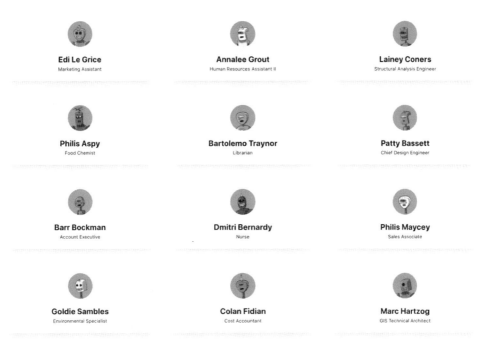

Figure 7.4 – Employee directory home page in light mode

In my case, I had the system preference set to **light theme**, so Chakra UI rendered the page using its light theme by default. We can always change that by clicking on the **Toggle theme** button in the `TopBar` component:

Figure 7.5 – Employee directory home page in dark mode

We now only need to create a single employee page.

Let's create a new file called `pages/users/[username].js`; here, we'll use the Next.js built-in methods to statically render each page at build time.

We can start by importing the `users.js` file and create all the static paths using the Next.js `getStaticPaths` function:

```
import users from '../../data/users';


export function getStaticPaths() {
  const paths = users.map((user) => ({
    params: {
```

```
            username: user.username
        }
    }));

    return {
        paths,
        fallback: false
    };
}
```

With the `getStaticPaths` function, we're telling Next.js that we need to render a new page for each user found in the users' array.

We're also telling Next.js to display a 404 page if the requested path hasn't been generated at build time; we do that by using the `fallback: false` property.

If set to `true`, that property tells Next.js to try to render a page on the server side if it hasn't been rendered at build time. That's because we may want to get the pages from a database or external API, and we don't want to rebuild the whole website every time we create a new page. So, when we set `fallback` to `true`, Next.js will rerun the `getStaticProps` function on the server side, render the page, and serve it as a static page.

In this case, we don't need this feature as we're taking our data from a static JavaScript file, but we'll use the feature in later chapters.

Let's move on by writing the `getStaticProps` function:

```
export function getStaticProps({ params }) {
    const { username } = params;

    return {
        props: {
            user: users.find((user) => user.username ===
                username)
        }
    };
}
```

With that function, we're querying the specific user that we want to display on the page by filtering the users' array.

Before we move on to writing the page content, let's import the required Chakra UI and Next.js dependencies:

```
import Link from 'next/link';
import {
  Avatar,
  Box,
  Center,
  Text,
  Image,
  Button,
  Flex,
  useColorModeValue
} from '@chakra-ui/react';
```

We can finally write our UserPage component. We will be wrapping everything inside a Chakra UI <Center> component, which uses flexbox under the hood to center all the child elements.

We'll then use other Chakra UI built-in components such as <Image>, <Flex>, <Avatar>, <Text>, and so on, to create our component:

```
function UserPage({ user }) {
  return (
    <Center
      marginTop={['0', '0', '8']}
      boxShadow="lg"
      minHeight="fit-content">
      <Box>
        <Box position="relative">
          <Image
            src={user.cover_image}
            width="fit-content"
            height="250px"
            objectFit="cover" />
          <Flex
```

```
      alignItems="flex-end"
      position="absolute"
      top="0"
      left="0"
      backgroundColor={
        useColorModeValue('blackAlpha.400',
          'blackAlpha.600')
      }
      width="100%"
      height="100%"
      padding="8"
      color="white">
      <Avatar size="lg" src={user.avatar} />
      <Box marginLeft="6">
        <Text as="h1" fontSize="xx-large"
          fontWeight="bold">
          {user.first_name} {user.last_name}
        </Text>
        <Text as="p" fontSize="large"
          lineHeight="1.5">
          {user.job_title}
        </Text>
      </Box>
    </Flex>
  </Box>
  <Box
    maxW="container.xl"
    margin="auto"
    padding="8"
    backgroundColor={useColorModeValue('white',
      'gray.700')}>
    <Text as="p">{user.description}</Text>
    <Link href="/" passHref>
      <Button marginTop="8" colorScheme="whatsapp"
        as="a">
        Back to all users
```

```
            </Button>
          </Link>
        </Box>
      </Box>
    </Center>
  );
}


export default UserPage;
```

We can notice other great Chakra UI features, such as the `as` prop used in the `Back to all users` button:

```
<Button marginTop="8" colorScheme="whatsapp" as="a">
```

Here, we're telling Chakra UI to render the `Button` component as an `<a>` HTML element. That way, we can use the `passHref` prop in its parent Next.js `Link` component to pass its `href` value to the button, making a more accessible UI; in doing so, we will create an actual `<a>` element with a proper `href` property attached to it.

We can now run the development server and test the final result:

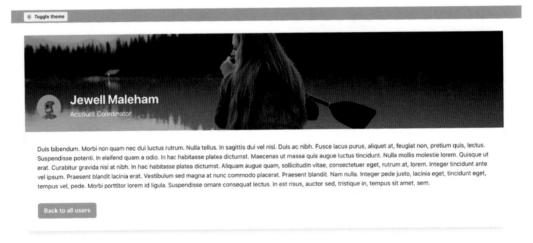

Figure 7.6 – Single employee in light mode

By clicking on the **Toggle theme** button, we can also access the dark version of our user interface, which looks like this:

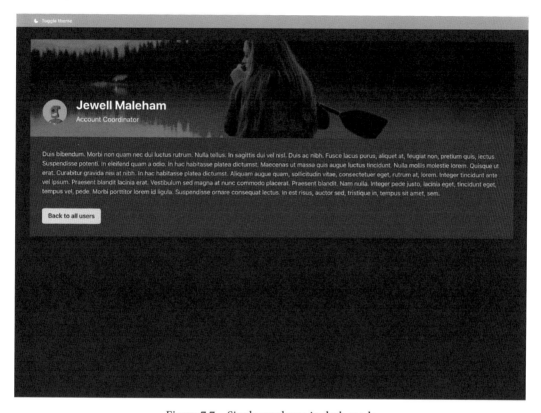

Figure 7.7 – Single employee in dark mode

We have also used responsive styles, so we can test our UI by resizing the browser page:

Image 7.8 – Single employee page (mobile view)

As you can see, implementing a responsive user interface with Chakra UI's built-in components was straightforward.

If you want to dig deeper into all the existing components, hooks, and utilities, you can learn more at `https://chakra-ui.com`.

Conclusive words about Chakra UI

Chakra UI is a great modern UI library, and I personally use it on many of the projects I work on. It's open source and free to use, with a great community that works every day to optimize it and make it even more accessible, performant, and complete.

It also provides a premium set of pre-made UI components built by the Chakra UI core team. If you're interested, you can look at them at `https://pro.chakra-ui.com/ components`.

In the next section, we will change our focus to another popular yet completely different UI library: TailwindCSS.

Integrating TailwindCSS in Next.js

TailwindCSS is a utility-first CSS framework that allows you to build any user interface using pre-made CSS classes that map CSS rules in a straightforward way.

Unlike Chakra UI, Material UI, and many other UI frameworks, it just provides CSS rules; the framework gives no JavaScript scripts or React components, so we'll need to write them by ourselves.

Its main strengths are the following:

- *Framework agnostic*: You can use TailwindCSS in React, Vue, Angular, and even in plain HTML and JavaScript. It's just a set of CSS rules.

- *Themeable*: Just like Chakra UI, you can customize all the TailwindCSS variables to make them match your design tokens.

- *Dark and light theme support*: You can easily enable or disable the dark theme by modifying a specific CSS class from the `<html>` element.

- *Highly optimized*: TailwindCSS is formed of many CSS classes, but it's able to prune the unused ones at build time, reducing the final bundle size, as unused CSS classes get removed.

- *Mobile-ready*: You can use specific CSS classes' prefixes to apply certain rules to mobile, desktop, or tablet screens only.

In this section, we will see how to integrate, customize, and optimize TailwindCSS in Next.js by rebuilding the same project we did in the last section. That way, the differences between Chakra UI and TailwindCSS will be even more evident.

Let's create a new project and install all the required dependencies:

```
npx create-next-app employee-directory-with-tailwindcss
```

TailwindCSS only requires three devDependencies, so let's enter the newly created project and install them:

```
yarn add -D autoprefixer postcss tailwindcss
```

As we've already seen, TailwindCSS doesn't ship with any JavaScript utility, so, unlike Chakra UI, we will need to manage the dark/light theme switch ourselves. However, we can take advantage of the next-themes library to help us manage the themes, so let's install that package:

```
yarn add next-themes
```

Now that we have all the dependencies installed, we need to set up the basic TailwindCSS configuration files. We can do that by using the tailwindcss init command:

```
npx tailwindcss init -p
```

This will create two different files:

- tailwind.config.js: This file will help us configure the TailwindCSS theme, unused CSS purge, dark mode, plugins, and more.
- postcss.config.js: **TailwindCSS** uses **PostCSS** under the hood and ships with a pre-configured postcss.config.js that we can always edit as we prefer.

First of all, we want to configure TailwindCSS to remove unused CSS from the final build. We can do that by opening the tailwind.config.js file and editing it as follows:

```
module.exports = {
  purge: ['./pages/**/*.{js,jsx}',
    './components/**/*.{js,jsx}'],
  darkMode: 'class',
  theme: {
    extend: {},
  },
```

```
  variants: {
    extend: {},
  },
  plugins: [],
};
```

As you can see, we're telling TailwindCSS to check every file ending with `.js` or `.jsx` inside both `pages/` and `components/` directories and remove all the CSS classes that are not used inside of any of those files.

We also set the `darkMode` property to `'class'`. That way, the framework will look at the `<html>` class element to determine whether we need to render the components using dark or light mode.

We now only need to include the default `tailwind.css` CSS file on every single page of our application, and we're ready to start. We can do that by importing `'tailwindcss/tailwind.css'` inside our `pages/_app.js` file:

```
import 'tailwindcss/tailwind.css';

function MyApp({ Component, pageProps }) {
  return <Component {...pageProps} />
}

export default MyApp;
```

We can now start to include specific TailwindCSS classes. Keeping the `pages/_app.js` file open in our code editor, we can begin by importing `ThemeProvider` from the `next-themes` package, which will help us manage the dark/light theme switch, and wrap every other component inside of it:

```
import { ThemeProvider } from 'next-themes';
import TopBar from '../components/TopBar';
import 'tailwindcss/tailwind.css';

function MyApp({ Component, pageProps }) {
  return (
    // attribute="class" will set a "dark" CSS class
    // to the main <html> tag
    <ThemeProvider attribute="class">
```

```
        <div
          className="dark:bg-gray-900 bg-gray-50 w-full min-
            h-screen"
        >
          <TopBar />
          <Component {...pageProps} />
        </div>
      </ThemeProvider>
    );
  }

export default MyApp;
```

As you can see, we're following the same steps we did with Chakra UI. We're importing the `TopBar` component (which will be common to all the pages on our website) and wrapping the Next.js `<Component />` component inside a container.

We'll see how to write the `TopBar` component in just a moment; for now, let's concentrate on the `<div>` that is wrapping the `<Component />` component:

```
<div className="dark:bg-gray-900 bg-gray-50 w-full min-h-
screen">
```

We used four different CSS classes; let's break them down:

- `dark:bg-gray-900`: When the theme is set to dark mode, the background color for this `<div>` will be set to `bg-gray-900`, a TailwindCSS variable that maps to the #111927 HEX color.

- `bg-gray-50`: By default (so in light mode), the background color for this div will be set to `bg-gray-50`, which maps to the #f9fafb HEX color.

- `w-full`: This means "full width," so the `<div>` will have the `width` property set to `100%`.

- `min-h-screen`: This CSS class stands for *set the min-height property to the whole screen height*, shorthand for `min-height: 100vh`.

We can now create a new `/components/TopBar/index.js` file and add the following content:

```
import ThemeSwitch from '../ThemeSwitch';

function TopBar() {
  return (
    <div className="w-full p-2 bg-green-500">
      <div className="w--10/12 m-auto">
        <ThemeSwitch />
      </div>
    </div>
  );
}

export default TopBar;
```

Here, we're creating the full-width horizontal green bar (`className="w-full p-2 bg-green-500"`) with 0.5rem of padding (`p-2` class) and `#12b981` as the background color (`bg-green-500`).

Inside that `<div>`, we're placing another centered `<div>` with 75% width (`w-10/12`).

We're then importing the `ThemeSwitch` button, which still needs to be created. Let's do that by creating a new file under `components/ThemeSwitch/index.js`:

```
import { useTheme } from 'next-themes';

function ThemeSwitch() {
  const { theme, setTheme } = useTheme();
  const dark = theme === 'dark';

  const toggleTheme = () => {
    setTheme(dark ? 'light' : 'dark');
  };

  if (typeof window === 'undefined') return null;

  return (
```

```
    <button
      onClick={toggleTheme}
      className="
        dark:bg-green-900 dark:bg-opacity-20 dark:text-
          gray-50
        bg-green-100 text-gray-500 pl-2 pr-2 rounded-md
          text-xs
        p-1"
    >
      Toggle theme
    </button>
  );
}


export default ThemeSwitch;
```

This component is pretty straightforward; we use the `useTheme` hook packed with the `next-themes` library and change the theme value to `light` or `dark`, depending on the current set theme.

One thing to notice is that we're doing that on the client side only (by writing `typeof window === 'undefined'`). In fact, this hook adds a `theme` entry in the browser's `localStorage`, which of course, is not accessible on the server side.

For that reason, the `ThemeSwitch` component will be rendered on the client side only.

Talking about the `<button>` CSS classes, we can see that we're building a rounded button with a green background. The green tonality, by the way, will be different depending on the currently selected theme.

Now let's write the `UserCard` component. Create a new file under `components/UserCard/index.js` and add the following content:

```
import Link from 'next/link';


function UserCard(props) {
  return (
    <Link href={`/user/${props.username}`} passHref>
      <div
        className="
```

```
                    dark:bg-gray-800 bg-gray-100 cursor-pointer
                    dark:text-white p-4 rounded-md text-center
                      shadow-xl"
              >
            <img
              src={props.avatar}
              alt={props.username}
              className="w-16 bg-gray-400 rounded-full m-auto"
            />
            <div className="mt-2 font-bold">
              {props.first_name} {props.last_name}
            </div>
            <div className="font-light">{props.job_title}</div>
          </div>
        </Link>
    );
}


export default UserCard;
```

Except for the CSS class names, this component is not that different from the Chakra UI one.

> **Image Optimizations**
>
> As you can see, we're not currently optimizing the images, and we're serving them using the default `<img />` HTML element. Unfortunately, that can make our website slower and lead to a lousy SEO score.
>
> Try to configure automatic image optimization and serve them using the Next.js `<Image />` component!
>
> Can't remember how to do it? You can go over *Chapter 3, Next.js Basics and Built-In Components*.

We're now ready to write the home page for our ACME employee directory. First, make sure to have the same `users.js` file we used in the previous section positioned under `data/users.js`.

If you need to download it again, you can do it by copying the content from here:
`https://github.com/PacktPublishing/Real-World-Next.js/blob/main/07-using-ui-frameworks/with-tailwindcss/data/users.js`.

Now we can open the `pages/index.js` file, import both the `users.js` file and the `UserCard` component, then put everything together to create a user grid as we did with Chakra UI:

```
import UserCard from '../components/UserCard';
import users from '../data/users';


export default function Home() {
  return (
    <div className="sm:w-9/12 sm:m-auto pt-16 pb-16">
      <h1 className="
        dark:text-white text-5xl font-bold text-center
      ">
        ACME Corporation Employees
      </h1>
      <div className="
        grid gap-8 grid-cols-1 sm:grid-cols-3 mt-14
        ml-8 mr-8 sm:mr-0 sm:ml-0
      ">
        {users.map((user) => (
          <div key={user.id}>
            <UserCard {...user} />
          </div>
        ))}
      </div>
    </div>
  );
}
```

As you can see, here we're starting to use some responsive directives:

```
<div className="sm:w-9/12 sm:m-auto pt-16 pb-16">
```

The `sm:` prefix is used to apply a specific rule when the window width is greater than or equal to `640px`.

By default, TailwindCSS classes are mobile-first, and if we want to apply a specific class to wider screens, we will need to prefix those classes with one of the following prefixes: `sm:` (640px), `md:` (768px), `lg:` (1024px), `xl:` (1280px), or `2xl:` (1536px).

We can now run the development server and head to the home page. We will see the following result:

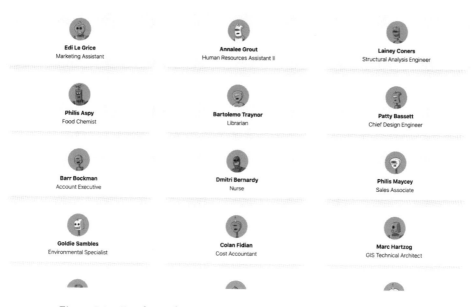

Figure 7.9 – Employee directory built with TailwindCSS (light theme)

We can also switch the theme to **dark** by clicking on the button on the green bar at the top of the screen:

Figure 7.10 – Employee directory built with TailwindCSS (dark theme)

If you compare the visual results of the Chakra UI implementation and the TailwindCSS one, you will see how similar they look!

Let's complete our website by creating the single-user page. If you haven't already, create a new page called `pages/user/[username].js`, and start by importing the required dependencies:

```
import Link from 'next/link';
import users from '../../data/users';
```

We can now write the `getStaticPaths` function:

```
export function getStaticPaths() {
  const paths = users.map((user) => ({
    params: {
      username: user.username
    }
```

```
    }));

  return {
    paths,
    fallback: false
  };
}
```

And let's write the `getStaticProps` function:

```
export function getStaticProps({ params }) {
  const { username } = params;

  return {
    props: {
      user: users.find((user) => user.username ===
        username)
    }
  };
}
```

You may have noticed that those functions are the same as we wrote in the Chakra UI section. In fact, with this implementation, we only change the way we render the page content; all the server-side data fetching and manipulation will remain the same.

We're finally ready to write the single-user page component. Here, we will be creating a similar structure to the one we wrote with Chakra UI, but of course, using TailwindCSS classes and standard HTML elements:

```
function UserPage({ user }) {
  return (
    <div className="pt-0 sm:pt-16">
      <div className="
        dark:bg-gray-800 text-white w-12/12
        shadow-lg sm:w-9/12 sm:m-auto">
        <div className="relative sm:w-full">
          <img
            src={user.cover_image}
            alt={user.username}
```

```
                className="w-full h-96 object-cover object-
                    center"
            />
            <div className="
                bg-gray-800 bg-opacity-50 absolute
                flex items-end w-full h-full top-0 left-0 p-8">
                <img
                    src={user.avatar}
                    alt={user.username}
                    className="bg-gray-300 w-20
                        rounded-full mr-4"
                />
                <div>
                    <h1 className="font-bold text-3xl">
                        {user.first_name} {user.last_name}
                    </h1>
                    <p> {user.job_title} </p>
                </div>
            </div>
        </div>
        <div className="p-8">
            <p className="text-black dark:text-white">
                {user.description}
            </p>
            <Link href="/" passHref>
                <button className="
                    dark:bg-green-400 dark:text-gray-800
                        bg-green-400
                    text-white font-semibold p-2
                    rounded-md mt-6">
                Back to all users
                </button>
            </Link>
        </div>
    </div>
</div>
```

```
    );
}
```

```
export default UserPage;
```

And we're done! We've rewritten our entire application by using TailwindCSS.

At the time of writing, the original TailwindCSS stylesheet size is around 4.7 MB. After building the website for production by just running `yarn build`, the final TailwindCSS file will be about 6 KB.

You can quickly test this by commenting on the `purge` property inside of the `tailwind.config.js` file.

So far, we've seen two different (yet very modern) approaches to styling a web application, and they both have their pros and cons.

While they share some ideas about how to write styles for any website, Chakra UI has the advantage of providing pre-built React components, which can come in handy when you want to integrate the library in your Next.js/React application and make it more dynamic with ease.

Luckily, the TailwindCSS team came up with the innovative idea of providing a dynamic interface to TailwindCSS (and possibly any other UI framework): Headless UI.

In the next section, we will look at Headless UI and how it can make things easier for us when building modern, performant, and optimized web applications with Next.js.

Integrating Headless UI

As we saw in the previous section, TailwindCSS only provides CSS classes to be used inside any web component.

If we want to implement something dynamic, such as a modal, a switch button, and so on, we need to write some JavaScript logic on our own.

Headless UI solves this problem by providing the opposite of TailwindCSS: dynamic components without any CSS class or style. That way, we're free to use TailwindCSS or any other CSS framework to style pre-built components in a straightforward way.

Headless UI is a free and open source project created by the *Tailwind Labs* team (the same organization behind TailwindCSS), and if you're interested, you can browse the source code at the following URL: `https://github.com/tailwindlabs/headlessui`.

Integrating Headless UI and TailwindCSS is not very different from integrating TailwindCSS alone. We can set up a new project and install all the TailwindCSS dependencies just like we did in the previous section.

After that, we can install Headless UI itself. We will also install `classnames`, a simple and widely used utility that will help us create dynamic CSS class names:

```
yarn add @headlessui/react classnames
```

We will now develop a simple menu component by using Headless UI and TailwindCSS.

Let's go to the `pages/index.js` file and import Headless UI, `classnames`, and Next. js' `Link` component:

```
import Link from 'next/link';
import { Menu } from '@headlessui/react';
import cx from 'classnames';
```

Now, inside the same page, let's create an array of menu elements. We will be using them to populate the menu with mocked data:

```
const entries = [
  {
    name: 'Home',
    href: '/'
    enabled: true,
  },
  {
    name: 'About',
    href: '/about',
    enabled: true,
  },
  {
    name: 'Contact',
    href: '/contact',
    enabled: false,
  },
];
```

We can now destructure the Headless UI `Menu` component and take all the components we need to build our menu:

```
const { Button, Items, Item } = Menu;
```

Every menu entry will be wrapped inside an `Item` component. Given that every menu entry will behave the same way, we can create a generic `MenuEntry` component and apply it to our array of entries:

```
const MenuEntry = (props) => (
  <Item disabled={!props.enabled}>
    {(({ active }) => (
      <Link href={props.href} passHref>
        <a>{props.name}</a>
      </Link>
    )}
  </Item>
);
```

As you can see, Headless UI will pass an `active` state to all the elements inside of `Item`. We will use that state to show the user which element of the menu is currently active.

We now only need to wrap everything together inside the `Menu` component:

```
export default function Home() {
  return (
    <div className="w-9/12 m-auto pt-16 pb-16">
      <Menu>
        <Button>My Menu</Button>
        <Items>
          {entries.map((entry) => (
            <MenuEntry key={entry.name} {...entry} />
          ))}
        </Items>
      </Menu>
    </div>
  );
}
```

If we now launch the development server, we will see an utterly unstyled button at the top right of our screen. We can click on this button to reveal – and then hide – its content.

We can now proceed to style our menu, beginning with the `MenuEntry` component:

```
const MenuEntry = (props) => (
  <Item disabled={!props.enabled}>
    {(({ active }) => {
      const classNames = cx(
        'w-full', 'p-2', 'rounded-lg', 'mt-2', 'mb-2',
        {
          'opacity-50': !props.enabled,
          'bg-blue-600': active,
          'text-white': active,
        });

      return (
        <Link href={props.href} passHref>
          <a className={classNames}>{props.name}</a>
        </Link>
      );
    }}
  </Item>
);
```

Moving on to the main component, we can simply add the CSS classes required for styling `Button` and `Item` components. We want the menu button to be purple with white text, and the drop-down menu to have rounded corners with a nice box shadow, so let's add the following classes:

```
export default function Home() {
  return (
    <div className="w-9/12 m-auto pt-16 pb-16">
      <Menu>
        <Button className="
          bg-purple-500 text-white p-2 pl-4 pr-4 rounded-lg
        "> My Menu </Button>
        <Items className="
          flex flex-col w-52 mt-4 p-2 rounded-xl shadow-lg
```

```
            ">
                {entries.map((entry) => (
                    <MenuEntry key={entry.name} {...entry} />
                ))}
            </Items>
        </Menu>
    </div>
    );
}
```

We can also apply a transition to our menu, making the reveal/hide part smoother. We just need to import the `Transition` component from Headless UI and wrap the menu items inside it:

```
import { Menu, Transition } from '@headlessui/react';

// ...

export default function Home() {
  return (
    <div className="w-9/12 m-auto pt-16 pb-16">
      <Menu>
        <Button className="
          bg-purple-500 text-white p-2 pl-4 pr-4 rounded-lg
        "> My Menu </Button>
        <Transition
          enter="transition duration-100 ease-out"
          enterFrom="transform scale-95 opacity-0"
          enterTo="transform scale-100 opacity-100"
          leave="transition duration-75 ease-out"
          leaveFrom="transform scale-100 opacity-100"
          leaveTo="transform scale-95 opacity-0">
          <Items className="
            flex flex-col w-52 mt-4 p-2
              rounded-xl shadow-lg
          ">
            {entries.map((entry) => (
```

```
            <MenuEntry key={entry.name} {...entry} />
        ))}
      </Items>
    </Transition>
  </Menu>
</div>
);
}
```

We just styled our first headless component with TailwindCSS, but we can use our own CSS rules or any other CSS framework!

Just like Chakra UI, TailwindCSS provides a series of premium components, and many of those components rely on Headless UI for managing their interactions. If you're interested in that, you can learn more at `https://tailwindui.com`.

Summary

In this chapter, we have seen three different and modern approaches for building user interfaces with Next.js, React, and even plain HTML.

In the following chapters, where we will be working on real-world web applications, we will be using the lessons learned in these sections to speed up the UI development, always keeping an eye on performance, accessibility, and developer experience.

If you're interested in learning more about the differences between Chakra UI and TailwindCSS specifically, you can read the official guide on the Chakra UI website: `https://chakra-ui.com/docs/comparison`.

Both libraries provide excellent support for implementing beautiful user interfaces, and even though they share some features, they are quite different in practice.

Chakra UI exposes a fantastic set of components, but they are only available for React and Vue. What if your project uses Angular or Svelte?

TailwindCSS, on the other hand, is 100% framework-agnostic: you can use it for writing the frontend of any web application independently of the technology you're using.

In my opinion, there is no clear winner: choosing either of these libraries is entirely up to personal taste.

In the next chapter, we will change our focus to the backend of our applications, learning how to dynamically serve a Next.js web application from a custom Node.js server.

8
Using a Custom Server

Next.js is an incredibly powerful framework. In the first seven chapters of this book, we've been able to create some nice server-side rendered web applications without really caring about tweaking and customizing the web server. Of course, there are few chances for us to discuss implementing a Next.js application inside an Express.js or Fastify server in a real-life scenario, but knowing how to do so is likely to be handy on many occasions.

Talking for myself, in the past years, I've created dozens of large-scale web applications using Next.js, and I rarely needed to use a custom server. However, in some cases, it is inevitable.

We will look at the following topics in detail:

- What using a "custom server" means, when we might need to use it, and what are the options.

- How to use Express.js and Next.js together

- How to use Fastify and Next.js together

- What are the requirements for deploying a custom server?

By the end of this chapter, you'll be able to determine when to use a custom server, what its advantages and downsides are, and what problems it can solve.

Technical requirements

To run the code examples in this chapter, you need to have both Node.js and npm installed on your local machine.

If you prefer, you can use an online IDE such as `https://repl.it` or `https://codesandbox.io`; they both support Next.js, and you don't need to install any dependency on your computer. As with the other chapters, you can find the codebase for this chapter on GitHub: `https://github.com/PacktPublishing/Real-World-Next.js`.

About using a custom server

As we've already seen, Next.js ships with its own server, so we don't need to configure a custom one to get started with writing web applications with this framework. Still, there are some cases where we may want to serve a Next.js app from a custom web server, such as Express.js or Fastify, and the framework makes this possible by exposing some straightforward APIs that we'll be looking into in just one moment. But before looking at the implementation, let's answer an important question: *do we really need a custom server?*

The short answer is, most of the time, *no*. Next.js is such a complete framework that we rarely need to customize the server-side logic via Express.js, Fastify, or any other server-side framework. But sometimes, it is just inevitable, as it can solve specific problems.

Some common use cases for a custom server are as follows:

- **Integrating Next.js into an existing server**: Suppose you're refactoring an existing web application to adopt Next.js; you may want to maintain as much server-side logic as possible, your middlewares, and routes. In that case, you can progressively add Next.js by choosing which pages of your websites will be served from the framework and which ones will be rendered by something else.

- **Multi-tenancy**: Even though Next.js supports multiple domains and conditional rendering depending on the current hostname (look at `https://github.com/leerob/nextjs-multiple-domains` if you're interested in a native solution), there are cases where you may need more control and a simplified workflow for handling up to thousands of different domains. If you're interested in an Express.js/Fastify multi-tenant middleware for Next.js, you can take a look at `https://github.com/micheleriva/krabs`.

- **You want more control**: Even though Next.js provides everything you need for creating a robust and complete user experience, there are cases where your app is growing in complexity and you want to organize the backend code using different approaches, such as adopting the MVC philosophy, where Next.js is just the "view" part of the process.

While a custom server could solve some problems, it also has some downsides. For instance, you cannot deploy a custom server to Vercel, the platform created by the Next.js authors, which is highly optimized for the framework. Also, you'll need to write and maintain more code, which can be a significant downside if you're working on a side project, in a small team, or for a small company.

In the next section, we'll see how to write a custom server for Next.js using one of the most popular web frameworks for Node.js: Express.js.

Using a custom Express.js server

Writing a custom Express.js server to render Next.js pages is easier than you might think. Let's create a new project and install the following dependencies:

```
yarn add express react react-dom next
```

Once we've installed these four packages, we can start writing a custom Express.js server. Let's create an `index.js` file inside the project root and start by importing the required dependencies:

```
const { parse } = require('url');
const express = require('express');
const next = require('next');
```

We now need to instantiate the Next.js app, and we can do that by adding the following code right after the import statements:

```
const dev = process.env.NODE_ENV !== 'production';
const app = next({ dev });
```

Let's complete our server by writing the `main` function, which takes every incoming GET request and passes it to Next.js for server-side rendering:

```
async function main() {
  try {
```

```
    await app.prepare();

    const handle = app.getRequestHandler();
    const server = express();

    server
      .get('*', (req, res) => {
        const url = parse(req.url, true);
        handle(req, res, url);
      })
      .listen(3000, () => console.log('server ready'));
  } catch (err) {
    console.log(err.stack);
  }
}

main();
```

Let's focus on the `main` function body and see what's going on.

First of all, we wait for the Next.js app to be ready for rendering. Then, we instantiate a `handle` constant, which will handle the incoming requests on behalf of Next.js. We then create the Express.js server and ask it to handle all the GET requests using the Next.js request handler.

We can now create a home page by creating a new `pages/` directory and a `pages/index.js` file with the following content:

```
export default function Homepage() {
  return <div> Homepage </div>;
}
```

If we try to run `node index.js`, and then go to `http://localhost:3000`, we will see the **Homepage** text displayed on the screen. We did it!

We can also test dynamic routes by creating a new `pages/greet/[user].js` file with the following content:

```
export function getServerSideProps(req) {
  return {
```

```
      props: {
        user: req.params.user,
      },
    };
  }


export default function GreetUser({ user }) {
  return (
    <div>
      <h1>Hello {user}!</h1>
    </div>
  );
}
```

Going to `http://localhost:3000/greet/Mitch`, we will see a friendly **Hello Mitch!** message printed on the screen. As you can see, implementing dynamic routes is incredibly easy!

From this point, we can continue working on Next.js as we always did. There aren't many differences compared to what we did in the previous chapters, but what would be the point of having a custom server if we did not exploit its full potential?

We've seen that a custom server may be helpful when we have an existing web application that we wish to progressively migrate to Next.js.

Start adding some more functionality by refactoring the server as follows:

```
server
  .get('/', (req, res) => {
    res.send('Hello World!');
  })
  .get('/api/greet', (req, res) => {
    res.json({ name: req.query?.name ?? 'unknown' });
  })
  .listen(3000, () => console.log('server ready'));
```

As you can tell, we're not serving any page with Next.js right now. So instead, we just serve a home page, and a fake API at `/api/greet`.

We now want to create a new /about page and serve it using Next.js. But first, we need to create the Next.js-powered page under the /pages/about route:

```
export default function About() {
    return <div> This about page is served from Next.js </div>;
}
```

Now, we can go back to our index.js file and edit the main function, as follows:

```
server
    .get('/', (req, res) => {
        res.send('Hello World!');
    })
    .get('/about', (req, res) => {
        const { query } = parse(req.url, true);
        app.render(req, res, '/about', query);
    })
    .get('/api/greet', (req, res) => {
        res.json({ name: req.query?.name ?? 'unknown' });
    })
    .listen(3000, () => console.log('server ready'));
```

We're now using a different function for rendering a Next.js page: app.render.

This function takes the following arguments: Express.js' request and response, the page to render, and the parsed query string.

But as soon as we start the server and head over to http://localhost:3000/about, we will notice a blank page. If we inspect the network call for this page, we will see the following situation:

Name	Status	Type	Initiator	Size	Time	Waterfall
about	200	document	Other	881 B	7 ms	
webpack.js?ts=1627824916875	404	script	about	272 B	5 ms	
main.js?ts=1627824916875	404	script	about	272 B	6 ms	
_app.js?ts=1627824916875	404	script	about	272 B	10 ms	
about.js?ts=1627824916875	404	script	about	272 B	10 ms	
_buildManifest.js?ts=1627824916875	404	script	about	272 B	9 ms	
_ssgManifest.js?ts=1627824916875	404	script	about	272 B	8 ms	
react-refresh.js?ts=1627824916875	404	script	about	272 B	10 ms	

Figure 8.1 – Next.js scripts are not found

What's happening here? Next.js renders the page properly, as you can tell by inspecting the HTML output, but the page is entirely white!

We forgot to tell Express.js that every static asset whose path starts with _next/ needs to be handled by Next.js itself. This is because all those static assets (typically JavaScript files) are responsible for importing React into the browser, handling hydration, and managing all the Next.js frontend-specific features.

We can quickly fix that by adding the following route:

```
// ...

await app.prepare();

const handle = app.getRequestHandler();
const server = express();

server
  .get('/', (req, res) => {
    res.send('Hello World!');
  })
  .get('/about', (req, res) => {
    const { query } = parse(req.url, true);
    app.render(req, res, '/about', query);
  })
  .get('/api/greet', (req, res) => {
    res.json({ name: req.query?.name ?? 'unknown' });
  })
  .get(/_next\/.+/, (req, res) => {
    const parsedUrl = parse(req.url, true);
    handle(req, res, parsedUrl);
  })
  .listen(3000, () => console.log('server ready'));
```

Given that we cannot predict Next.js static asset names, we will use a regular expression (/_next\/.+/) matching every file whose path starts with _next/. We then use the Next.js handle method for serving those files.

We can now start our server and see that it is working as expected.

As we've seen before, from now, the developer experience will remain the same while developing Next.js-powered pages. We still have access to both the _app.js and _document.js files, we can still use the built-in Link component, and so on.

In the next section, we will see how to integrate Next.js with another incredibly popular Node.js web framework: Fastify.

Using a custom Fastify server

Fastify is an incredible web framework for Node.js. As the name suggests, it can be attractive as it is really, really fast when compared to other web frameworks, such as Express.js, Koa, and Hapi. If you're interested in learning more about its performance, you can find the official benchmarks in the following repository: https://github.com/fastify/benchmarks.

This web framework is developed and maintained by some of Node.js' core developers, such as Matteo Collina (Node.js technical steering committee member). So, as you can imagine, the people behind Fastify perfectly know how the runtime works and have made the framework as optimized as possible.

But Fastify is not just about the performance: it also enforces excellent best practices to keep the developer experience as good as possible. It also has a robust plugin system that allows everyone to write their own plugin or middleware with ease. If you haven't already, I highly recommend checking it out at https://github.com/fastify/fastify.

Fastify provides an official plugin for managing Next.js-rendered routes: fastify-nextjs. You can find its source code here: https://github.com/fastify/fastify-nextjs.

Let's create a new empty project and install the following dependencies to see it in action:

```
yarn add react react-dom fastify fastify-nextjs next
```

We can now create the same three pages we made in the past section.

A simple home page under /pages/index.js can be implemented as follows:

```
export default function Homepage() {
  return <div> Homepage </div>;
}
```

An "about" page under `/pages/about.js` can be implemented as follows:

```
export default function About() {
  return <div> This about page is served from Next.js </div>;
}
```

Lastly, a dynamic page used for greeting a user under `/pages/greet/[user].js` can be implemented as follows:

```
export function getServerSideProps(req) {
  return {
    props: {
      user: req.params.user,
    },
  };
}


export default function GreetUser({ user }) {
  return (
    <div>
      <h1>Hello {user}!</h1>
    </div>
  );
}
```

We can finally code our Fastify server, and it will be straightforward compared to the Express.js one. Let's create an `index.js` file inside of the project's root and add the following content:

```
const fastify = require('fastify')();

fastify
  .register(require('fastify-nextjs'))
  .after(() => {
    fastify.next('/');
    fastify.next('/about');
    fastify.next('/greet/:user');
  });
```

```
fastify.listen(3000, () => {
  console.log('Server listening on http://localhost:3000');
});
```

Starting the server, we will be able to render all the pages we specified in our `index.js` file! As you can notice, this implementation is even easier than the Express.js one. We just invoke the `fastify.next` function to render a Next.js page, and we don't even need to worry about Next.js' static assets; Fastify will take care of them on our behalf.

From this point, we can start writing different routes serving different contents, such as JSON responses, HTML pages, and static files:

```
fastify.register(require('fastify-nextjs')).after(() => {
  fastify.next('/');
  fastify.next('/about');
  fastify.next('/greet/:user');
  fastify.get('/contacts', (req, reply) => {
    reply
      .type('html')
        .send('<h1>Contacts page</h1>');
  });
});
```

As you can see, integrating Next.js with Fastify is incredibly easy. From this point, just like with Express.js, we can do whatever we want, just like we're writing a common Next.js web application.

We can create both `_app.js` and `_document.js` files to customize our Next.js pages' behavior, integrate any UI library, and do all the things we've already seen in the previous chapters.

Summary

In this chapter, we've seen how to integrate Next.js with two of the most popular web frameworks for Node.js: Express.js and Fastify. It is possible to integrate Next.js with other web frameworks, and the implementation won't be different from what we've seen in the previous sections.

One thing to consider when using a custom server of any kind (be it Express.js, Fastify, or any other framework) is that we cannot deploy it to some providers, such as Vercel or Netlify.

Technically speaking, many providers (Vercel, Netlify, Cloudflare, and so on) provide a great way to serve Node.js-powered applications: serverless functions. However, since this is quite an advanced topic, we will discuss it in depth in *Chapter 11, Different Deployment Platforms*.

As we'll see in *Chapter 11, Different Deployment Platforms*, Next.js is a framework highly optimized to run on Vercel, the infrastructure provided by the company behind the creation (and maintenance) of the framework. Using a custom server, we lose the ability to deploy to this infrastructure, making things a bit less optimized and integrated.

Still, there are other awesome options out there, such as DigitalOcean, Heroku, AWS, and Azure. From this point, we can deploy our custom Next.js server on all of those services that support a Node.js environment.

Starting from *Chapter 11, Different Deployment Platforms*, we will discuss Next.js deployments in more depth. But for now, we just want to concentrate on its features and integrations.

Talking about its integrations specifically, once we write a page, some middleware, or a component for our Next.js application, we want to test whether it works properly before deploying it to production. In the next chapter, we'll discuss implementing unit and end-to-end tests using two of the most commonly used testing libraries out there: Jest and Cypress.

9
Testing Next.js

Testing is an essential part of the whole development workflow. It gives you more assurance that you're not introducing bugs into your code, as well as that you're not breaking any existing features.

Testing Next.js specifically is not different from testing any other React app or Express.js, Fastify, or Koa application. In fact, we can divide the testing phases into three different stages:

- Unit testing
- End-to-end testing
- Integration testing

We will look at those concepts in detail in this chapter's sections.

If you already have previous experience in writing a React application, you're likely to re-utilize your knowledge for testing a Next.js-based website.

In this chapter, we will look in detail at the following:

- An introduction to testing and testing frameworks
- Setting up a testing environment
- How to use some of the most popular test runners, frameworks, and utility libraries

By the end of this chapter, you'll be able to set up a testing environment using a test runner and a testing library and run tests before sending the code to production.

Technical requirements

To run the code examples in this chapter, you need to have both Node.js and npm installed on your local machine.

If you prefer, you can use an online IDE such as `https://repl.it or https://codesandbox.io`; they both support Next.js, and you don't need to install any dependency on your computer. As with the other chapters, you can find the code base for this chapter on GitHub: `https://github.com/PacktPublishing/Real-World-Next.js`.

An introduction to testing

As we've seen during this chapter's introduction, testing is an essential part of any development workflow and can be divided into three separate testing phases:

- *Unit testing*: These tests aim to make sure that every single function in your code is working. They do that by testing the codebase's functions individually against correct and incorrect inputs, asserting their results and possible errors to ensure they're working expected.

- *End-to-end testing*: This testing strategy reproduces a typical user interaction with your application, ensuring that the app responds with a specific output once a given action occurs, just like we would do by testing the website manually on a web browser. For instance, if we build a form, we want to automatically guarantee that it is working correctly, validating the input, and performing a specific action on the form's submission. Also, we want to test that the user interface is rendering as we intended by using particular CSS classes, mounting certain HTML elements, and so on.

- *Integration testing*: In this case, we want to ensure that separate parts of our application, such as functions and modules, are cohesively working together. For instance, we want to assert that composing two functions results in a certain output, and so on. Unlike unit tests, where we test our functions individually, with integration tests, we ensure that a whole group of aggregated functions and modules are producing a correct output when given a different set of inputs.

There might be other testing phases and philosophies, but in the following sections, we will be concentrating on the ones we've mentioned here, as they are the essential parts of the testing workflow, and I strongly encourage you to adopt all of those phases when shipping your code to production.

As said in the introduction for this chapter, testing Next.js is not different than testing a React application or an **Express.js/Fastify/Koa** web server. We need to choose the proper test runner and libraries and ensure that our code is working as expected.

When talking about test runners, we refer to tools responsible for executing every test found in the code base, collecting the coverage, and displaying the test results in the console. If the test runner process fails (and exits with a non-zero exit code), the tests are considered to have failed.

The Node.js and JavaScript ecosystems offer a large set of choices for test runners, but starting from the next section, we will be concentrating on the two most popular alternatives out there: **Jest** (for unit and integration tests) and **Cypress** (for **e2e**, short for **end-to-end**, tests).

Running unit and integration tests

In this section, we will write some integration and unit tests by using one of the most popular test runners in the JavaScript ecosystem: Jest.

Before installing all the dependencies we need, clone the following repository, which already contains a small web application that we'll be using as an example for writing our tests: `https://github.com/PacktPublishing/Real-World-Next.js/tree/main/09-testing-nextjs/boilerplate`.

It's a simple website with the following features:

- Two pages: a home page containing all the articles in our blog and a single article page.
- The article page URL implements the following format: `<article_slug>-<article-id>`.
- There are some utility functions that create the page's URL, retrieve the article ID from the article URL, and so on.
- Two REST APIs: one for getting all the articles and one for getting a specific article given an ID.

Now let's enter the project we've cloned and install the following dependency:

```
yarn add -D jest
```

Jest is the only dependency that we'll need for our tests, as it acts both as a testing framework and as a test runner. It provides an extensive set of features that will make our development (and testing) experience pleasant.

Given that we're writing our functions and components using ESNext" features, we want to tell Jest to use the default Next.js babel preset for transpiling those modules correctly. We can do that by creating a `.babelrc` file in our project's root and adding the following content:

```
{
    "presets": ["next/babel"]
}
```

The `next/babel` preset comes pre-installed with Next.js, so we don't need to install anything, and we're ready to go.

We can start using it without any other configuration, as it comes pre-configured for running every file ending with `.test.js` or `.spec.js`.

Still, there are different approaches for how to write and where to place those files. For example, some people prefer to have a test file close to the source file, and others prefer to have all the tests inside a `tests/` directory. Of course, neither of those approaches is wrong: it's up to your taste.

> **Pay Attention When Writing Next.js Pages' Tests**
>
> Next.js serves every `.js`, `.jsx`, `.ts`, and `.tsx` file placed inside of the `pages/` directory as an application page. Therefore, *you should never place any test file inside that directory*, or Next.js will try to render it as an application page. We will see how to test Next.js pages in the next section while writing end-to-end tests.

Let's write our first test, starting from the easiest part of our code base: the utility functions. We can create a new file, `utils/tests/index.test.js`, and start by importing all the functions that we can find in our `utils/index.js` file:

```
import {
  trimTextToLength,
  slugify,
  composeArticleSlug,
  extractArticleIdFromSlug
} from '../index';
```

We can now write the first test for the `trimTextToLength` function. This function takes two arguments: a string and the length under which we will be cutting it, adding an ellipsis at its end. We use this function to show a sneak peek of the article body to tempt the reader to read the whole article.

For instance, pretend we have the following string:

```
const str = "The quick brown fox jumps over the lazy dog";
```

If we apply `trimTextToLength` to it, we should see the following output:

```
const str = "The quick brown fox jumps over the lazy dog";
const cut = trimTextToLength(str, 5);
cut === "The q..." // true
```

We can translate the preceding function description into code as follows:

```
describe("trimTextToLength", () => {
test('Should cut a string that exceeds 10 characters', () => {
    const initialString = 'This is a 34 character long
     string';
    const cutResult = trimTextToLength(initialString, 10);
    expect(cutResult).toEqual('This is a ...');
  });
});
```

As you can see, we're using some of Jest's built-in functions, such as `describe`, `test`, and `expect`. They all have their specific function, and we can summarize them as follows:

- `describe`: Creates a group of related tests. For example, we should include tests regarding the same functions or modules inside of that function.

- `test`: Declares a test and runs it.

- `expect`: This is the function that we use to compare our function's outputs against a fixed number of results.

As we've seen, we can add several tests into the `describe` group so that we can test our function against multiple values:

```
describe("trimTextToLength cuts a string when it's too long, ()
=> {
  test('Should cut a string that exceeds 10 characters', ()
    => {
    const initialString = 'This is a 35 characters long
     string';
```

```
        const cutResult = trimTextToLength(initialString, 10);
        expect(cutResult).toEqual('This is a ...');
    });


    test("Should not cut a string if it's shorter than 10
    characters",
        () => {

            const initialString = '7 chars';
            const cutResult = trimTextToLength(initialString,
             10);
            expect(cutResult).toEqual('7 chars');

        }
    );
});
```

Moving on to the `slugify` function, let's try to write its own tests:

```
describe('slugify makes a string URL-safe', () => {
  test('Should convert a string to URL-safe format', () =>
    {
    const initialString = 'This is a string to slugify';
    const slugifiedString = slugify(initialString);
    expect(slugifiedString).
      toEqual('this-is-a-string-to-slugify');


    });
  test('Should slugify a string with special
    characters', () => {
    const initialString = 'This is a string to
    slugify!@#$%^&*()+';
    const slugifiedString = slugify(initialString);
    expect(slugifiedString).
      toEqual('this-is-a-string-to-slugify');
    });
});
```

Now, try to implement the tests for the remaining functions on your own. If you have any doubt, you can find the complete test implementation here: `https://github.com/PacktPublishing/Real-World-Next.js/blob/main/09-testing-nextjs/unit-integration-tests/utils/tests/index.test.js`.

Once we've written all the remaining tests, we're finally ready to run our test suite. To make it easier and standard, we can create a new script inside of our `package.json` file:

```
"scripts": {
  "dev": "next dev",
  "build": "next build",
  "start": "next start",
  "test": "jest"
},
```

And that's all we need! We can now type `yarn test` in the console and admire the following output:

```
λ → yarn test
yarn run v1.22.10
$ jest
 PASS  utils/tests/index.test.js
  cutTextToLength cuts a string when it's too long
    ✓ Should cut a string that exceeds 10 characters (2 ms)
    ✓ Should not cut a string if it's shorter than 10 characters
  slugify makes a string URL-safe
    ✓ Should convert a string to URL-safe format
    ✓ Should slugify a string with special characters
  composeArticleSlug should create a complete article URL given a title and an ID
    ✓ Should create a complete article URL (1 ms)
    ✓ Should create a complete article URL with special characters
  extractArticleIdFromSlug should correctly extract the ID out of an article URL
    ✓ Should correctly extract the ID out of an article URL

Test Suites: 1 passed, 1 total
Tests:       7 passed, 7 total
Snapshots:   0 total
Time:        0.599 s, estimated 1 s
Ran all test suites.
✨  Done in 1.39s.
```

Figure 9.1 – Unit test output

We can now move on to writing a more complex test. If you open the `components/ArticleCard/index.js` file, you will see a simple React component that creates a link to a Next.js page.

In that case, we want to test that our `composeArticleSlug` and `trimTextToLength` functions (used in that component) integrate correctly by producing the expected output. We also want to test that the displayed text will match a fixed result when given an article as input.

Sadly, Jest alone is not enough for testing React components. We will need to mount and render them to test their output, and specific libraries do that incredibly well.

The most popular options out there are **react-testing-library** and **Enzyme**. In this example, we will be using `react-testing-library`, but feel free to experiment with Enzyme and see which approach you prefer.

Let's install the `react-testing-library` package by running this:

```
yarn add @testing-library/react
```

Now let's move on to create a new file named `components/ArticleCard/tests/index.test.js`.

Before moving on to the test implementation, let's consider something. We now need to test our `ArticleCard` component against a REST API, but we won't be running the server during the test's execution. Right now, we're not testing that our API is responding with the correct JSON containing the article, we're just testing that given an article as input, the component will produce a fixed output.

That said, we can easily create a mock containing all the information we expect an article to contain, and give it as an input to our component.

Let's create a new file, `components/ArticleCard/tests/mock.js`, with the following content (or just copy it from this book's GitHub repository under `09-testing-nextjs/unit-integration-tests/components/ArticleCard/tests/mock.js`):

```
export const article = {
  id: 'u12w3o0d',
  title: 'Healthy summer melon-carrot soup',
  body: 'Lorem ipsum dolor sit amet, consectetur adipiscing
    elit. Morbi iaculis, felis quis sagittis molestie, mi
    sem lobortis dui, a sollicitudin nibh erat id ex.',
  author: {
    id: '93ksj19s',
    name: 'John Doe',
  },
```

```
    image: {
        url: 'https://images.unsplash.com/photo-1629032355262-
        d751086c475d',
        author: 'Karolin Baitinger',
    },
};
```

If you try to run the Next.js server, you will see that the APIs inside of `pages/api/` will return either an array of articles or a single article in the same format we used for the mock.

We're finally ready to write our tests. Open the `components/ArticleCard/tests/index.test.js` file and start by importing the react-testing-library functions, the components, mocks, and utilities we want to test:

```
import { render, screen } from '@testing-library/react';
import ArticleCard from '../index';
import { trimTextToLength } from '../../../utils';
import { article } from '../tests/mock';
```

Now let's write our first test case. If we open the `ArticleCard` component, we will see that there's a Next.js Link component wrapping the entire card. This link's `href` should be in the format `/articles/<article-title-slugified>-id`.

As a first test case, we will test that there's one link, where the `href` attribute is equal to `/articles/healthy-summer-meloncarrot-soup-u12w3o0d` (which is the title we can see in our mock, plus the article ID):

```
describe('ArticleCard', () => {
    test('Generated link should be in the correct format', ()
        => {
            const component = render(<ArticleCard {...article} />);
            const link = component.getByRole('
            link').getAttribute('href');
            expect(link).toBe(
            '/articles/healthy-summer-meloncarrot-soup-u12w3o0d'
        );
    });
});
```

We're using the react-testing-library `render` method to mount and render the component, then we get the link and extract its `href` attribute. We eventually test this attribute value against a fixed string, which is the expected value.

Still, there is a problem with our test. If we try to run it, we will see the following error appearing in the console:

```
The error below may be caused by using the wrong
test environment, see https://jestjs.io/docs/
configuration#testenvironment-string.
Consider using the "jsdom" test environment.
```

That's because react-testing-library relies on the browser's document global variable, which is unavailable in Node.js.

We can quickly solve this problem by changing the Jest environment for this test file to JSDOM, a library that emulates a large part of the browser's features for testing purposes. We don't need to install anything; we can just add the following comment at the top of our testing file, right before the `import` statements, and Jest will do the rest:

```
/**
 * @jest-environment jsdom
 */
```

If we now run `yarn test` in the terminal, the tests will succeed as expected.

Inside the `ArticleCard` component, we show a brief extract of the article body to tempt the reader to read the entire piece. It uses the `trimTextToLength` function to trim the article body to a maximum length of 100 characters, so we expect to see those first 100 chapters inside the rendered component.

We can proceed with writing a test as follows:

```
describe('ArticleCard', () => {
  test('Generated link should be in the correct format', ()
    => {
      const component = render(<ArticleCard {...article} />);
      const link = component.getByRole('link')
        .getAttribute('href');
      expect(link).toBe(
        '/articles/healthy-summer-meloncarrot-soup-u12w3o0d'
      );
```

```
  });
    test('Generated summary should not exceed 100
    characters',
      async () => {
        render(<ArticleCard {...article} />);
        const summary = screen.getByText(
          trimTextToLength(article.body, 100)
        );
      expect(summary).toBeDefined();
    });
  });
```

In this case, we render the whole component, then generate the article summary and expect it to exist inside our document.

That was an elementary example of how we can test our code base by using Jest and react-testing-library. When writing a real-world application, we also want to test our components against incorrect data to see if they can handle any errors correctly, either by throwing an error, showing a message on the screen, and so on.

Testing is not an easy topic, but it must be taken seriously as it can help us avoid shipping broken code or introducing regressions (for example, breaking a component that was previously working fine) into the existing code base. It is such a complex matter that there's also an entire book on how to test React components using react-testing-library: *Simplify Testing with React Testing Library* by Scottie Crump, published by Packt.

If you're interested in learning more and digging deep into React testing, I strongly suggest reading this book.

That said, there is still one piece missing in our tests. We're not testing the full-page renders, whether the APIs send back correct data, and whether we can navigate correctly between pages. But that's what end-to-end tests are all about, and we will discuss this in the next section.

End-to-end testing with Cypress

Cypress is a powerful testing tool that can test anything that runs on a web browser.

It enables you to write and run unit, integration, and end-to-end tests efficiently by running them on Firefox and Chromium-based browsers (for example, Google Chrome).

So far, we have written tests for understanding whether our functions and components are working as expected. Now it's time to test whether the entire application is working correctly.

To get started with Cypress, we just need to install it as a `dev` dependency in our project. We will be using the same project as the latest section, but if you want to get started from a clean project, you can clone the following repository and get started from there: `https://github.com/PacktPublishing/Real-World-Next.js/tree/main/09-testing-nextjs/unit-integration-tests`.

Let's install Cypress by typing the following command into the terminal:

```
yarn add -D cypress
```

Once Cypress is installed, we can edit our main `package.json` file by adding the following script:

```
"scripts": {
  "dev": "next dev",
  "build": "next build",
  "start": "next start",
  "test": "jest",
  "cypress": "cypress run",
},
```

We now need to create a Cypress configuration file. Let's write a `cypress.json` file in the project root containing the following content:

```
{
  "baseUrl": http://localhost:3000
}
```

Here, we're telling Cypress where to look when running tests; in our case, `localhost:3000`. Now that we're all set, let's move on to writing our first tests!

By convention, we will be putting our end-to-end tests inside a folder called `cypress/`, placed at the root level of the repository.

We will start with an easy test to verify that our REST APIs are working correctly.

If you open the `pages/api/` folder, you will see two different APIs:

- `articles.js`, which returns a list of articles:

```
import data from '../../data/articles';
export default (req, res) => {
  res.status(200).json(data);
};
```

- `article/index.js`, which takes an article ID as a query string parameter and returns the single article with that ID:

```
import data from '../../../data/articles';
export default (req, res) => {
  const id = req.query.id;
  const requestedArticle = data.find(
    (article) => article.id === id
  );
  requestedArticle
    ? res.status(200).json(requestedArticle)
    : res.status(404).json({ error: 'Not found' });
};
```

Let's create our first Cypress test file, named `cypress/integration/api.spec.js`, and add the following content:

```
describe('articles APIs', () => {
  test('should correctly set application/json header', ()
    => {
    cy.request('http://localhost:3000/api/articles')
      .its('headers')
      .its('content-type')
      .should('include', 'application/json');
  });
});
```

The APIs are slightly different from the Jest ones, but we can still see that they share the same philosophy. We use them to describe the response coming from the server, testing it against a fixed value.

In the preceding example, we're just testing that the HTTP headers include the
`content-type=application/json header`.

We can proceed by testing the status code, which should be equal to `200`:

```
describe('articles APIs', () => {
  test('should correctly set application/json header', ()
    => {
    cy.request('http://localhost:3000/api/articles')
      .its('headers')
      .its('content-type')
      .should('include', 'application/json');
  });
  test('should correctly return a 200 status code', () => {
    cy.request('http://localhost:3000/api/articles')
      .its('status')
      .should('be.equal', 200);
  });
});
```

Moving on to a more complex test case, we can test the API output to be an array
of objects, where each object must contain a minimum set of properties. The test
implementation would look like this:

```
test('should correctly return a list of articles', (done) => {
  cy.request('http://localhost:3000/api/articles')
    .its('body')
    .each((article) => {
      expect(article)
        .to.have.keys('id', 'title', 'body', 'author',
          'image');
      expect(article.author).to.have.keys('id', 'name');
      expect(article.image).to.have.keys('url', 'author');
      done();
    });
});
```

As you can see, we're using the `.to.have.keys` method to test that returning object contains all the keys specified in the function argument.

Another thing to notice is that we're doing that in an `each` loop. For that reason, we will need to call the `done` method (highlighted in the code snippet) once we've tested all the desired properties, as Cypress cannot control when the code inside of the `each` callback has returned.

We can proceed by writing another couple of tests to see if we can get a single article given a fixed article ID:

```
test('should correctly return a an article given an ID', (done)
=> {
  cy.request('http://localhost:3000/api/article?id=u12w3o0d')
    .then(({ body }) => {
      expect(body)
        .to.have.keys('id', 'title', 'body', 'author',
          'image');
      expect(body.author).to.have.keys('id', 'name');
      expect(body.image).to.have.keys('url', 'author');
      done();
    });
});
```

And we can also test that the server returns a 404 status code when the article is not found. To do that, we will need to change our request method a bit as Cypress, by default, throws an error when a status code greater than or equal to 400 is encountered:

```
test('should return 404 when an article is not found', () => {
  cy.request({
    url: 'http://localhost:3000/api/article?id=unexistingID',
    failOnStatusCode: false,
  })
  .its('status')
  .should('be.equal', 404);
});
```

Now that we have written the tests, we're ready to run them, but there's still a problem. If we try to run yarn cypress, we will see the following error on the console:

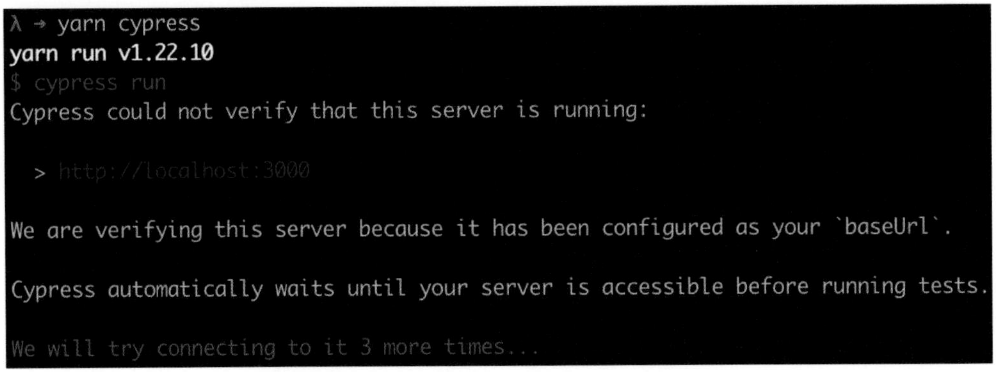

```
λ → yarn cypress
yarn run v1.22.10
$ cypress run
Cypress could not verify that this server is running:

  > http://localhost:3000

We are verifying this server because it has been configured as your `baseUrl`.

Cypress automatically waits until your server is accessible before running tests.

We will try connecting to it 3 more times...
```

Figure 9.2 – Cypress cannot connect to the server

In fact, Cypress runs our tests against a real server, which is not reachable at the moment. We can quickly solve that by adding the following dependency:

```
yarn add -D start-server-and-test
```

This will help us by building and starting the server, and once it's reachable, it will run Cypress. To do that, we will need to edit our package.json file too:

```
"scripts": {
  "dev": "next dev",
  "build": "next build",
  "start": "next start",
  "test": "jest",
  "cypress": "cypress run",
  "e2e": "start-server-and-test 'yarn build && yarn start'
    http://localhost:3000 cypress"
},
```

If we now try to run yarn e2e, we will see that the tests are passing correctly!

Let's create one last test file where we'll be testing the navigation between pages. We can call it cypress/integration/navigation.spec.js, and we can add the following content:

```
describe('Navigation', () => {
  test('should correctly navigate to the article page', ()
    => {
```

```
      cy.visit('http://localhost:3000/');
      cy.get('a[href*="/articles"]').first().click();
      cy.url().should('be.equal',
      'http://localhost:3000/articles/healthy-summer-meloncarrot-
        soup-u12w3o0d');
      cy.get('h1').contains('Healthy summer melon-carrot
        soup');
  });
  test('should correctly navigate back to the homepage', ()
    => {
    cy.visit('http://localhost:3000/articles/
      healthy-summer-meloncarrot-soup-u12w3o0d');
    cy.get('a[href*="/"]').first().click();
    cy.url().should('be.equal', 'http://localhost:3000/');
    cy.get('h1').contains('My awesome blog');
  });
});
```

In the first test case, we're asking Cypress to visit our website's home page. Then, we look for all the links where the `href` property contains `/articles`. We then click on the first occurrence and expect the new URL to be equal to a fixed value (`http://localhost:3000/articles/healthy-summer-meloncarrot-soup-u12w3o0d`).

We also test that the `<h1>` HTML element contains the correct title. But what does this test tell us?

- We can navigate between pages; links aren't broken. Then, of course, we should add more and more tests for links, but we just want to look at the concept right now.

- The Next.js server correctly asks and serves the correct data, since we can spot the right title inside the rendered page.

In the second test case, we ask Cypress to visit a single article page, then click on a link to go back to the home page. Again, we test the new URL is correct, and the `<h1>` HTML element contains the right title for the home page.

Of course, these are not complete tests, as we might want to check whether the behavior of the website is consistent between browsers (especially if we do a lot of client-side rendering), that an existing form gets validated correctly, giving accurate feedback to the user, and so on.

Like unit and integration testing, end-to-end testing is a vast and complex topic that we must deal with before shipping code to production, as it can ensure greater quality for our product, with fewer bugs and more control over regressions.

If you're interested in learning more about Cypress, I suggest you read the book *End-to-End Web Testing with Cypress*, by Waweru Mwaura, published by Packt.

Summary

In this chapter, we've seen how to write unit, integration, and end-to-end tests using some of the most popular libraries and test runners out there, such as Cypress, Jest, and react-testing-library.

As mentioned multiple times during the chapter, testing is essential for any application development and release process. It should be taken seriously as it can be the difference between a successful and an unsuccessful product.

In the next chapter, we will focus on a different yet crucial topic: SEO and performance. Even if our code base is 100% tested, well-designed, and working great, we need to consider its SEO score and performance. In many cases, we want as many people as possible to be browsing our applications, and we must take care of search engine optimization to reach a large audience to validate our product.

10
Working with SEO and Managing Performance

SEO (short for **Search Engine Optimization**) and performances are two topics that go hand in hand during the development process as a whole.

Even though there have been multiple enhancements on the Next.js side to improve performances and facilitate SEO best practices, we still need to know where our application could potentially create any problems that would result in poor search engine indexing and a lousy user experience.

In this chapter, we will cover the following topics in detail:

- Choosing the proper rendering method for your application (SSR, SSG, CSR).
- When an application will typically fail on the performance aspect
- How to use the Vercel Analytics module
- Tools that help us to write SEO-friendly web applications

By the end of this chapter, you'll be able to optimize your web application for SEO and performance by learning some of the best practices and tools for dealing with such complex topics.

Technical requirements

To run the code examples in this chapter, you need to have both Node.js and npm installed on your local machine.

If you prefer, you can use an online IDE such as `https://repl.it` or `https://codesandbox.io`; they both support Next.js, and you don't need to install any dependency on your computer. As for the other chapters, you can find the code base for this chapter on GitHub: `https://github.com/PacktPublishing/Real-World-Next.js`.

SEO and performance – an introduction

Since the rise of the first big search engines, web developers have struggled to find a way to optimize their web applications to get better positioning in search results on Google, Bing, Yandex, DuckDuckGo, and many other popular search engines.

With the evolution of frontend web frameworks, things became even more complicated. While React, Angular, Vue (and many others) provide a fantastic way to deal with complex UIs, they make things a bit harder for web spiders, the bots responsible for indexing websites into a search engine. They need to execute JavaScript, wait for the UI to render, and eventually index highly dynamic web pages. In addition, many contents would be initially hidden, as they get generated dynamically by JavaScript on the frontend directly following user interaction.

That caused many problems and made countless developers regret *the good old days* when the web was essentially server side rendered, where JavaScript was used to add just a touch of dynamism inside the UI.

OK, I exaggerated a bit. Developers eventually faced the fact that React, Angular, Vue, and all the other fellow frameworks bring such significant innovation to the web development sphere, and they wouldn't give up on them.

Next.js is, in part, a response to those problems. While there are frameworks that only care about SEO and performance by generating all the web pages statically at build time (with all the limitations that this can bring, as seen in *Chapter 2, Exploring Different Rendering Strategies*), Next.js lets you decide which page needs to be statically generated and server side rendered, and which components need to be rendered exclusively on the client side.

In *Chapter 2, Exploring Different Rendering Strategies*, we described the differences between those rendering methods. In the next section, we will discuss some real-world examples of how to choose a rendering strategy when it comes to rendering a web page using Next.js.

Rendering strategies, from a performance and SEO perspective

Depending on the website or web application you want to build, you may consider different rendering strategies.

Every rendering strategy has its pros and cons, but the great thing about Next.js is that you don't have to compromise. Instead, you can choose the best rendering strategy for every single page in your web application.

Let's pretend Next.js doesn't exist for a moment. Pretty scary, isn't it?

We want to build a web application using React, but we have to compromise between rendering strategies.

Client-side rendering is a great starting point. The application would be deployed as a JavaScript bundle that dynamically generates the HTML content once it gets downloaded to the web browser. The performances will be outstanding, as all the computation will be done on the client side. In addition, the user experience will be amazing, as the customers would feel as if they were using a native app. On the other hand, you'd have to struggle with SEO, as client-side rendering makes life harder for search engine bots.

On second thought, we may consider server-side rendering. We would render all the content that is important for SEO purposes on the server side, allowing the client to generate the rest. This could be the best option security-wise, as we can hide many data fetch, validation, and sensitive API calls on the backend. That's a good alternative but has some drawbacks. With client-side rendering, we've seen how the app could be bundled into a unique JavaScript file. With SSR, we will need to set up, maintain, and scale a server. With an increase in traffic, it would get slower, more expensive, and harder to maintain. Time to look for a third option.

Our last option is to generate the whole website at build time statically. We would achieve the best possible performance, while SEO scores would increase significantly, but we'd still have some significant drawbacks.

If our SEO-sensitive content changes frequently, we may need to re-render the whole website multiple times in a few hours. That could be a significant issue on large websites, as building can require quite a long time. Also, it would be harder to handle user security, as every sensitive API call (occurring after the building phase) or computation would happen on the client side exclusively.

Let's recap our options:

- **Client-side rendering (CSR)**: Great performance, highly dynamic content, but lousy SEO and security
- **Server-side rendering (SSR)**: Better SEO, excellent security, but possibly inferior performance, and more challenging to manage the server
- **Static site generation (SSG)**: Best possible performance, best possible SEO score, but lacking security and bad for highly dynamic content

Now we can finally stop pretending that Next.js doesn't exist and start appreciating the possibilities that this framework is giving us.

We don't have to choose one single rendering methodology to implement our web app. We can choose them all.

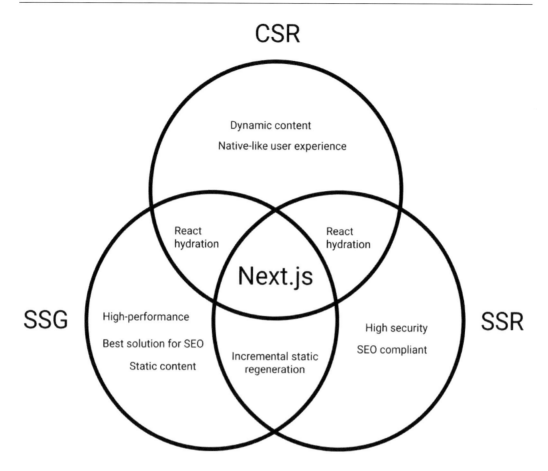

Figure 10.1 – Next.js rendering strategies

One of the key features of Next.js is the ability to choose whether to render a page on the server or generate it at build time (or even on the client side entirely).

Given that possibility, we can start reasoning about our website as a composition of different sections rendered in many different ways, depending on the purpose of each individual section.

In the next section, we will see how to choose the right rendering approach in a real-world website example.

The reasoning behind a real-world website example

Let's pretend we're building a photography website. Users can upload their pictures and receive feedback and votes from the other users on the platform. When a user logs in, the home page will display a list of images posted by the user-followed profiles. Clicking on any of these pictures will open the picture detail page where we can read the comments, feedback, and history behind the photo.

Given this information, we can start to think about how we want to render these website sections.

First, we know that the home page content changes depending on how the user browses it. We can then exclude statically generating the main list of pictures on the home page at build time, as the content is highly dynamic.

We have the following options:

- We statically render the home page with some placeholders for the images, which will be loaded later after React hydration on the client side, depending on whether the user is logged in and following anyone on the website.

- We can render the page on the server side. Thanks to session cookies, we may already know if the user is logged in, and we can pre-render this list on the server before sending the page to the client.

One thing is for sure: we don't really care about SEO when dealing with this specific list of pictures. Google bots will never log in to this website, as there's no reason to index custom content that is different for each user.

Talking about performance, we should consider a couple of points before deciding how we want to render the home page. If the API used for generating a customized stream of pictures is fast enough and the images are highly optimized, we can surely pre-render the whole list on the server side. Otherwise, we could create some good-looking skeleton loading placeholders that can entertain the user while we're waiting for the API to respond and the images to render on the frontend.

The worst-case scenario is that the API is slow, and the images are not optimized, hence we need to be prepared for that eventuality. We then decide to generate the whole page statically at build time, but we'll wait for React hydration to make the API call and generate the optimized images (maybe using the Next.js built-in image component, as seen in *Chapter 3, Next.js Basics and Built-In Components*).

So, the final verdict is SSG and CSR. We'll statically generate the home page and create the list of images on the client side.

In the next section, we will see the best way to handle the image detail page.

Rendering the image detail page

Moving on to the following sections of our websites, we want to create a single image page template. Here, we will render the photo posted by a user, its description, some tags, and all the comments and feedback given by other users.

In that case, we want this page to be indexed by search engines, as its content doesn't depend on user sessions or any other variable of that kind.

Again, we must choose how we want to render this page. We already know that SEO is essential, so we exclude full client-side rendering as an option. We have to choose between statically generating this page at build time or server-side rendering it with each request.

We know that either choice will help us with SEO, but the wrong decision here would affect the performance of this website as soon as it needs to scale. It's time to compare the pros and cons of SSG and SSR for this specific use case.

Static site generation pros and cons for dynamic pages

Static site generation provides many pros for that kind of application:

- Once we generate a static page during the build process, the server won't need to re-render it on each request. That brings less load to the server, which leads to cheaper infrastructure costs and effortless scalability under high loads.

- The picture author may want to change some of the static content following generation. However, at this point, we don't want to wait for the next build to occur: we can just use incremental static regeneration for re-rendering the static page on the server once every (let's say) 30 minutes if anything changes.

- Page performances will be the best possible.

- Dynamic parts such as comments and like counts (that might not be important for SEO) can be rendered later on the client side.

- When a user wants to add a new picture, they don't have to wait for the next build for their image to appear on the website. In fact, we can set the `fallback: true` parameter inside the returning object of the `getStaticPaths` function to let Next.js statically render a new page at request time.

There is just one big disadvantage when rendering this kind of web page at build time: if you have thousands of pages, it will take a lot of time for your website to build. That's something to keep in mind when choosing SSG for dynamic routes. How many dynamic pages are we likely to support in the future? How much would it take for the build process to generate them?

Now let's move on looking at the pros and cons of server-side rendering for the single picture detail page.

Server-side rendering pros and cons for dynamic pages

Server-side rendering provides a couple of important pros when compared to static site generation for this specific page.

The first one is that if a user changes the content of a page, we don't have to wait for incremental static regeneration to occur. We can see the changes reflected on the production page as soon as the picture author changes any information about their photo.

The second pro is even more critical. As seen before, SSG can take up to several minutes to complete when generating a large number of static pages. Server-side rendering solves this problem by just rendering the page at request time, making the whole deployment pipeline faster.

If you think about large-scale websites such as Google and Facebook, you can easily understand why generating those pages at build time could be a problem. It can work fine if you want to render dozens or hundreds of pages, but it will become a huge bottleneck if you generate millions or even billions of them.

In our case, we expect to host thousands of pictures, with each picture having a detail page. Therefore, we will eventually decide to adopt server-side rendering for them.

Another option would be statically generating the most popular pages at build time (let's say the first thousand pages), then using the "fallback" property to generate them at runtime.

We now only need to define the rendering strategy for private routes, where users can change their own profile details. We will cover that right in the next section.

Private routes

As the adjective "private" suggests, private pages are not meant to be reached by everybody. Instead, they should be accessible by logged-in users only and contain the essential information needed to manage their account settings (username, password, email, and so on).

That said, we won't really care about SEO, but we'll focus on security instead. The data contained in those pages is sensitive, and we want to protect it at all costs.

This is one of those rare cases where we want to sacrifice some performance to improve our security.

We could quickly generate the private routes statically and then make all the required API calls on the client side, but this could expose some personal (or private) data if not handled correctly. So instead, we will adopt the server-side rendering strategy to detect anonymous users right before rendering the page and redirect them away. Also, if the user making the request is logged in, we can preload all of their data on the backend and pass it to the client side via `getServerSideProps`, which drastically improves security while transmitting data to the client.

Now that we've defined how to manage private routes, we've completed the basic rendering strategy analysis, so it's time for a quick recap. We'll see that in the next section.

A quick recap regarding our decisions

In the previous sections, we made some decisions based on the kind of pages that we'll need to render for our photography website.

This analysis is critical and should be considered for every website we will be working on in the future. If we need to add new pages to an existing Next.js website, we will need to perform a similar analysis to understand the best solution possible to get the best performances, security, and SEO compliance.

For our photography website, we came up with the following structure:

- **Home page**: We will statically generate the whole home page except for the custom list of images, which will be rendered on the client side depending on the user browsing it.

- **Image detail page**: We can either choose to server-side render it (as this will allow us to optimize the page for SEO and guarantees an excellent way of scaling our website up to millions of different image detail pages) or statically generate the most popular pages at build time and then use the "fallback" property to generate missing pages at runtime.

- **Private pages**: We will server side render them to determine whether a user is logged in before rendering the page. Also, we will be able to fetch all the private data on the server side, hiding that API call from the frontend.

In *Chapter 13, Building an E-Commerce Website with Next.js and GraphCMS*, for example, we will need to make this kind of decision to build a real-world Next.js e-commerce website. However, if you want to practice before getting into that, I'd suggest you think about how you would recreate your favorite websites.

Facebook, Google, YouTube, Amazon – they all have specific needs, security requirements, and SEO specifications. So, how would you handle that? How are they dealing with those features?

In the next section, we will concentrate on improving SEO by using some open source tools that will help us deal with search engine bots.

Working with SEO

SEO in Next.js is not different from any other framework. Search engine bots make no difference; they only care about website content and quality. So, even though Next.js tries to simplify things, we still need to respect specific rules and develop our websites on the basis of the search engine specifications to get a good indexing score.

Given the rendering possibilities that Next.js provides for us, we already know that particular decisions can negatively impact the final SEO score (for example, rendering important data on the client side). We talked about that in the previous sections, so we won't go deep into it again.

There are specific SEO metrics that might be a bit out of our control when developing the website. Domain authority, referring domains, page impressions, click-through rate, and organic market share are just a few of them. Even though we are unlikely to improve those metrics during the development process (as they are the product of good content management on the website), we should do our best to improve whatever we can by coding the website. This includes a series of optimizations and developments that include (but are not limited to) the following:

- *Creating an SEO-friendly routing structure*: A well-made routing system is essential for search engine bots to index a website correctly. URLs should always be human-friendly and composed according to a certain logic. For example, if we're creating a blog, we should use a URL structure to help the user identify the page content by just looking at the page URL. While something like `https://myblog.com/posts/1` can be easier to work with, it makes things harder for blog users (and search engines too!) since, by looking at the page address, we can't tell what the content is about. `https://myblog.com/posts/how-to-deal-with-seo` is a better URL, which tells us that on this page, we're talking about SEO and how to deal with it.

- *Fill the pages with correct and complete metadata*: In *Chapter 3, Next.js Basics and Built-In Components*, we've already seen how to deal with metadata. This is essential data that we should always include in our pages, with no exception. There are great libraries such as `next-seo` (`https://github.com/garmeeh/next-seo`) that can drastically reduce the development time required to manage the metadata during the development process.

- *Optimize your images*: We've already talked about how we can optimize images. The built-in image component has been developed in cooperation with the Google Chrome team to give better support for images, and that is also reflected in some SEO metrics (such as Cumulative Layout Shift and First Contentful Paint).

- *Generate a proper sitemap*: Once we're ready to deploy a website, we can submit the sitemap to search engines to help them index our content. A well-made sitemap is essential for any website as it allows the creation of a neat, structured path for search engines to follow to index the site. As for today, there's no built-in solution in Next.js for creating a sitemap, but there are several great libraries, including `nextjs-sitemap-generator` (`https://github.com/IlusionDev/nextjs-sitemap-generator`), that can help to create it.

- *Use the correct HTML tags*: Using semantic HTML tags to build a website is essential as they tell the search engine bots how to index the content in terms of priority and importance. As an example, while we always want our content to be indexed, using `<h1>` HTML tags for every text content is not the best choice for SEO. We always need to find the right balance in order for our HTML tags to be meaningful for users and search engine bots.

Dealing with SEO is not an easy task. It has always been challenging and can only become harder in the future as new technologies and rules rise. The good thing is that every rule is the same for every website, so you can bring your experience with other frameworks, CMSes, and development tools to Next.js with ease, as it can only help you create more optimized websites with less effort.

One other metric that can impact SEO is the performance of the website. Again, this is a crucial topic, and we will look into that in the next section.

Dealing with performance

Performance and SEO are two important aspects of any web application. Performance, in particular, can affect the SEO score, as a lousy-performing website will lower the SEO score.

At the beginning of this chapter, we've already seen how choosing the right rendering strategy can help us improve performance, but sometimes, we have to compromise between a slightly lower performance in favor of security, business logic, and suchlike.

Another thing that can potentially increase (or decrease) performance is the deployment platform. For instance, if you're deploying a Next.js static website to a CDN such as Cloudflare or AWS Cloudfront, you're likely to get the best possible performance. On the other hand, deploying a server-side rendered application to a small, cheap server will probably give you some trouble once the website starts to scale and the server is not prepared for handling all the incoming requests, leading to bad performance. We will discuss this topic in depth in *Chapter 11, Different Deployment Platforms*. As for now, keep in mind that this is another big topic to consider during performances analysis.

When we talk about performance, we don't always refer to server-side metrics; even the frontend performance is essential, and if not carefully handled, this can lead to lousy SEO scores and a bad user experience.

With the release of Next.js 10, the Vercel team has announced a new built-in function to be used in our pages: `reportWebVitals`.

It has been developed in collaboration with Google and allows us to collect valuable information about our frontend performances, including the following:

- **Largest contentful paint (LCP)**: This measures the loading performance, which should occur within 2.5 seconds of the initial page load.

- **First input delay (FID)**: This measures how much time it takes for the page to be interactive. It should take less than 100 milliseconds.

- **Cumulative layout shift (CLS)**: This measures visual stability. Remember when we talked about images? A heavy picture might take a long time to load. Once it appears, it would shift the layout, causing the user to lose track of the section they were looking at. The image is a typical example, but other elements could be involved in this: ADV banners, third-party widgets, and so on.

When we deploy our Next.js website, we can enable the platform to track those values to help us understand the performance of our web application on real-world data. Vercel will give us a well-made dashboard that will keep track of deployments and how new features affect overall website performance. Let's look at the following example dashboard:

Figure 10.2 – Vercel analytics dashboard

As you can see, the preceding dashboard shows the average data for a whole website. While CLS and FID values are well implemented, we can clearly see that FCP and LCP can be improved.

If you're unwilling to host your web application on Vercel, you can still collect that data by implementing the `reportWebVitals` function on your `_app.js` page. Let's make a simple example:

```
export const reportWebVitals = (metrics) => console.
  log(metrics);
export default function MyApp({ Component, pageProps }) {
  return <Component {...pageProps} />;
}
```

Thanks to this one-line function, we will see the following output in the console every time we enter a new page:

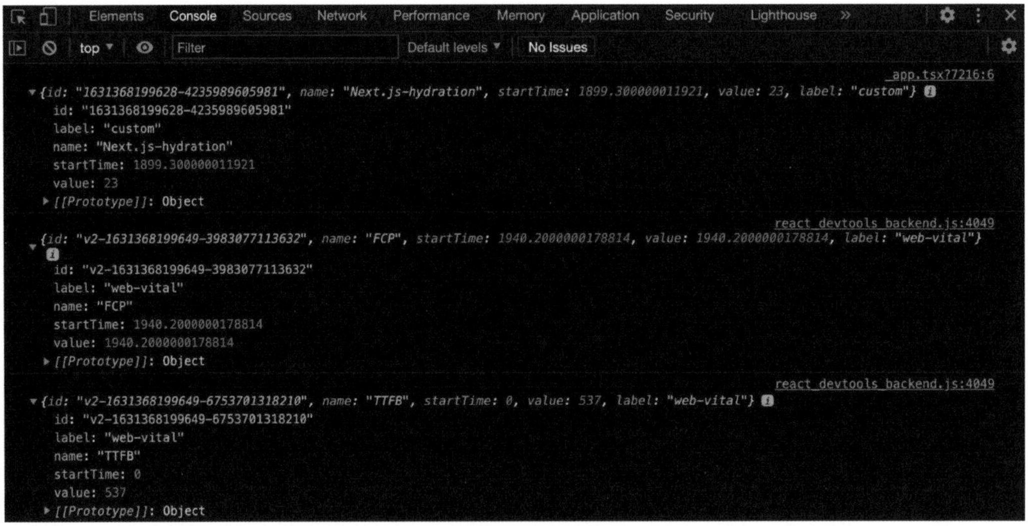

Figure 10.3 – Web vitals

We can then decide to send this data to any external service, such as Google Analytics or Plausible, to collect this helpful information:

```
export const reportWebVitals = (metrics) =>
  sendToGoogleAnalytics(metric);
export default function MyApp({ Component, pageProps }) {
  return <Component {...pageProps} />;
}
```

If you want to learn more about web vitals, the official website maintained by Google is always up to date with the latest improvements and rules: `https://web.dev/vitals`. I strongly suggest you read this before getting started with collecting and measuring frontend performances in your web application.

Summary

In this chapter, we've seen how to reason in relation to our pages regarding SEO, performance, and security. Even though those topics are quite complex, the primary purpose of this chapter was to give a kind of framework of thinking. In fact, those topics are likely to evolve in the future, as the web itself is moving forward fast with new performance metrics, SEO rules, and security standards.

In the next chapter, we will continue talking about these topics from another perspective. We will see how to deploy our web applications and choose the right hosting platform with respect to our needs.

11
Different Deployment Platforms

In the previous chapters, we saw how Next.js works, how to optimize it for SEO, how to deal with performance, how to adopt UI frameworks, and how to fetch data on both the client and server sides, eventually being able to create a fantastic web application. But then, we have a problem: how should we ship it to production? There are many different hosting providers, cloud platforms, and even **Platform as a Service** (**PaaS**) solutions out there; how do we pick one?

In this chapter, we will see how to choose the right deployment platform.

We will look at the following in detail:

- How choosing the right deployment platform could affect performance
- How to decide between different cloud solutions
- What are the most popular alternatives for hosting a Next.js app?

By the end of this chapter, you'll be able to deploy any Next.js application to any host, knowing how to choose the right provider from the most popular hosting solutions.

Technical requirements

To run the code examples in this chapter, you need to have both Node.js and npm installed on your local machine.

If you prefer, you can use an online IDE, such as `https://repl.it` or `https://codesandbox.io`; they both support Next.js, and you don't need to install any dependency on your computer. As with the other chapters, you can find the code base for this chapter on GitHub: `https://github.com/PacktPublishing/Real-World-Next.js`.

A brief introduction to different deployment platforms

While thinking about a new web application, we have many things to consider. For example, how do we want to render its pages, which styling method do we want to adopt, where does data come from, how do we manage the application state, and where do we want to deploy the application itself?

Focusing on that last part, we could split one problem into two: *where* do we want to deploy our application and *how* do we want to do it?

In fact, most of the time, choosing a deployment platform also means selecting a slightly different deployment method. There are specific cloud platforms, such as Vercel, Netlify, and Heroku, where the deployment process is standardized and incredibly simplified to be accessible for everyone. With other cloud providers, such as AWS, Azure, and DigitalOcean, you have complete control over the whole deployment process. Unfortunately, in many cases, you have to implement this process on your own or use third-party software.

The number of cloud infrastructures has drastically increased over the last few years, and the competition has brought some great innovation to this sector. Even though there are many alternatives, we will be focusing on the most popular ones, as we're more likely to find more documentation and support for them.

In the next section, we will discuss the most prominent platform to deploy a Next.js application to: *Vercel*.

Deploying to the Vercel platform

Develop, preview, ship is not just a motto. It's the perfect description of the company that developed Next.js (alongside many other open source libraries) and an excellent cloud infrastructure for deploying and serving web applications.

With Vercel, you almost don't need to configure anything. You can deploy your web application from the command line using their CLI tool, or create an automatic deployment after a push to the main Git branch.

One thing to know before getting started with Vercel is that the platform is built specifically for static sites and frontend frameworks. Unfortunately, that means that *custom Node.js servers are not supported.*

But at this point, you might be wondering whether only statically generated or client-side-rendered Next.js websites are supported. The short answer is *no*. In fact, Vercel supports server-side-rendered pages by serving them via *serverless functions*.

> **What Does "Serverless Function" Mean?**
>
> When talking about "serverless functions," we refer to a single function (written in any programming language) that gets invoked on a managed infrastructure. In fact, it's called "serverless" because we just have to write the function without really thinking about the server executing it. Unlike traditional servers, where we typically pay an hourly rate (for example, we could pay $1 for every hour, even when the server is not processing any data), serverless functions have a different pricing model: we pay them a fraction of a cent for each execution, depending on the execution duration, memory usage, and other similar metrics. For example, at the time of writing, AWS Lambda (the most popular serverless environment) costs *$0.20 for every million requests* and $0.0000000021 for every millisecond of duration (when allocated 128 MB of memory). As you can imagine, this pricing model can be really attractive compared to more traditional alternatives, as you only pay for what you actually use.

Vercel does an incredible job of setting up serverless functions for us when deploying a Next.js application, so we don't have to worry about them; we just have to concentrate on the web application we're building.

Deploying an application to Vercel is pretty straightforward. We can proceed in two different ways:

- *By linking our GitHub, GitLab, or Bitbucket repository to Vercel.* Every time we create a pull request, Vercel will deploy a preview application to test the features we just developed before publishing them to production. Once we merge or push to our main branch, Vercel will automatically deploy the application to production.

- *We can do everything manually from the command line.* For example, we can decide to create a preview application, preview it locally, or publish it to production directly from our terminal using the Vercel CLI tool, where typing `vercel --prod` is enough to promote the app to production.

Either way, the developer experience is outstanding, so feel free to test both deployment strategies and find your favorite one.

Among all the possible alternatives for deploying and serving Next.js applications, Vercel is probably one of the easiest ones. Also, it allows you to gain access to the analytics module (do you remember we talked about it in *Chapter 10, Working with SEO and Managing Performance?*), which can be incredibly useful to measure frontend performances over time. That will help us keep an eye on frontend optimization, which other platforms don't do (also, it's something fundamental!).

If you're looking for something comparable to Vercel, a good alternative you may consider is Netlify. The whole deployment workflow is quite similar to Vercel's one, and the developer experience is just as phenomenal. However, I'd encourage you to consider the pricing model differences before deciding on either platform.

Both Vercel and Netlify also work incredibly well when deploying a static website. But there, the competition with other platforms will grow; we'll see some alternatives in the next section.

Deploying a static site to a CDN

When talking about a **CDN** (short for **content delivery network**), we refer to a geographically distributed network of data centers used to achieve high availability and performance when serving content to users in any part of the world.

To keep it simple, let's give an example. I currently live near Milan, Italy, and I want my web application to be used in potentially any part of the world. So, where should I host it from a geographical point of view?

Certain providers, such as Amazon AWS, DigitalOcean, and Microsoft Azure (and many more), will let you choose a specific data center to serve your application from. For example, I could select AWS *eu-south-1* (Milan, Italy), *ap-northeast-2* (Seoul, South Korea), or *sa-east-1* (São Paulo, Brazil). If I choose to serve my web application from Milan, Italian users will notice a very low latency when trying to reach the web application; it is geographically located very close to them. The same could happen for French, Swiss, and German users, but for people living in Asia, Africa, or the Americas, it will be the opposite. The further you are from the data center, the greater the latency, leading to lousy performance, poor client-to-server request latency, and so on. If we think of static assets, such as images, CSS, or JavaScript files, this will be even clearer.

Heavy file size + data center distance = bad download performance. It's quite easy, isn't it?

CDNs solve this specific problem by providing a whole infrastructure distributed in (almost) every continent. Once you deploy your static asset to a CDN, it will be replicated across all the regions in the network, making it available closer to your users in any part of the world.

If you look at Next.js' statically generated websites, you will quickly notice that there is no need for a server to render the pages at request time. Instead, the website is entirely generated and statically rendered at build time, so we eventually end up with a collection of static HTML, CSS, and JavaScript files that can be deployed to a CDN.

If we're in that situation, then we're in luck. We're about to achieve the best possible performances by serving static HTML pages from a CDN. But which CDN should I choose? We'll find it out in the next section.

Choosing a CDN

When looking for a CDN to deploy our web application, we will find many different alternatives. Prominent players in this area are (but are not limited to) *Amazon AWS*, *Microsoft Azure CDN*, and *Cloudflare*. Of course, there are many other alternatives, but these are the ones I've tried and had great experiences with, so I feel confident recommending them to you.

The CDN deployment adds some configuration steps, but spending a bit more time to achieve the best possible performance might be worth it.

Talking about AWS, for instance, the procedure won't be as straightforward as the Vercel one. We would need to build a pipeline (with either GitHub Actions or GitLab Pipelines, and so on) to statically generate the web application, then to push it to **AWS S3** (a service used for storing static assets), and eventually use a **CloudFront** (AWS CDN) distribution to let users reach these static assets over HTTP requests. We would also need to link our CloudFront distribution to a domain name, and we can do that using **AWS Route 53** (an AWS proprietary DNS service).

Cloudflare, in comparison, makes things a bit easier. It has a more straightforward UI, called Cloudflare Pages, that can help us link our project to a Git repository and automatically deploy a new website version every time we push new code to any branch. Of course, every time we push some code to the main branch, it will be published in production; if we want to preview some features living on feature branches, we can just push our code there and wait for Cloudflare to publish a preview deployment, just like Vercel does.

Microsoft Azure provides another exciting approach. We can enter the Azure portal (the Azure administration dashboard), create a new resource, select "static web app" as the resource type, and enter the required data to configure it. After that, we can link our GitHub account, making automatic deployments available just like we did on Cloudflare and Vercel. Azure will create a GitHub workflow file for us so the build phase will run on GitHub and push the content to Azure as soon as it succeeds.

Now, you might be wondering how to choose the best CDN among the ones listed previously. Well, they're all excellent, but there's a way to determine which one best suits our needs.

AWS, for instance, might look like the most complicated one. But if we already have an AWS infrastructure, it would make things easier for us to set up a deployment there. The same applies to Microsoft Azure, where we might already have existing projects running on this platform, and we don't want to move just one web application outside of it.

Cloudflare, instead, can be the perfect solution for all static websites that don't need to rely on other services, except for serverless functions (Cloudflare offers a serverless function service called Cloudflare Workers) and other similar services that you can find at `https://developers.cloudflare.com`.

Even though there are ways to execute serverless functions decoupled from the static website (by using AWS Lambda, Azure Functions, Cloudflare Workers, and so on), there are times when we need to create dozens or even hundreds of serverless functions. Organizing such deployments can be challenging, especially if we're working in a small team without support from someone who's really into DevOps.

Other times, we just need server-side rendering alongside statically generated pages, and we need to deploy an application where we can use Node.js code at runtime. One interesting approach is to deploy the website in a completely serverless fashion.

There is an open source project called **serverless-next.js** (`https://github.com/serverless-nextjs/serverless-next.js`) that can help us achieve that result. It works as a *"Serverless component"* (in that case, *Serverless* is the name of an npm library used to deploy code to any serverless platform) that will configure a deployment on AWS by adapting it to the following rules:

- SSR pages and API routes will be deployed and served by AWS Lambda (serverless functions).

- Static pages, client assets, and public files will be deployed to S3 and automatically served by CloudFront.

This approach will lead to a kind of hybrid deployment where we always try to achieve the best possible performances of each type of request. SSR and API pages (which need a Node.js runtime) will be served by a serverless function, everything else from a CDN.

Don't worry if that sounds complex because it isn't. But if you feel like it would be an over-engineered part of your application life cycle (and you still need server-side rendering and API routes), you may want to consider other approaches. We will discuss how to deploy an SSR Next.js application to any platform correctly in the next section.

Deploying Next.js on any server

So far, we've seen some alternatives for deploying our Next.js application to CDNs and managed infrastructures, such as Vercel and Netlify. Still, there is another alternative that we haven't considered yet; what if we want to deploy our application to our private server?

Even though this is a common situation, it is also the most complex one by far. While platforms such as Vercel, Netlify, and Heroku manage the server for us, sometimes we may want to host our application on a private server where we have to control everything independently.

Let's have a quick recap of what the previously mentioned managed platforms can do for us:

- Automatic deployments

- Rollback to previous deployments

- Automatic deployments for feature branches

- Automatic server configuration (Node.js runtime, reverse proxy, and so on)
- Built-in scaling capabilities

By choosing a custom server, we have to implement all these features on our own. But is it worth it? Well, it depends. When working in a large company that already has a significant infrastructure up and running on a given cloud provider (be it Amazon AWS, Google Cloud, Microsoft Azure, and so on), it might make sense for us to identify the best solution for deploying our Next.js application in the same infrastructure.

If we're working on a side project or a small business website or starting a new web application from scratch, we could consider alternatives, such as managed platforms or CDNs, but we've already talked about that.

Let's pretend for a moment that the choice has been made, and we have to deploy our application to either Amazon AWS, Google Cloud, or Microsoft Azure. How do we approach deployment and hosting from there?

The first thing to consider is how we want to serve our application. Starting with an empty server means that we have to manually set up a bunch of stuff to make it ready to serve a Node.js application. That includes (but is not limited to) the following:

- *The Node.js runtime*: Node.js is not pre-installed on every operating system, so we'll need to install it to serve API and server-side-rendered pages.

- *A process manager*: If you have already worked with Node.js in the past, you may know that if the main process crashes, the entire application will stay down until we manually restart it. That is due to the Node.js single-threaded architecture, and it's unlikely to change in the future, so we need to be prepared for this possibility. A popular approach to solving that problem is using a process manager such as PM2 (`https://github.com/Unitech/pm2`), which monitors the Node.js processes and manages them to keep the application up and running. It also provides many other additional features for handling any Node.js program, so if you're interested in that, I'd recommend you read the official documentation at `https://pm2.keymetrics.io`.

- *A reverse proxy*: Even though we could easily set up any Node.js application to manage incoming HTTP requests, it is a best practice to put it behind a reverse proxy such as NGINX, Caddy, or Envoy. This adds an extra layer of security, other than valuable features we don't want to compromise on, but also means we have to maintain a reverse proxy on our server.

- *Setting up firewall rules*: We need to open the firewall to accept incoming HTTP requests to the :443 and :80 ports.

- *Setting up an efficient deployment pipeline*: We could use Jenkins, CircleCI, or even GitHub Actions. But this is another thing to take care of.

Once we're done setting up the whole environment, we should also consider that we may need to replicate that same environment on another server as soon as we need to scale our infrastructure to accept more and more incoming requests. It might be pretty easy to replicate it on a new server, but what if we need to scale on dozens of new machines? And what if we need to upgrade the Node.js runtime or the reverse proxy on all of them? Things are getting more complicated and time-consuming, so we may want to look for an alternative approach, and that's what we're going to talk about in the next section: how to deploy our Next.js application to any server by using Docker.

Running Next.js in a Docker container

Docker, and virtualization in general, has changed forever the way we build and deploy our applications. It provides a set of useful utilities, commands, and configurations to make our build reproducible on any server, making our application available on almost every operating system by creating a virtual machine running our program (or web application).

In Case You Are New to Docker

Docker is an important tool to consider when building and deploying any computer program (a web application, database, or anything else). If you're new to this technology, I highly recommend reading the official Docker documentation at https://www.docker.com before starting to use it. If you're interested in a hands-on approach to learning Docker, I'd also recommend you read *Mastering Docker – Fourth Edition* by Russ McKendrick (https://www.packtpub.com/product/mastering-docker-fourth-edition/9781839216572); it provides a complete guide to getting started and understanding Docker.

Running Next.js in Docker is relatively straightforward. A very basic Dockerfile is composed of the following commands:

```
FROM node:16-alpine
```

```
RUN mkdir -p /app
```

```
WORKDIR /app

COPY . /app/

RUN npm install
RUN npm run build

EXPOSE 3000

CMD npm run start
```

It's almost effortless, isn't it? Let's break it down into small steps:

1. First, declare which image we want to run our server in. In this case, we're choosing `node:14-alpine`.

2. It is a best practice to create a new working directory, so as a first step, create it and name it `/app`.

3. Choose `/app` as our working directory.

4. Copy all the content of our local directory into the Docker working directory.

5. Install all the required dependencies.

6. Build Next.js inside the container's working directory.

7. Expose port `3000` to be reached from outside the container.

8. Run the start script for booting the Next.js built-in server.

We can test the previous Dockerfile by creating a new, empty Next.js app running the following command in a new directory:

```
npx create-next-app my-first-dockerized-nextjs-app
```

Let's create a Dockerfile with the content we just discussed. We should also create a `.dockerignore` file containing `node_modules` and the Next.js output directory so that we won't be copying them into the container:

```
.next
node_modules
```

We can now proceed by building the Docker container:

```
docker build -t my-first-dockerized-nextjs-app .
```

We're tagging it with a custom name, in this case, `my-first-dockerized-nextjs-app`.

Once the build succeeds, we can run the container as follows:

```
docker run -p 3000:3000  my-first-dockerized-nextjs-app
```

We are finally able to reach our web application at `http://localhost:3000`!

Starting from that simple configuration, we will be able to deploy our application to any managed container service (such as AWS ECS or Google Cloud Run), any Kubernetes cluster, or any machine with Docker installed.

Using containers in production has many benefits, as we only need a very simple configuration file for setting up the virtualization of a Linux machine to run our application in. Whenever we need to duplicate, scale, or reproduce our build, we can simply do that by sharing the Dockerfile and executing it, making the whole process incredibly straightforward, scalable, and easy to maintain.

That said, do we always need Docker? Let's discuss this in the summary for this chapter, right in the next section.

Summary

In this chapter, we've seen different deployment platforms for our Next.js application. There's no perfect solution for building and deploying Next.js apps, as it depends on the specific use case and challenges that every project brings.

Vercel, Netlify, and Heroku (just to quote some) are all excellent alternatives for quickly deploying a Next.js application to production. On the other hand, Cloudflare Pages, AWS S3 and AWS CloudFront, and Microsoft Azure CDN can really provide excellent performance for our static sites, which competes with all the other great solutions we've seen in this chapter when it comes to serving a statically generated website.

Docker is probably one of the most flexible solutions. It allows us to deploy our application everywhere, making it easy to replicate the production environment on every machine.

Again, there's no "perfect" solution for deploying a Next.js application, as the competition in this field is extremely strong, and many companies provide excellent solutions to simplify our lives as developers and make our browsing experience always better as users.

The best suggestion I can give when deciding where to deploy a Next.js application is to consider the following aspect: how big is the team I'm working in? While solutions such as Vercel, Netlify, Heroku, and Cloudflare are well suited for both little and big teams, there are other providers where the required knowledge, skillset, and capacity are way higher. Setting up an AWS EC2 instance or a custom machine on DigitalOcean or Google Cloud gives us much more control over the whole application life cycle, but the cost (in terms of configuration, setup, and required time) is considerable.

On the other hand, when working in big companies where there's a dedicated DevOps team that can take care of the release process for the application, they might prefer to adopt custom solutions where they have more and more control.

But even if we're working alone, we can choose to deploy our applications to a custom cloud infrastructure. If we're doing that, we should make sure we're not unintentionally reinventing the wheel by recreating infrastructures that Vercel, Netlify, Cloudflare, and so on can provide even on a free plan.

We've made some significant progress so far. We learned the basics of the framework and how to integrate it with different libraries and data sources, and now we also know how to choose a deployment platform for any need.

Starting from the next chapter, we will build some real-world applications that will allow us to understand the real-world challenges we will face when creating production-ready web applications in Next.js.

Part 3:
Next.js by Example

In this part, we will write some production-grade apps using all the methods and strategies we've explored in the past chapters. We will manage production-ready authentication, consume GraphQL APIs, and integrate Stripe, a payment service.

We will also see the next steps for becoming even more confident with Next.js by developing some example apps and learning how to stay up to date regarding this fast-evolving framework.

This section comprises the following chapters:

12
Managing Authentication and User Sessions

In the previous chapters, we've seen how to work with some of the fundamental Next.js features. We learned how to choose between rendering strategies and how those can influence SEO and performance. We also learned how to style our application using built-in and external styling methods and libraries, managing the application state, integrating with external APIs, and many other valuable things.

Starting with this chapter, we will begin to learn and develop real-world applications by combining the lessons learned in the past sections with industry-standard strategies to keep our applications secure, performant, and highly optimized in every aspect.

In this chapter, we will see how to manage user session and authentication, an essential part of every highly dynamic web application.

We will cover the following topics in detail:

- How to integrate our application with a custom authentication service
- How to use industry-standard service providers such as Auth0, NextAuth.js, and Firebase
- How to keep sessions between page changes
- How to keep user data secure and private

By the end of this chapter, you will be able to authenticate users and manage their sessions on any Next.js app, be aware of the differences between different authentication strategies, and even adopt a custom one.

Technical requirements

To run the code examples in this chapter, you need to have both Node.js and npm installed on your local machine. If you prefer, you can use an online IDE such as `https://repl.it` or `https://codesandbox.io`; they both support Next.js, and you don't need to install any dependency on your computer. As for the other chapters, you can find the code base for this chapter on GitHub: `https://github.com/PacktPublishing/Real-World-Next.js`.

A brief introduction to user sessions and authentication

When talking about user authentication, we refer to that process that identifies a specific user, letting them read, write, update, or delete any protected content, depending on their authorization level.

A typical example could be a simple blogging system: we can publish, edit, or even delete content only after authenticating ourselves.

There are many different authentication strategies, but the most common are:

- **Credentials-based authentication**: This method allows us to log in to a system using personal credentials, commonly, an email address and a password.
- **Social login**: We can log in to a system using our social accounts (Facebook, Twitter, LinkedIn, and so on).

- **Passwordless login**: Over recent years, this has become a pretty popular authentication method. Platforms such as Medium and Slack will send you what's called a "magic link" to your email address, letting you enter your account without typing any password.

- **Single sign-on (SSO)**: If you've worked in a big company, you may have experienced this. Services such as Okta provide a way of using unique credentials for many different services, centralizing user authentication over their own service. Once you log in to an SSO system, it will redirect you to the desired website, granting your identity.

But once we log in to a system, we want it to remember us, so we don't have to authenticate ourselves on every page change during our navigation. This is where session management kicks in.

Again, there are many ways to manage user sessions. If you're familiar with PHP, you may know that it provides a built-in method for controlling the user session. Let's look at the following code snippet:

```php
<?php
  session_start();

  $_SESSION["first_name"] = "John";
  $_SESSION["last_name"]  = "Doe";
?>
```

This is a typical example of server-side session management.

It creates a session cookie and keeps track of all the properties linked to that session. So, for example, we could associate a logged-in user email or username with that session, and every time we render a page, we can do it depending on the authenticated user data.

We can refer to this strategy as a *stateful session* as the user state is kept on the server side and linked to the client via a specific session cookie.

While managing stateful sessions is relatively easy during the prototyping phase, things tend to get a bit more complex once you begin to scale in production.

In the previous chapter, we talked about deploying our application to Vercel, AWS, or any other managed hosting platform. Let's take Vercel as an example, as it is the most straightforward (yet optimized) one for hosting our Next.js web app. We've seen how every API and SSR page gets rendered on a serverless function, right? Now imagine, in that scenario, how is it possible to keep a server-side stateful session when we don't even have a server to manage?

Let's pretend we're rendering a welcome page for our users after they sign in. We can set a session cookie, but every instance of server-side stateful data will be canceled after the Lambda function terminates its execution. So how do we keep the session? What will happen once the users exit this page? The server-side session will be lost, and they will need to re-authenticate again.

This is where the concept of *stateless sessions* can really help.

Instead of setting a session cookie that links a server-side session to the frontend, we want to release some information that identifies the user on every new request. Every time the authenticated user sends a request to the backend, they must follow an authorization mechanism, such as passing a specific cookie or an HTTP header. On every new request, the server will take this information, validate it, recognize the user (if the passed cookie or header is valid), and then serve the desired content.

An industry-standard approach that follows this pattern is *JWT-based* authentication, but we will discuss this in the next section.

Understanding JSON web tokens

As written on the `https://jwt.io` website, a **JWT** (short for **JSON Web Token**) is an open, industry-standard *RFC 7519* method for representing claims securely between two parties.

To keep it simple, we can think of JWTs as three distinct base64-encoded JSON chunks of data.

Let's take the following JWT as an example:

```
eyJhbGciOiJIUzI1NiIsInR5cCI6IkpXVCJ9.eyJzdWIiOiI5MDhlYWZhNy03M-
WJkLTQyMDMtOGY3Ni1iNjA3MmNkMTFlODciLCJuYW1lIjoiSmFuZSBEb2UiL-
CJpYXQiOjE1MTYyMzkwMjJ9.HCl73CTg8960TvLP7i5mV2hKQlSJLaLAlmvHk-
38kL8o
```

If we pay enough attention, we can see three different chunks of data separated by periods.

The first part represents the JWT header. It contains two essential pieces of information: the token type and the algorithm used for signing it (we will talk more about that in just a second).

The second part is the payload. Here is where we put all the non-sensitive data that can help us identify our users. *Never store data such as passwords and bank details inside a JWT payload.*

The third and last part of a JWT token is its signature. This is what makes JWTs secure, and we will talk about that in detail later in this section.

If we decode our JWT token with any client library or a dedicated website such as `https://jwt.io`, we will see the following JSON data:

```
// First chunk
{
   "alg": "HS256", // Algorithm used to sign the token
   "typ": "JWT"      // Token type
}

// Second chunk
{
   "sub": "908eafa7-71bd-4203-8f76-b6072cd11e87", // JWT subject
   "name": "Jane Doe",                              // User name
   "iat": 1516239022                               // Issued at
}
```

The first chunk tells us that the given token is a JWT signed using the HS256 algorithm.

The second chunk gives us some helpful information about the user, such as the JWT subject (typically the user ID), the username, and the timestamp of when we issued the token.

> **JWT Payload Best Practices**
>
> The official *RFC7519* specifies some optional payload properties, such as `"sub"` (subject), `"aud"` (audience), `"exp"` (expiration time), and more. Even though they are optional, it is best practice to implement them in accordance with the official RFC specification, which can be found at `https://datatracker.ietf.org/doc/html/rfc7519#section-4`.

Once we need personal user data, we can set this JWT as a cookie or use it as a bearer token inside an HTTP authorization header. Once the server gets this data, it will verify the token, and here is where the third token section becomes essential.

As we have already seen, the third part of any JWT is its signature. Let's keep things easy again and make an elementary example of why (and how) we want to sign our JWT tokens.

It is pretty easy for anyone to decode a JWT token; it is just a base64-encoded JSON, so we can use JavaScript built-in functions to decode it, manipulate it (by adding an `"admin"`: `true` property, for example), and then encode it again in the required format.

It would be tremendous if it were so easy to hack a JWT token, right? The good news is: decoding, manipulating, and then encoding the token again is not enough. We also need to sign it using the same secret code used on the server that issued the JWT.

For instance, we could use the jsonwebtoken library to generate a token for our user as follows:

```
const jwt = require('jsonwebtoken');

const myToken = jwt.sign(
    {
        name: 'Jane Doe',
        admin: false,
    },
    'secretpassword',
);
```

We would end up with the following JWT token:

```
eyJhbGciOiJIUzI1NiIsInR5cCI6IkpXVCJ9.eyJuYW1lIjoiSmFuZSBEb2UiL-
CJhZG1pbiI6ZmFsc2UsImlhdCI6MTYzNDEzMTI2OH0.AxLW0CwWpsIUk71WNbb-
ZS9jTPpab8z4LVfJH6rsa4Nk
```

We now want to verify it, just to make sure that it works as expected:

```
const jwt = require('jsonwebtoken');

const myToken = jwt.sign(
    {
        name: 'Jane Doe',
        admin: false,
    },
    'secretpassword',
);


const tokenValue = jwt.verify(myToken, 'secretpassword');
```

```
console.log(tokenValue);
// => { name: 'Jane Doe', admin: false, iat: 1634131396 }
```

In that library, the `jwt.verify` method returns the decoded payload once the signature has been verified. If the verification fails, it will throw an error.

We can test this by copying and pasting the preceding JWT on the `https://jwt.io` home page. It will allow us to edit it freely, so we can try to set the `"admin": true` claim to our JWT:

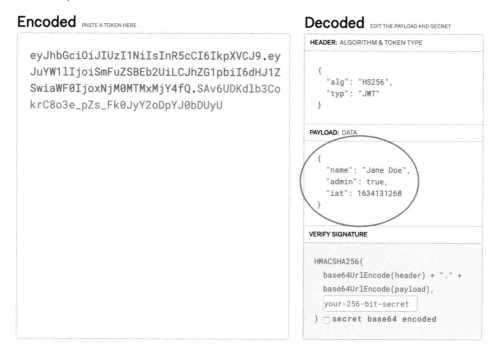

Figure 12.1 – Editing the JWT token on https://jwt.io

As you may notice, the web app will update the JWT token as soon as we type something in the header or payload section. Once we're done with our edits, we can finally test it with our script:

```
const tokenValue = jwt.verify(
'eyJhbGciOiJIUzI1NiIsInR5cCI6IkpXVCJ9.eyJuYW1lIjoiSmFuZS-
BEb2UiLCJhZG1pbiI6dHJ1ZSwiaWF0IjoxNjM0MTMxMjY4fQ.SAv6UDKdlb-
3CokrC8o3e_pZs_Fk0JyY2oDpYJ0bDUyU',
    'secretpassword',
);
```

Once we try to verify this token, we will see the following error to be thrown in the console:

```
JsonWebTokenError: invalid signature
```

And that's what makes a JWT secure: everyone could potentially read and manipulate it. But once you do it, you're not able to sign it using a valid signature as it remains secret and hidden on the server side.

In the next section, we will see a practical example of integrating JWT authentication into a Next.js app.

Custom authentication – the good, the bad, and the ugly

Let's make this clear from the outset: when possible, we should avoid implementing custom authentication strategies. There are several great providers (including Auth0, Firebase, AWS Cognito, and Magic.link, just to name a few) that are putting a lot of effort into making authentication secure, reliable, and optimized for many different situations. When investigating authentication strategies for a web app, I'd highly recommend looking into a well-established service provider as this is possibly one of the most critical aspects of a dynamic web application.

In this section, we're looking into creating a custom authentication mechanism for a simple reason: we just want to understand at a high level how authentication works, how to make it as secure as possible, and what the critical factors of a custom auth system are.

As we'll find out during this section, there will be several limitations when implementing custom authentication mechanisms. For instance, I'd highly discourage implementing client-side authentication on statically generated websites as it forces us to authenticate users on the client side exclusively, possibly exposing sensitive data to the network.

For that reason, we will create a new Next.js web application that will use the API routes for communicating with a data source (typically a database) and retrieving the user data.

So, let's start by creating a new, empty Next.js app:

```
npx create-next-app with-custom-auth
```

Once the boilerplate code is ready, we can start writing the login API. Please keep in mind that the following code is not meant to go to production; we're just taking a simplified, high-level overview of how authentication works.

Let's start by creating a `/pages/api/login.js` file by exporting the following function:

```
export default (req, res) => {}
```

This is where we will handle the user input and authenticate it.

The first thing we can do is to take the user input and filter the request method to accept POST requests only:

```
export default (req, res) => {
  const { method } = req;
  const { email, password } = req.body;

  if (method !== 'POST') {
    return res.status(404).end();
  }
}
```

> **Why Do We Need to Filter POST Requests?**
>
> By default, all the Next.js API routes accept any HTTP method. By the way, it is best practice to allow only specific methods on certain routes, for example, enabling POST requests when creating new content, GET when reading data, PUT when modifying something, or DELETE for deleting data.

We can now validate the user input. When validating an email and password, for example, we could check that the passed email is in a valid format and that the password is following a particular policy. That way, if any of the given data is not valid, we can just reply with a 401 status code (unauthorized) as we won't find any occurrence in the database for that email and password combination. That would also help us to avoid useless database calls.

Right now, we don't have a database, and we will rely on hardcoded values as we only want to understand authentication at a high level. That said, we will only check whether the request body contains an email and a password, so we can keep it simple:

```
export default (req, res) => {
  const { method } = req;
  const { email, password } = req.body;

  if (method !== 'POST') {
```

```
    return res.status(404).end();
  }


if (!email || !password) {
  return res.status(400).json({
    error: 'Missing required params',
  });
  }
}
```

If the email or password doesn't exist in the request body, we will return a 400 status code (bad request) with an error message explaining why the request failed.

If the request is sent using the HTTP POST method and provides both an email and password, we can process them using any authentication mechanism. For example, we could look up a user with that specific email in the database, retrieve their password, and then verify it on the server side or ask for an external authentication service to do that for us.

Right now, given that we're just taking an overview of custom authentication strategies, we will use an elementary function that checks the combination of email and password against two fixed strings. Again, this is not meant for production usage.

Inside the same pages/api/login.js file, we can create a very elementary function that can do that for us:

```
function authenticateUser(email, password) {
  const validEmail = 'johndoe@somecompany.com';
  const validPassword = 'strongpassword';


  if (email === validEmail && password === validPassword) {
    return {
      id: 'f678f078-fcfe-43ca-9d20-e8c9a95209b6',
      name: 'John Doe',
      email: 'johndoe@somecompany.com',
    };
  }


  return null;
}
```

In a production environment, we will never use such an authentication function. Instead, we will communicate with a database or external service to dynamically retrieve the user data.

We can finally combine the preceding function with our API handler. If the passed data is correct, we will get some user data back and send it to the client. Otherwise, we'll just send a 401 status code (unauthorized) with an error explaining that the passed data is incorrect:

```
export default (req, res) => {
  const { method } = req;
  const { email, password } = req.body;

  if (method !== 'POST') {
    return res.status(404).end();
  }

  if (!email || !password) {
    return res.status(400).json({
      error: 'Missing required params',
    });
  }

  const user = authenticateUser(email, password);

  if (user) {
    return res.json({ user });
  } else {
    return res.status(401).json({
      error: 'Wrong email of password',
    });
  }
};
```

At this point, we could start analyzing the risks of this approach. Let's pretend for a moment that we will log in from the frontend, the server will reply with such information, and we will store it in a cookie. Once we need to get more data about (let's say) our user, we could just submit a request to the server, which will read the cookie, get the current user ID, and then query the database for their data.

Can you see the point of failure of such a solution?

Everyone could potentially edit their cookies by just using the developer tools built into every modern web browser. This means that everyone could just read the cookie, change it, and impersonate another user without even logging in.

> **Why Are We Talking about Cookies?**
>
> Cookies are a good solution for storing session data. We could use different browser features, such as `localStorage`, `sessionStorage`, or even `indexedDB`. The problem is, everyone could steal this data by just injecting a malicious script into your web page. When dealing with cookies, we can (and we should) set an `httpOnly` flag to `true` to make cookies available on the server side only. That adds an extra layer of security when storing this data. Even though we should be aware that every user can have access to cookies by inspecting them using the dev tools provided by modern browsers, we should never share sensitive information there.

This is where JWTs can help. We can simply edit our login handler to make it a bit more secure by setting a cookie containing a JWT before returning any data.

Let's start by installing the `jsonwebtoken` npm package:

```
yarn add jsonwebtoken
```

Let's create a new file, `lib/jwt.js`, and add the following content:

```
import jwt from 'jsonwebtoken';

const JWT_SECRET = 'my_jwt_password';

export function encode(payload) {
  return jwt.sign(payload, JWT_SECRET);
}

export function decode(token) {
  return jwt.verify(token, JWT_SECRET);
}
```

Now, going back to our `pages/api/login.js` file, we can edit it by encoding the user payload into a JWT:

```
import { encode } from '../../lib/jwt';

function authenticateUser(email, password) {
  const validEmail = 'johndoe@somecompany.com';
  const validPassword = 'strongpassword';

  if (email === validEmail && password === validPassword) {
    return encode({
      id: 'f678f078-fcfe-43ca-9d20-e8c9a95209b6',
      name: 'John Doe',
      email: 'johndoe@somecompany.com',
    });
  }

  return null;
}
```

One last thing: we said we wanted to set a cookie containing the JWT we just created. We can install a handy library that can help us achieve that:

```
yarn add cookie
```

Once installed, we can edit our `pages/api/login.js` file by setting the session cookie:

```
import { serialize } from 'cookie';

// ...

export default (req, res) => {
  const { method } = req;
  const { email, password } = req.body;

  if (method !== 'POST') {
    return res.status(404).end();
  }
```

```
if (!email || !password) {
  return res.status(400).json({
    error: 'Missing required params',
  });
}


const user = authenticateUser(email, password);


if (user) {
  res.setHeader('Set-Cookie',
    serialize('my_auth', user, { path: '/', httpOnly:
      true })
  );
  return res.json({ success: true });
} else {
  return res.status(401).json({
    success: false,
    error: 'Wrong email of password',
  });
}
};
```

As you can see, we're creating a cookie named my_auth, which will contain the user JWT. We won't pass the JWT to the client directly as we want to keep it hidden from any potential malicious script running on the client side.

We can inspect whether the procedure is working as expected by testing it with useful HTTP clients such as Postman or Insomnia (you can download Insomnia for free here: https://insomnia.rest):

Figure 12.2 – The login API response in Insomnia

If we move to the **Cookie** tab in the response section of our tool of choice (in my case, Insomnia), we can eventually see the authentication cookie:

Figure 12.3 – The authentication cookie in Insomnia

It's finally time to manage the authentication on the client side by creating a login form and a protected route, only visible after the login. So, let's start from there: let's create a new /pages/protected-route.js file with the following content:

```
import styles from '../styles/app.module.css';

export default function ProtectedRoute() {
  return (
    <div className={styles.container}>
      <h1>Protected Route</h1>
      <p>You can't see me if not logged-in!</p>
    </div>
  );
}
```

As you can tell by looking at the ProtectedRoute function, we're not preventing anonymous users from browsing that page; we'll get there in a moment, right after creating the login page.

Let's also create the /styles/app.module.css file, where we'll put all the styling for our app; we're not aiming to make an award-winning UI, so we'll just create a couple of simple styles there:

```
.container {
  min-height: 100vh;
  padding: 0 0.5rem;
  display: flex;
  flex-direction: column;
  justify-content: center;
  align-items: center;
  height: 100vh;
}
```

Now we can start concentrating on the login. Let's create a new page, /pages/login.js, and start writing the login UI:

```
import { useState } from 'react';
import { useRouter } from 'next/router';
import styles from '../styles/app.module.css';
```

```
export default function Home() {
  const [loginError, setLoginError] = useState(null);

  return (
    <div className={styles.container}>
      <h1>Login</h1>
      <form className={styles.form}
        onSubmit={handleSubmit}>
        <label htmlFor="email">Email</label>
        <input type="email" id="email" />

        <label htmlFor="password">Password</label>
        <input type="password" id="password" />

        <button type="submit">Login</button>

        {loginError && (
          <div className={styles.formError}>
            {loginError} </div>
        )}
      </form>
    </div>
  );
}
```

Before creating the missing `handleSubmit` function, let's add a couple of styles to the `styles/app.module.css` file:

```
.form {
  display: flex;
  flex-direction: column;
}

.form input {
  padding: 0.5rem;
  margin: 0.5rem;
  border: 1px solid #ccc;
```

```css
  border-radius: 4px;
  width: 15rem;
}

.form label {
  margin: 0 0.5rem;
}

.form button {
  padding: 0.5rem;
  margin: 0.5rem;
  border: 1px solid #ccc;
  border-radius: 4px;
  width: 15rem;
  cursor: pointer;
}

.formError {
  color: red;
  font-size: 0.8rem;
  text-align: center;
}
```

We can now write the handleSubmit function. Here, we will catch the form submit event, prevent the browser's default behavior (to submit a request to a remote API), and handle the two possible cases for our login: success and failure. If the login succeeds, we will redirect the user to our protected page. If it fails, we'll set an error inside our loginError state:

```javascript
export default function Home() {
  const router = useRouter();
  const [loginError, setLoginError] = useState(null);

  const handleSubmit = (event) => {
    event.preventDefault();
    const { email, password } = event.target.elements;
```

```
    setLoginError(null);
    handleLogin(email.value, password.value)
      .then(() => router.push('/protected-route'))
      .catch((err) => setLoginError(err.message));
  };

// ...
```

We're now missing one last function, the one that is responsible for making the login API request. We can create it outside the Home component since, during the testing phase, we may want to test it individually:

```
// ...

async function handleLogin(email, password) {
  const resp = await fetch('/api/login', {
    method: 'POST',
    headers: {
      'Content-Type': 'application/json',
    },
    body: JSON.stringify({
      email,
      password,
    }),
  });

  const data = await resp.json();

  if (data.success) {
    return;
  }

  throw new Error('Wrong email or password');
}

// ...
```

We can finally test our login page and see whether it's working correctly! If it does, we should get redirected to our private route; otherwise, we should see a friendly error message displayed under the form submit button.

Now it's time to protect our private page. If we aren't logged in, we shouldn't be able to see it. A similar thing should apply to the login page: once we're logged in, we shouldn't be able to see it.

Before proceeding any further with the implementation, we should decide how to implement authentication in our app.

We could render our pages on the server side to check the cookies on each request (remember? We don't want to access auth cookies on the client side!), or we could just render a loader on the frontend and wait for a hook to check whether we're logged in before rendering the actual page content.

What should we consider before making such a choice?

There are several scenarios where this choice could have an impact. For example, let's think of SEO; if we're building a blog where only logged-in users can (for example) post comments, that's not a big deal. We can send a statically generated page and wait for a hook to tell us whether the user is authenticated. Meanwhile, we could just render the public content (such as the article body, author, and tags), so the SEO wouldn't be impacted. The user will be able to comment as soon as the client knows that they're logged in.

Also, the performances would be great, as we could serve a statically generated page with dynamic data rendered on the client side exclusively.

As an alternative, we could simply get the user cookie on the server side, validate the JWT, and then render the page depending on the user authentication status; that might be a bit easier to implement (we can do that inside the `getServerSideProps` built-in function), but will undoubtedly add some delay, and will force us to render all the pages on the server side.

We will implement the first solution, where we'll need to create a custom hook to determine whether the user is logged in.

To do that, we'll first need to implement an API that parses our cookies and replies with the bare minimum information about our session. Let's do that by creating a `pages/api/get-session.js` file:

```
import { parse } from 'cookie';
import { decode } from '../../lib/jwt';
```

```
export default (req, res) => {
  if (req.method !== 'GET') {
    return res.status(404).end();
  }

  const { my_auth } = parse(req.headers.cookie || '');

  if (!my_auth) {
    return res.json({ loggedIn: false });
  }

  return res.json({
    loggedIn: true,
    user: decode(my_auth),
  });
};
```

We can now log in using the form we just created and then call the API over `http://localhost:3000/api/get-session`. We will see a result similar to the following:

```
{
  "loggedIn": true,
  "user": {
    "id": "f678f078-fcfe-43ca-9d20-e8c9a95209b6",
    "name": "John Doe",
    "email": "johndoe@somecompany.com",
    "iat": 1635085226
  }
}
```

If we call the same API within an incognito session, we would only get a `{ "loggedIn": false }` response.

We can use this API to determine whether the user is logged in by creating a custom hook. Let's do that by creating a `lib/hooks/auth.js` file with the following content:

```
import { useState, useEffect } from 'react';

export function useAuth() {
```

```
const [loggedIn, setLoggedIn] = useState(false);
const [user, setUser]         = useState(null);
const [loading, setLoading]   = useState(true);
const [error, setError]       = useState(null);

useEffect(() => {
   setLoading(true);
   fetch('/api/get-session')
     .then((res) => res.json())
     .then((data) => {
        if (data.loggedIn) {
           setLoggedIn(true);
           setUser(data.user);
        }
     })
     .catch((err) => setError(err))
     .finally(() => setLoading(false));
}, []);

return {
   user,
   loggedIn,
   loading,
   error,
};
}
```

The hook itself is pretty simple. As soon as it's loaded (so, when the `useEffect` React hook is triggered), it will make an HTTP call to our `/api/get-session` API. Once the API succeeds (or fails), it will return the user status, errors (if any), and set the `loading` status to `false`, so we will know that it's time to re-render the UI.

We can finally implement this hook in our protected page by just importing it and displaying the private content depending on the authentication status:

```
import { useRouter } from 'next/router';
import { useAuth } from '../lib/hooks/auth';
```

```
import styles from '../styles/app.module.css';

export default function ProtectedRoute() {
  const router = useRouter();
  const { loading, error, loggedIn } = useAuth();

  if (!loading && !loggedIn) {
    router.push('/login');
  }

  return (
    <div className={styles.container}>
      {loading && <p>Loading...</p>}
      {error && <p> An error occurred. </p>}
      {loggedIn && (
        <>
          <h1>Protected Route</h1>
          <p>You can't see me if not logged-in!</p>
        </>
      )}
    </div>
  );
}
```

We can now try to reach our private page and see whether it is working correctly once logged in! First, there should be a little moment where we can spot the "loading" text; then, we should see the protected route content.

We could adopt a similar approach for hiding the login page from a logged-in user; let's open the pages/login.js file and edit it as follows:

```
import { useState } from 'react';
import { useRouter } from 'next/router';
import { useAuth } from '../lib/hooks/auth';
import styles from '../styles/app.module.css';

// ...
```

Once we import the `useAuth` hook, we can start writing the component logic. We won't render the login form until we know whether the user is logged in:

```
// ...

export default function Home() {
  const router = useRouter();
  const [loginError, setLoginError] = useState(null);
  const { loading, loggedIn } = useAuth();

  if (loading) {
    return <p>Loading...</p>;
  }

  if (!loading && loggedIn) {
    router.push('/protected-route');
    return null;
  }

// ...
```

Here, we're telling our login page to behave the other way around when compared to the protected route page. We will wait for the hook to complete the loading phase, and when it ends, we will check whether the user is logged in. If they're logged in, we will simply redirect them to the protect page using the Next.js `useRouter` hook.

We successfully implemented a very simple (and not ready for production, by any means) login strategy for our web page, but what did we miss? What are the problems that come next? Should we pursue writing custom authentication strategies?

Well, I think it is not worth it unless we're working in a big and expert team.

This section of the book is entitled *Custom authentication – the good, the bad, and the ugly,* so let's divide some considerations into those three categories:

The good: We may all appreciate writing a custom authentication system because it teaches us a lot about security and gives us complete control over the whole authentication workflow.

The bad: We would take a considerable risk. Writing robust authentication mechanisms is not easy, and companies invest a lot in providing secure authentication strategies. It's hard for a company working outside this business to meet the same security levels as Auth0, Okta, Google, or Amazon AWS.

The ugly: Even if we could create a robust authentication system, we would have to implement many custom processes manually – resetting the password and user registration workflows, two-factor authentication, and transactional emails, just to name a few. It would require a lot of extra jobs and will lead to replicating an existing service without meeting the same level of security and reliability, as it is tough to match Auth0, Google, or AWS standards.

In the next section, we will see how to implement authentication for any Next.js app using an industry-standard, well-known authentication provider: Auth0.

Implementing authentication using Auth0

In the previous section, we've seen how to implement an elementary and straightforward authentication method. I won't repeat this enough: what we saw was just a high-level overview and shouldn't be used for any production-ready product.

When building production-ready web apps, we're likely to adopt external authentication methods, which are secure and reliable.

There are many different auth providers (AWS Cognito, Firebase, Magic.link, and so on), and I believe they're all doing a fantastic job protecting their users. In this chapter, we will be using a popular, secure, and affordable authentication provider, taking advantage of its generous free plan: Auth0.

If you want to follow along with this chapter, you can create a free account on `https://auth0.com` (no credit card is required for free plan users).

Auth0 will manage the most complex steps of any authentication strategy and will give us some friendly APIs to play with.

Thanks to this authentication provider, we don't have to worry about any of the following:

- User registration
- User login
- Email verification
- Forgot password flow
- Reset password flow

Nor will we have to worry about many other critical parts of any authentication strategy.

So, let's start by creating a new Next.js app:

```
npx create-next-app with-auth0
```

Now, log in to Auth0 and create a new application:

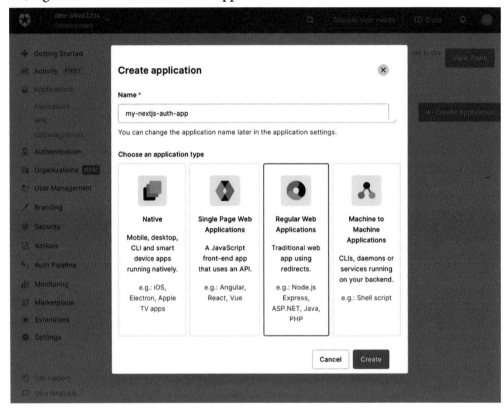

Figure 12.4 – Creating a new Auth0 application

Once we create our application, Auth0 will ask us which technology are we going to use. We can select **Next.js** and Auth0 will redirect us to an excellent tutorial on how to adopt their authentication mechanism in this framework.

If we go to **Settings**, we will be able to set up our callback URLs. Those URLs represent the pages to which our users will be redirected once they complete specific actions, such as login, logout, and registration.

At this point, we need to set the *Allowed Callback URLs* by adding `http://localhost:3000/api/auth/callback`, and the *Allowed Logout URLs* by setting `http://localhost:3000/`.

This will authorize us to adopt Auth0 for local development after every Auth0-related operation (such as login, registration, and password reset), as Auth0 will redirect us to the URL where the action originated.

So, for example, if we want to log in on `https://example.com`, after the login action, Auth0 will automatically redirect us to `https://example.com/api/auth/callback`, which needs to be authorized in the section we just saw.

Given that our local development URL is likely to be `http://localhost:3000` (which is the default for Next.js), we may need to authorize other staging or production URLs inside the *Allowed Callback URLs* and *Allowed Logout URLs* sections. Of course, we can always do that by adding more URLs and separating them with a comma.

Once we're done setting up the redirect URLs, we can start setting up our local environment.

First of all, we will need to create an environment file for the local environment. So, let's create it and name it `.env.local`, and then add the following content:

```
AUTH0_
SECRET=f915324d4e18d45318179e733fc25d7aed95ee6d6734c8786c03
AUTH0_BASE_URL='http://localhost:3000'
AUTH0_ISSUER_BASE_URL='https://YOUR_AUTH0_DOMAIN.auth0.com'
AUTH0_CLIENT_ID='YOUR_AUTH0_CLIENT_ID'
AUTH0_CLIENT_SECRET='YOUR_AUTH0_CLIENT_SECRET'
```

Remember that we should never commit the environment file as it contains sensitive data that could compromise our application's security.

As you can see, we're setting five essential environment variables:

- AUTH0_SECRET: A randomly generated string used by Auth0 as a secret key to encrypt the session cookie. You can generate a new, secure, random secret by running `openssl rand -hex 32` in the terminal.

- AUTH0_BASE_URL: The base URL of our application. For the local development environment, it will be `http://localhost:3000`. If you want to start the application on a different port, make sure to update the `.env.local` file to reflect this change.

- AUTH0_ISSUER_BASE_URL: The URL of your Auth0 app. You can find it at the beginning of the **Settings** section we just visited for setting the callback URLs (labeled as **domain** in the Auth0 dashboard).

- `AUTH0_CLIENT_ID`: The client ID for the Auth0 application. You can find yours right under the **Domain** setting.

- `AUTH0_CLIENT_SECRET`: The client secret for the Auth0 application. You can find it under the **client ID** setting in the Auth0 dashboard.

Once we've set all those environment variables, we can create an API route for Auth0 in our Next.js application. Remember when we talked about how many things we should implement when writing down a custom authentication strategy? Login, logout, password reset, user registration... Auth0 handles everything for us, and it does it by asking us to create just a straightforward API route under `/pages/api/auth/[...auth0].js`.

Once we have created this page, we can add the following content to it:

```
import { handleAuth } from '@auth0/nextjs-auth0';
```

```
export default handleAuth();
```

If you haven't already done so, you can install the official Auth0 Next.js SDK by running the following command:

```
yarn add @auth0/nextjs-auth0
```

Once we start our Next.js server, the `handleAuth()` method will create the following routes for us:

- `/api/auth/login`, the route that will allow us to log in to our application

- `/api/auth/callback`, the callback URL where Auth0 will redirect us right after logging in successfully

- `/api/auth/logout`, where we can log out from our web application

- `/api/auth/me`, an endpoint where we can fetch our own information in JSON format once we log in

To make our session persistent among all the web application pages, we can wrap our components in the official Auth0 `UserProvider` context. We can do that by opening our `pages/_app.js` file and adding the following content:

```
import { UserProvider } from '@auth0/nextjs-auth0';
```

```
export default function App({ Component, pageProps }) {
```

```
  return (
    <UserProvider>
      <Component {...pageProps} />
    </UserProvider>
  );
}
```

We can now try to visit our application login page by browsing `http://localhost:3000/api/auth/login`. We should eventually see the following page:

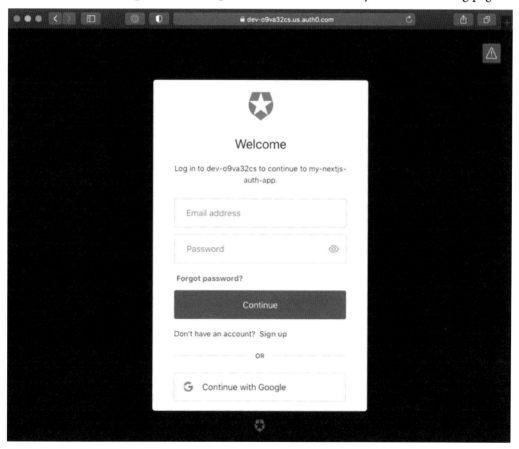

Figure 12.5 – The default Auth0 login page

We don't have an account yet, as this is the first time we access the login page. We can click on **Sign up** and create a new account.

Once we create it, we will get redirected to the application home page and receive an email to confirm our mail address.

Now that we're logged in, we can display some helpful information on our frontend depending on the logged-in user; let's start from something straightforward and just show a greeting message.

We can do that by opening the /pages/index.js file and adding the following content:

```
import { useUser } from '@auth0/nextjs-auth0';

export default function Index() {
  const { user, error, isLoading } = useUser();

  if (isLoading) {
    return <div>Loading...</div>;
  }

  if (error) {
    return <div>{error.message}</div>;
  }

  if (user) {
    return (
      <div>
        <h1> Welcome back! </h1>
        <p>
          You're logged in with the following email
            address:
          {user.email}!
        </p>
        <a href="/api/auth/logout">Logout</a>
      </div>
```

```
    );
  }


  return (
    <div>
      <h1> Welcome, stranger! </h1>
      <p>Please <a href="/api/auth/login">Login</a>.</p>
    </div>
  );
}
```

As you can see, this pattern is quite similar to the one we used while implementing our custom authentication mechanism. We statically generate the page, then wait for the client to fetch the user information, and once we have it, we print the private content on screen.

You can now try to log in and out from the application to test that it's working correctly.

Once we log in and out, we might wonder: how can we customize the authentication form? What if we want to keep the data on our own database? We'll discuss this in the next section.

Customizing Auth0

So far, we have built a straightforward authentication mechanism using Auth0. However, when compared to the custom one, it is clear how many advantages it could bring: secure authentication flow, fully featured auth management, and suchlike, to name just a few.

One thing that we might be missing is how much control we had when building the custom authentication strategy; we could control every authentication step, the look and feel of the form, and the required data needed to create a new account... how can we do that with Auth0?

Talking about the login/registration form aspect, we can customize it by navigating to the **Branding** section in our Auth0 dashboard:

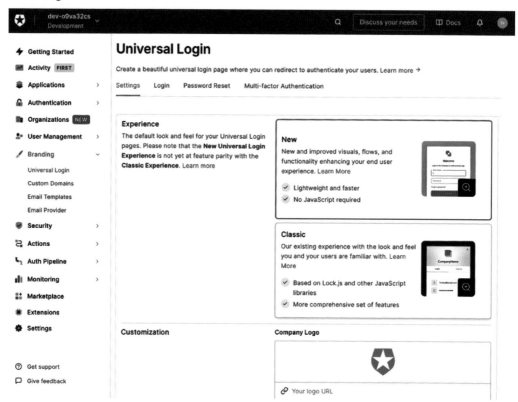

Figure 12.6 – The Auth0 branding section

Here, we can edit the HTML form directly to follow our application style. We can also customize the email templates to be consistent with our web application look and feel.

Another important topic is how Auth0 stores the user data. By default, it keeps all the login data on their own databases, but once inside the Auth0 dashboard, we can go to the authentication/database/custom database page and set up some custom scripts to grant access to an external database, where we have complete control over data ownership.

We could also set up a series of webhooks so that every time a new user registers, logs in, deletes their account, and so on, an external REST API (managed by us) gets notified, and we can replicate the data changes on external services and databases.

Auth0 gives us a lot of possibilities to customize the whole authentication experience, and it's one of the most complete providers out there. It also grants a generous free plan, where we can test a lot of its features for free before deciding whether it fits all our needs. So, if you're willing to build a production-ready app, I'd highly recommend looking into Auth0 for managing authentication safely.

Summary

In this chapter, we've seen how using a third-party authentication provider can save us from many issues when dealing with complex and sensitive topics such as private data management and user sessions.

So, the final question could be: when does it make sense to implement a custom authentication strategy? In my humble opinion, we should avoid writing custom authentication mechanisms in almost any scenario, unless we're working with an expert team capable of detecting security flaws and identifying vulnerabilities in the whole authentication flow.

There are many good alternatives to Auth0 (NextAuth.js, Firebase, AWS Cognito, and so on), and it is just too risky to replicate their battle-tested features.

If you're not comfortable working with external providers, you can also use any web framework and its built-in authentication strategies. For example, suppose you feel comfortable using Ruby on Rails, Laravel, or Spring Boot. In that case, these are all excellent alternatives over external authentication providers. They will also give you all the flexibility and security you may need with a lot of support from the community and constant security releases and fixes.

Another option could be to use a headless CMS for managing users and their data; open source CMSs such as Strapi, for example, handle authentication natively and allow us to take advantage of their own authentication mechanisms supported by the community and the company that is developing the CMS.

In any case, implementing custom authentication is a very instructive task as it teaches you a lot about how security mechanisms work and how you should protect against malicious users. For example, in the next chapter, we will be building an e-commerce website using GraphCMS; imagine that we're implementing a custom authentication mechanism here, letting malicious users exploit a vulnerability and access users' private data. Would it be worth the risk?

13
Building an E-Commerce Website with Next.js and GraphCMS

During our journey exploring Next.js, we've learned a lot. We've explored different rendering methodologies, styling techniques, integrations, and even deployment strategies.

Now it's time to start creating something worth going to production, taking advantage of everything we have learned so far.

In this chapter, we will see how to adopt Next.js to build e-commerce storefronts from scratch.

We will look at the following in detail:

- What GraphCMS is and how to adopt it
- How to integrate payment methods such as Stripe
- How to deploy an e-commerce website

By the end of this chapter, you will be able to describe a Next.js e-commerce architecture, find the right SEO and performance tradeoff, and deploy your Next.js instance on the right cloud platform.

Technical requirements

To run the code examples in this chapter, you need to have both Node.js and npm installed on your local machine.

If you prefer, you can use an online IDE, such as `https://repl.it` or `https://codesandbox.io`; they both support Next.js and you don't need to install any dependency on your computer. As with the other chapters, you can find the code base for this chapter on GitHub: `https://github.com/PacktPublishing/Real-World-Next.js`.

Creating e-commerce websites for the modern web

Since the internet started to spread at the end of the 90s, it opened a world of possibilities for online businesses. As a result, many companies began to develop **software-as-a-service (SaaS)** products to help people build their own online shopping platforms.

Today, there are several significant players in this area: Shopify, Big Cartel, WordPress (using WooCommerce or other plugins), and Magento, just to name a few.

There are also companies, such as PayPal and Stripe, that make it incredibly easy to integrate payment methods on any platform, paving the ground for custom e-commerce creation, where our imagination is the only limit.

When talking about "limits" in e-commerce creation, I'm referring to the fact that certain SaaS platforms can make it hard for us developers to customize the UI, payment flow, and so on.

Shopify, as an example, solved this problem by creating a new server-side-rendered React.js framework called **Hydrogen**, which ships with pre-built components and Hooks to communicate with its GraphQL APIs, allowing developers to create unique user experiences on the frontend with ease.

Next.js, released Next.js Commerce, a highly customizable starter kit for effortlessly creating e-commerce experiences, being able to integrate with many different platforms.

Next.js Commerce doesn't add anything new to the Next.js framework. Instead, it acts as a template for starting a new e-commerce website, knowing that we can customize every single part of it with extreme ease. We will not touch upon the customization capabilities in practice; however, we will still deploy an incredibly performant and optimized online shop.

We can use Next.js commerce with any headless backend service. It doesn't matter whether we're using Shopify, BigCommerce, Saleor, or any other service, as long as they expose some APIs to communicate with the backend.

Starting from the next section, we will be using one of the best headless CMS platforms out there, which can manage any aspect of a modern e-commerce platform, from product inventory to content translations, always keeping an API-first approach: GraphCMS.

Setting up GraphCMS

There are many different competitors in the e-commerce world; all of them offer a great set of functionalities for building modern and performant solutions, but there's always a kind of tradeoff when it comes to analyzing back-office features, frontend customization capabilities, APIs, integrations, and so on.

In this chapter, we will be using GraphCMS for a simple reason: it's easy to integrate, offers a generous free plan, and requires no setup for complex release pipelines, databases, or whatever. We just need to open an account and take advantage of the massive set of free features to build a fully working e-commerce website.

It also provides an e-commerce starter template with pre-built (yet fully customizable) contents, which translates to a pre-built GraphQL schema ready to consume on the frontend to create product pages, catalogs, and so on.

We can start by creating a new GraphCMS account by going to `https://graphcms.com`. Once we log into our dashboard, we will see that GraphCMS prompts us to create a new project, and we will choose among several pre-made templates. We can select the **Commerce Shop** template, which will generate some mock content for us.

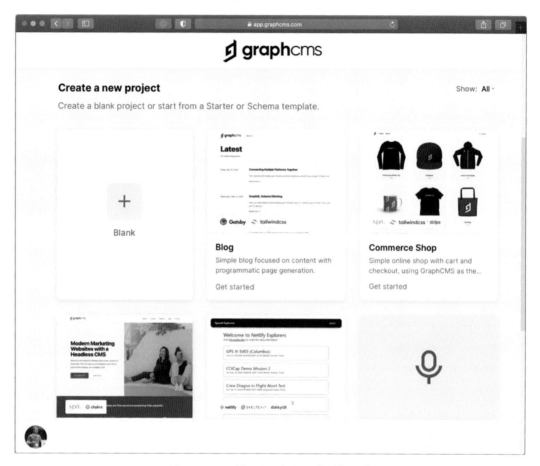

Figure 13.1 – The GraphCMS dashboard

Once we have created the project by selecting **Commerce Shop** as a template, we can browse the **Content** section in our GraphCMS dashboard and see what mock data we have.

We will see many useful and prepopulated sections, such as products, product variants, categories, and reviews; we will use this data in our Next.js commerce application shortly.

Now that we have our content, we need to create a Next.js application to display it on the frontend by using the powerful GraphCMS GraphQL APIs:

```
npx create-next-app with-graphcms
```

Once we have created the app, we can start thinking about how we want the UI to be. In this case, we want to keep things easy, and we'll use Chakra UI for styling our components. Let's install it and set it up inside our Next.js application:

```
yarn add @chakra-ui/react @emotion/react@^11 @emotion/
styled@^11 framer-motion@^4
```

Let's open our _app.js file and add the Chakra provider:

```
import { ChakraProvider } from '@chakra-ui/react';

function MyApp({ Component, pageProps }) {
  return (
    <ChakraProvider>
      <Component {...pageProps} />
    </ChakraProvider>
  );
}

export default MyApp;
```

Now that we've set up an elementary Next.js application, we can start thinking about linking GraphCMS to it.

As said before, GraphCMS exposes excellent GraphQL APIs, so we need to connect to it by using that protocol. We've already discussed how to connect to any GraphQL endpoint using Apollo in *Chapter 4, Organizing the Code base and Fetching Data in Next.js*. For the sake of simplicity, we'll now use a more straightforward library for connecting to GraphCMS: graphql-request.

We can install it by using Yarn:

```
yarn add graphql-request graphql
```

Now let's create a basic GraphQL interface to connect GraphCMS to our storefront. First, let's create a new file called `lib/graphql/index.js` and add the following content:

```
import { GraphQLClient } from 'graphql-request';

const { GRAPHCMS_ENDPOINT, GRAPHCMS_API_KEY = null } =
  process.env;
const authorization = `Bearer ${GRAPHCMS_API_KEY}`;

export default new GraphQLClient(GRAPHCMS_ENDPOINT, {
  headers: {
    ...(GRAPHCMS_API_KEY && { authorization} }),
  },
});
```

What's happening here?

As you can see, we will need to create a couple of environment variables: GRAPHCMS_ ENDPOINT and GRAPHCMS_API_KEY. The first one contains the GraphCMS endpoint URL, and the second is an optional API key for accessing protected data.

In fact, GraphCMS allows you to expose its data publicly, which can be handy in certain situations. In other cases, though, we want our data to be accessible to authorized clients only, so we need to use an API key.

We can retrieve those environment variables values by going to **Settings** then **API Access** on our GraphCMS dashboard.

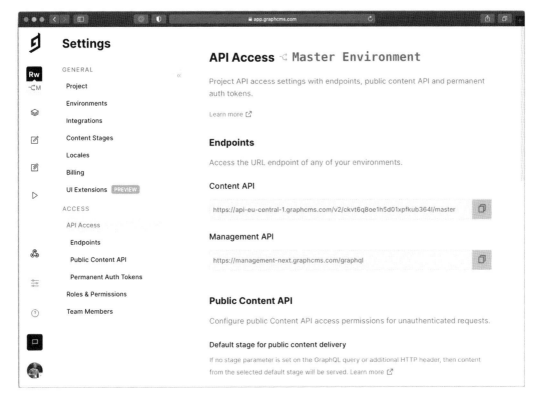

Figure 13.2 – API access management in GraphCMS

We can now take the **Content API** value and put it as a GRAPHCMS_ENDPOINT value inside the .env.local file in our codebase. Of course, if this file does not exist, we can create it from scratch:

```
GRAPHCMS_ENDPOINT=https://api-eu-central-1.graphcms.com/v2/
ckvt6q8oe1h5d01xpfkub364l/master
```

We now need to set the API key, which allows us to perform mutations on the CMS (for example, save an order once it's paid). We can use the default **Mutation** token created by GraphCMS for us under **Permanent Auth Tokens** in the **API Access** section. Once we retrieve it, we can simply add it as the GRAPHCMS_API_KEY value in our .env.local file.

We're now ready to go! We have a connection with the CMS, so we can read, write, and even update or delete data via GraphQL APIs. In the next section, we will use them to create the storefront and the product detail page.

Creating the storefront, cart, and product detail pages

GraphCMS offers a well-made, rock-solid, open source template for creating e-commerce websites, which can be found at this URL: `https://github.com/GraphCMS/graphcms-commerce-starter`.

We're not adopting this starter template because we want to fully understand the reasoning behind certain technical decisions and how to approach the problems that can appear during the development phase.

That said, we can focus on developing the first essential components for our storefront.

We will wrap our entire application in a Chakra UI box so that every page will have a similar layout. We can do that by opening the `_app.js` file and adding the following components:

```
import { Box, Flex, ChakraProvider } from '@chakra-ui/react';

function MyApp({ Component, pageProps }) {
  return (
    <ChakraProvider>
      <Flex w="full" minH="100vh" bgColor="gray.100">
        <Box maxW="70vw" m="auto">
          <Component {...pageProps} />
        </Box>
      </Flex>
    </ChakraProvider>
  );
}

export default MyApp;
```

Now, we can start thinking about how we want to show our products on the home page. However, before doing that, we may want to check the data provided via GraphQL APIs by the CMS, and we can easily do that by going into the **API Playground** section of our dashboard. Here, we can write our GraphQL queries, taking advantage of the **Explorer** functionality to help us create highly customizable GraphQL queries with ease.

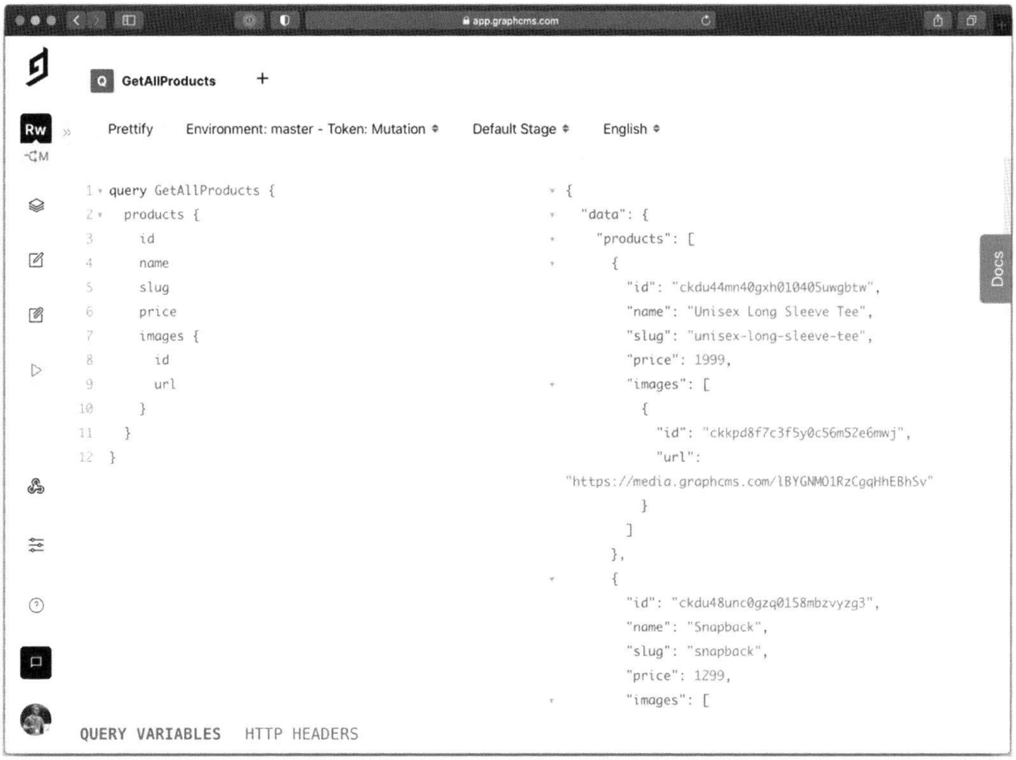

Figure 13.3 – GraphCMS API Playground

In the query shown in the preceding screenshot, we're retrieving all the publicly available products. We can use this exact query in our Next.js app, so let's create a new `/lib/graphql/queries/getAllProducts.js` file and add the following content:

```
import { gql } from 'graphql-request';

export default gql`
  query GetAllProducs {
    products {
      id
      name
```

```
        slug
        price
        images {
            id
            url
        }
    }
  }
`;
```

We're now ready to fetch all the products to populate our home page. To generate a static page at build time, let's head to our `pages/index.js` page and retrieve the products inside the `getStaticProps` function:

```
import graphql from '../lib/graphql';
import getAllProducts from '../lib/graphql/queries/
getAllProducts';

export const getStaticProps = async () => {
    const { products } = await graphql.request(getAllProducts)
    return {
      props: {
        products,
      },
    };
};
```

At this point, we might be wondering how to handle cases where we create a new product and want to display it immediately on the home page. Here, we have two options:

- Use `getServerSideProps` instead of `getStaticProps`, which will dynamically generate the page on each request, but we already know its downsides, as seen in *Chapter 10, Working with SEO and Managing Performance.*

- Use incremental static regeneration so that after a given period, the page gets regenerated, including any new API changes.

We'll proceed with the second option by adding the following property to our returning `getStaticProps` object:

```
import graphql from '../lib/graphql';
import getAllProducts from '../lib/graphql/queries/
getAllProducts';

export const getStaticProps = async () => {
  const { products } = await graphql.request(getAllProducts)
  return {
    revalidate: 60, // 60 seconds
    props: {
      products,
    },
  };
};
```

We're now ready to display all the products on our home page. We'll do that by creating a new component under `/components/ProductCard/index.js`, exposing the following function:

```
import Link from 'next/link';
import { Box, Text, Image, Divider } from '@chakra-ui/react';

export default function ProductCard(props) {
  return (
    <Link href={`/product/${props.slug}`} passHref>
      <Box
        as="a"
        border="1px"
        borderColor="gray.200"
        px="10"
        py="5"
        rounded="lg"
        boxShadow="lg"
        bgColor="white"
        transition="ease 0.2s"
        _hover={{
```

```
      boxShadow: 'xl',
      transform: 'scale(1.02)',
    }}>
    <Image src={props.images[0]?.url} alt={props.name} />
    <Divider my="3" />
    <Box>
      <Text fontWeight="bold" textColor="purple"
        fontSize="lg">{props.name}
      </Text>
      <Text textColor="gray.700">€{props.price/ 100}</Text>
    </Box>
  </Box>
</Link>
  );
}
```

As you can see, this is a straightforward component that displays a product card containing the product image, name, and price.

If you look at the used props (highlighted in the preceding code snippet), you will notice a one-to-one correspondence with the data we're getting back from GraphCMS. That's another slight advantage of using GraphQL: it allows you to model your data while querying it, making it incredibly easy to build components, functions, and even algorithms around it.

Now that we have our ProductCard component, we can import it into our home page and use it to display all the products fetched from the CMS:

```
import { Grid } from '@chakra-ui/layout';
import graphql from '../lib/graphql';
import getAllProducts from '../lib/graphql/queries/
getAllProducts';
import ProductCard from '../components/ProductCard';


export async const getStaticProps = () => {
  // ...
}
```

```
export default function Home(props) {
    return (
<Grid gridTemplateColumns="repeat(4, 1fr)" gap="5">
    {props.products.map((product) => (
    <ProductCard key={product.id} {...product} />
        ))}
</Grid>
    );
}
```

If we now launch our development server and head to `http://localhost:3000`, we will be able to see our storefront.

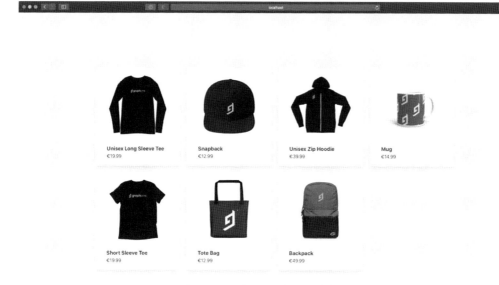

Figure 13.4 – Our first Next.js-based storefront

Now that we have a working storefront, we need to create a single product page.

As for the home page, we will use SSG + ISR to build all the product pages, which will help us maintain great performance and improve SEO and user experience.

We can do that by creating a new file under `pages/product/[slug].js`, where we can start writing the following function definitions:

```
export async function getStaticPaths() {}
```

```
export async function getStaticProps() {}
```

```
export default function ProductPage() {}
```

As you may have guessed, we will need to generate a new page for each product, and we can do that by using Next.js' reserved `getStaticPaths` function.

Inside that function, we will query for all the products in our CMS, then generate the dynamic URL paths for each one; that way, at build time, Next.js will generate all the pages we need in our website.

The other two functions should already sound familiar, so we will implement them later.

We now need to write a GraphQL query for getting all the products in GraphCMS. To keep it simple, we can reuse the query we wrote for the home page, which is already fetching all the products, including their slugs (which will be part of the product URL).

Let's update our product page by making a request to GraphCMS for all the products in the inventory:

```
import graphql from '../../lib/graphql';
import getAllProducts from '../../lib/graphql/queries/
getAllProducts';

export async function getStaticPaths() {
  const { products } = await
    graphql.request(getAllProducts);

  const paths = products.map((product) => ({
    params: {
      slug: product.slug,
    },
  }));

  return {
    paths,
```

```
        fallback: false,
    };
}
```

With this edit, we're returning an object containing all the pages we need to generate at build time. In fact, the returning object will look like this:

```
{
    paths: [
        {
            params: {
                slug: "unisex-long-sleeve-tee"
            }
        },
        {
            params: {
                slug: "snapback"
            }
        },
        // ...
    ]
    fallback: false
}
```

As you may guess, this will help Next.js to match a given `/product/[slug]` route with the correct product slug.

At this point, we need to create a GraphQL query to get the single product details. We can create a new file under `lib/graphql/queries/getProductDetail.js` and add the following content:

```
import { gql } from 'graphql-request';

export default gql`
    query GetProductBySlug($slug: String!) {
    products(where: { slug: $slug }) {
        id
        images(first: 1) {
        id
```

```
        url
    }
        name
        price
        slug
        description
    }
  }
`;
```

With this query, we will get all the products whose slug matches the $slug query variable. Given that the slug property is unique in GraphCMS, it will return an array with just one result if the requested products exist or an empty array if it doesn't.

We're now ready to import this query and edit the getStaticProps function:

```
import graphql from '../../lib/graphql';
import getAllProducts from '../../lib/graphql/queries/
getAllProducts';
import getProductDetail from '../../lib/graphql/queries/
getProductDetail';

export async function getStaticProps({ params }) {
  const { products } = await
    graphql.request(getProductDetail, {
    slug: params.slug,
  });

  return {
    props: {
      product: products[0],
    },
  };
}
```

Now we only need to create the product page layout, containing an image of our product, a title, a brief description, the price, and a quantity selector. To do that, we can edit the `ProductPage` function in the following way:

```
import { Box, Flex, Grid, Text, Image, Divider, Button,
  Select } from '@chakra-ui/react';


// ...


function SelectQuantity(props) {
  const quantity = [...Array.from({ length: 10 })];
  return (
  <Select  placeholder="Quantity"
    onChange={ (event)  =>props.onChange(event.target.value)}>
      {quantity.map((_, i) => (
    <option key={i + 1} value={i + 1}>
      {i + 1}
    </option>
    ))}
  </Select>
  );
}


export default function ProductPage({ product }) {
  return (
    <Flex rounded="xl" boxShadow="2xl" w="full" p="16"
      bgColor="white">
    <Image height="96" width="96" src={product.images[0].url}/>
    <Box ml="12" width="container.xs">
    <Text as="h1" fontSize="4xl" fontWeight="bold">
      {product.name}
    </Text>
    <Text lineHeight="none" fontSize="xl" my="3"
    fontWeight="bold" textColor="blue.500">
      €{product.price / 100}
    </Text>
    <Text maxW="96" textAlign="justify" fontSize="sm">
```

```
        {product.description}
      </Text>
      <Divider my="6" />
      <Grid gridTemplateColumns="2fr 1fr" gap="5"
        alignItems="center">
      <SelectQuantityonChange={() => {}} />
      <Button colorScheme="blue">
        Add to cart
      </Button>
      </Grid>
      </Box>
      </Flex>
    );
}
```

If we now launch the development server and open a single product page, we will see the following content:

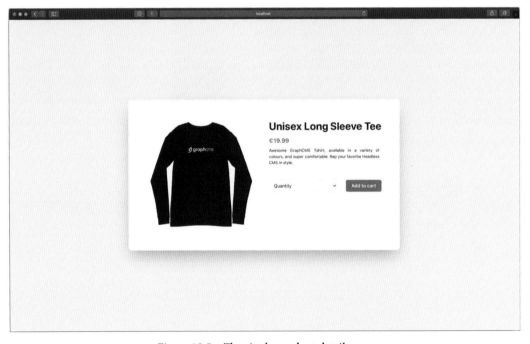

Figure 13.5 – The single product detail page

Now that we can navigate from the home page to a product page, we need to build a navigation bar that can allow us to go back to the storefront or go to the shopping cart to review the product we want to purchase and then make the payment.

We can easily create a navigation bar by opening a new file under `components/NavBar/index.js` and adding the following content:

```js
import Link from 'next/link';
import { Flex, Box, Button, Text } from '@chakra-ui/react';
import { MdShoppingCart } from 'react-icons/md';

export default function NavBar() {
  return (
    <Box position="fixed" top={0} left={0} w="full"
    bgColor="white" boxShadow="md">
    <Flex width="container.xl" m="auto" p="5"
      justifyContent="space-between">
    <Link href="/" passHref>
    <Text textColor="blue.800" fontWeight="bold"
      fontSize="2xl" as="a">
        My e-commerce
    </Text>
    </Link>
    <Box>
    <Link href="/cart" passHref>
      <Button as="a">
        <MdShoppingCart />
      </Button>
    </Link>
    </Box>
    </Flex>
    </Box>
  );
}
```

We will also need to install the `react-icons` library, which, as the name suggests, is an excellent package containing hundreds of well-made and useful icons for our React-based projects:

```
yarn add react-icons
```

We now only need to update our `_app.js` file by including the newest `NavBar` component so that it will be rendered on all the application pages:

```
import { Box, Flex, ChakraProvider } from '@chakra-ui/react';
import NavBar from '../components/NavBar';

function MyApp({ Component, pageProps }) {
  return (
    <ChakraProvider>
    <Flex w="full" minH="100vh" bgColor="gray.100">
    <NavBar />
    <Box maxW="70vw" m="auto">
      <Component {...pageProps} />
    </Box>
    </Flex>
    </ChakraProvider>
  );
}

export default MyApp;
```

We can finally navigate from the storefront to the product page and back!

Now that the website is taking shape, we want to add products to our shopping basket. We discussed a similar scenario in *Chapter 5, Managing Local and Global States in Next.js*.

We will need to create a React context to hold the shopping list until the user pays.

First, we will need to create a new file under `lib/context/Cart/index.js`. Here, we will write the following script:

```
import { createContext } from 'react';

const CartContext = createContext({
  items: {},
```

```
    setItems: () => {},
});
```

```
export default CartContext;
```

We now need to wrap the entire app under this context, so we need to open the _app.js file and edit it as follows:

```
import { useState } from 'react';
import { Box, Flex, ChakraProvider } from '@chakra-ui/react';
import NavBar from '../components/NavBar';
import CartContext from '../lib/context/Cart';

function MyApp({ Component, pageProps }) {
  const [items, setItems] = useState({});

  return (
    <ChakraProvider>
    <CartContext.Provider value={{ items, setItems }}>
    <Flex w="full" minH="100vh" bgColor="gray.100">
    <NavBar />
      <Box maxW="70vw" m="auto">
        <Component {...pageProps} />
      </Box>
    </Flex>
    </CartContext.Provider>
    </ChakraProvider>
  );
}
```

```
export default MyApp;
```

This is quite similar to the context we created in *Chapter 5, Managing Local and Global States in Next.js*, right?

We now need to link the single product page to the context to add products to the shopping cart. Let's open the components/ProductCard/index.js file and link the context to the **select quantity** and **add to cart** actions:

```
import { useContext, useState } from 'react';
import CartContext from '../../lib/context/Cart';
// ...

export default function ProductPage({ product }) {
  const [quantity, setQuantity] = useState(0);
  const { items, setItems } = useContext(CartContext);

  const alreadyInCart = product.id in items;

  function addToCart() {
      setItems({
      ...items,
      [product.id]: quantity,
    });
  }

  return (
    <Flex rounded="xl" boxShadow="2xl" w="full" p="16"
      bgColor="white">
    <Image height="96" width="96" src={product.images[0].url} />
    <Box ml="12" width="container.xs">
      <Text as="h1" fontSize="4xl" fontWeight="bold">
        {product.name}
      </Text>
      <Text lineHeight="none" fontSize="xl" my="3"
        fontWeight="bold" textColor="blue.500">
          €{product.price / 100}
      </Text>
      <Text maxW="96" textAlign="justify" fontSize="sm">
          {product.description}
      </Text>
      </Text>
      <Divider my="6" />
```

```
      <Grid gridTemplateColumns="2fr 1fr" gap="5"
        alignItems="center">
        <SelectQuantity
          onChange={(quantity)=>setQuantity
            (parseInt(quantity))}
        />
        <Button colorScheme="blue" onClick={addToCart}>
              {alreadyInCart ? 'Update' : 'Add to cart'}
        </Button>
      </Grid>
    </Box>
  </Flex>
    );
}
```

We can also make things more exciting and dynamic by showing how many products we have in our shopping cart. We can do this by linking the NavBar component to the same CartContext by adding a few lines:

```
import { useContext } from 'react';
import Link from 'next/link';
import { Flex, Box, Button, Text } from '@chakra-ui/react';
import { MdShoppingCart } from 'react-icons/md';
import CartContext from '../../lib/context/Cart';

export default function NavBar() {
  const { items } = useContext(CartContext);

  const itemsCount = Object
    .values(items)
    .reduce((x, y) => x + y, 0);

  return (
    <Box position="fixed" top={0} left={0} w="full"
      bgColor="white" boxShadow="md">
    <Flex width="container.xl" m="auto" p="5"
      justifyContent="space-between">
```

```
        <Link href="/" passHref>
        <Text textColor="blue.800" fontWeight="bold"
          fontSize="2xl" as="a">
            My e-commerce
        </Text>
        </Link>
<Box>
<Link href="/cart" passHref>
  <Button as="a">
    <MdShoppingCart />
<Text ml="3">{itemsCount}</Text>
  </Button>
</Link>
</Box>
</Flex>
</Box>
  );
}
```

Now that we have a way to add items to the shopping cart, we need to create the cart page itself. Let's create a new pages/cart.js, file where we will add the following component:

```
import { useContext, useEffect, useState } from 'react';
import { Box, Divider, Text } from '@chakra-ui/react';

export default function Cart() {
  return (
    <Box
      rounded="xl"
      boxShadow="2xl"
      w="container.lg"
      p="16"
      bgColor="white"
    >
      <Text as="h1" fontSize="2xl" fontWeight="bold">
        Cart
```

```
        </Text>
        <Divider my="10" />
        <Box>
            <Text>The cart is empty.</Text>
        </Box>
        </Box>
    );
}
```

This will be the shopping cart's page default state. When a user puts any product into the basket, we need to display it here.

To do that, we can easily use the cart context we just created, which will tell us the ID and quantity of each product:

```
import { useContext, useEffect, useState } from 'react';
import { Box, Divider, Text } from '@chakra-ui/react';
import cartContext from '../lib/context/Cart';


export default function Cart() {
  const { items } = useContext(cartContext);


  return (
    // ...
  );
}
```

We ended up having an object containing the IDs and the quantity for each product in the format { [product_id]: quantity }.

We will use the keys of this object to fetch all the required products from GraphCMS by using a new query, positioned under lib/graphql/queries/getProductsById.js:

```
import { gql } from 'graphql-request';


export default gql`
  query GetProductByID($ids: [ID!]) {
  products(where: { id_in: $ids }) {
    id
```

```
        name
        price
        slug
        }
    }
`;
```

Once we finish writing the query, we can move back to our cart.js file and implement it using a useEffect React Hook, so that we fetch all the products as soon as the page loads:

```
import { useContext, useEffect, useState } from 'react';
import { Box, Divider, Text } from '@chakra-ui/react';
import graphql from '../lib/graphql';
import cartContext from '../lib/context/Cart';
import getProductsById from '../lib/graphql/queries/
getProductsById';

export default function Cart() {
    const { items } = useContext(cartContext);
    const [products, setProducts] = useState([]);
    const hasProducts = Object.keys(items).length;

    useEffect(() => {
        // only fetch data if user has selected any product
        if (!hasProducts) return;

        graphql.request(getProductsById, {
            ids: Object.keys(items),
        })
          .then((data) => {
            setProducts(data.products);
        })
          .catch((err) =>console.error(err));
    }, [JSON.stringify(products)]);

    return (
```

```
    // ...
  );
}
```

As soon as we try to add a couple of products to the shopping basket and then move to the cart page, we will see the following error:

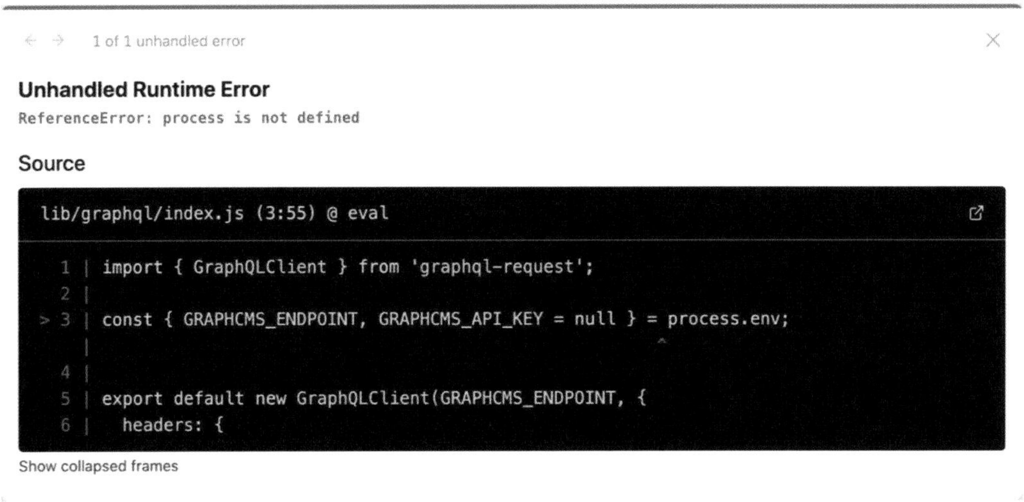

```
←  →     1 of 1 unhandled error                                                      ×

Unhandled Runtime Error
ReferenceError: process is not defined

Source
  lib/graphql/index.js (3:55) @ eval                                          ☐

  1 |  import { GraphQLClient } from 'graphql-request';
  2 |
> 3 |  const { GRAPHCMS_ENDPOINT, GRAPHCMS_API_KEY = null } = process.env;
    |                                                       ^
  4 |
  5 |  export default new GraphQLClient(GRAPHCMS_ENDPOINT, {
  6 |    headers: {

Show collapsed frames
```

Figure 13.6 – The browser can't find the process variable

Next.js is telling us that the `process` variable, containing all the environment variables, is not available on the browser. Thankfully, even if this variable is not officially supported by any browser, Next.js provides an excellent polyfill for us; we only need to make a couple of changes to make it effective.

First of all, we will need to rename the GRAPHCMS_ENDPOINT variable to NEXT_PUBLIC_GRAPHCMS_ENDPOINT. By prepending NEXT_PUBLIC_ to any environment variable, Next.js will add a `process.env` object, available on the browser, exposing only the public variables.

Let's make the change in the `.env.local` file, then move back to the `lib/graphql/index.js` file and make a small change there too:

```
import { GraphQLClient } from 'graphql-request';

const GRAPHCMS_ENDPOINT = process.env.NEXT_PUBLIC_GRAPHCMS_
ENDPOINT;
```

```
const GRAPHCMS_API_KEY = process.env.GRAPHCMS_API_KEY;

const authorization = `Bearer ${GRAPHCMS_API_KEY}`;

export default new GraphQLClient(GRAPHCMS_ENDPOINT, {
  headers: {
    ...(GRAPHCMS_API_KEY && { authorization }),
  },
});
```

Please note that we're not modifying the GRAPHCMS_API_KEY environment variable name, as it contains private data and should never be exposed.

Now that we have fixed this little issue, we're finally ready to compose our cart page.

First, we will need to write a function that calculates the final expense by summing the product prices multiplied by their quantity. We can do that by adding this function inside our component's body:

```
export default function Cart() {
  // ...

function getTotal() {
  if (!products.length) return 0;

  return Object.keys(items)
    .map(
      (id) =>
        products.find((product) => product.id === id).price
        * (items[id] / 100) // Stripe requires the prices to be
                            // integers (i.e., €4.99 should be
                            // written as 499). That's why
                            // we need to divide by 100 the
                            // prices
                            // we get from GraphCMS, which are
                            // already in the correct
                            // Stripe format

    )
```

```
      .reduce((x, y) => x + y)
      .toFixed(2);
  }

// ...
}
```

Now, we can update our component returning JSX by including the list of products that we added to the shopping cart:

```
  return (
    <Box
      rounded="xl"
      boxShadow="2xl"
      w="container.lg"
      p="16"
      bgColor="white">
    <Text as="h1" fontSize="2xl" fontWeight="bold">
      Cart
    </Text>
    <Divider my="10" />
    <Box>
      {!hasProducts ? (
    <Text>The cart is empty.</Text>
        ) : (
    <>
        {products.map((product) => (
    <Flex
      key={product.id}
      justifyContent="space-between"
      mb="4">
    <Box>
    <Link href={`/product/${product.slug}`} passHref>
    <Text
      as="a"
      fontWeight="bold"
      _hover={{
```

```
                    textDecoration: 'underline',
                    color: 'blue.500' }}>
                        {product.name}
                    <Text as="span" color="gray.500">
                        {''}
                        x{items[product.id]}
                    </Text>
                    </Text>
                    </Link>
                    </Box>
                    <Box>
                        €{(items[product.id] *
                        (product.price / 100)).toFixed(2)}
                    </Box>
                    </Flex>
                        ))}
                    <Divider my="10" />
                    <Flex
                        alignItems="center"
                        justifyContent="space-between">
                        <Text fontSize="xl" fontWeight="bold">
                        Total: €{getTotal()}
                        </Text>
                <Button colorScheme="blue"> Pay now </Button>
                    </Flex>
                    </>
                        )}
    </Box>
    </Box>
      );
    }
```

We're all set for managing the cart! We now need to process the payment by choosing a financial service, such as Stripe, PayPal, or Braintree.

In the next section, we will see how to implement the payment feature using Stripe.

Processing payments using Stripe

Stripe is one of the best financial services out there; it's straightforward to use and offers excellent documentation to understand how to integrate their APIs.

Before continuing with this section, make sure to open an account at `https://stripe.com`.

Once we have an account, we can log in and go to `https://dashboard.stripe.com/apikeys`, where we'll retrieve the following information: the publishable key and secret key. We will need to store them inside of two environment variables, following this naming convention:

```
NEXT_PUBLIC_STRIPE_SHARABLE_KEY=
STRIPE_SECRET_KEY=
```

Please double-check that you're not exposing the `STRIPE_SECRET_KEY` variable and that the `.env.local` file is not added to the Git history by including it in the `.gitignore` file.

Now let's install the Stripe JavaScript SDK inside of our project:

```
yarn add @stripe/stripe-js stripe
```

Once the two packages are installed, we can create a new file under `lib/stripe/index.js`, containing the following script:

```
import { loadStripe } from '@stripe/stripe-js';

const key = process.env.NEXT_PUBLIC_STRIPE_SHARABLE_KEY;

let stripePromise;

const getStripe = () => {
  if (!stripePromise) {
    stripePromise = loadStripe(key);
  }
```

```
    return stripePromise;
};
```

```
export default getStripe;
```

This script will ensure that we load Stripe only once, even if we come back to the cart page multiple times.

At this point, we will need to create an API page that creates a Stripe session. By doing that, Stripe will create a beautiful and secure checkout page to redirect our users to insert their payment and shipping details. Once the users place their orders, they will get redirected to a landing page of our choice, but we'll see that later on in this section.

Let's create a new API route under /pages/api/checkout/index.js, where we will write a very basic Stripe checkout session request:

```
import Stripe from 'stripe';

const stripe = new Stripe(process.env.STRIPE_SECRET_KEY);

export default async function handler(req, res) {

}
```

Once we have created this basic function, we need to understand what data Stripe requires to complete the session.

We will need to pass the following data in a particular order:

- All the products to purchase, containing names, quantities, prices, and (optionally) images
- All the available payment methods (credit cards, Alipay, SEPA Debit, or other payment methods, such as Klarna)
- Shipping rates
- Success and cancel redirect URLs for either case

We can start by considering the first point; we can easily pass the whole cart context object to this endpoint, including both product IDs to purchase and their quantity. We will need to then ask GraphCMS for product details, and we can do that by creating a new specific query under `lib/graphql/queries/getProductDetailsById.js`:

```javascript
import { gql } from 'graphql-request';

export default gql`
  query GetProductDetailsByID($ids: [ID!]) {
    products(where: { id_in: $ids }) {
      id
      name
      price
      slug
      description
      images {
        id
        url
      }
    }
  }
`;
```

Going back to our `/pages/api/checkout/index.js` API page, we can start by implementing the query to retrieve the product details:

```javascript
import Stripe from 'stripe';
import graphql from '../../../lib/graphql';
import getProductsDetailsById from '../../../lib/graphql/
queries/getProductDetailsById';

const stripe = new Stripe(process.env.STRIPE_SECRET_KEY);

export default async function handler(req, res) {
  const { items } = req.body;
  const { products } = await graphql
```

```
        .request(getProductsDetailsById, { ids: Object.keys(items)
});


}
```

Stripe requires a configuration object containing a property called `line_items`, which describes all the products ready for purchase. Now that we have all the product information, we can compose this property in the following way:

```
export default async function handler(req, res) {
  const { items } = req.body;
  const { products } = await graphql
    .request(getProductsDetailsById, { ids: Object.keys(items)
});

  const line_items = products.map((product) => ({
    // user can change the quantity during checkout
    adjustable_quantity: {
      enabled: true,
      minimum: 1,
    },
  price_data: {
  // of course, it can be any currency of your choice
    currency: 'EUR',
    product_data: {
      name: product.name,
      images: product.images.map((img) => img.url),
      },
  // please note that GraphCMS already returns the price in the
  // format required by Strapi: €4.99, for instance, should be
  // passed to Stripe as 499.
    unit_amount: product.price,
    },
    quantity: items[product.id],
  }));
```

As a reference, if a user buys a couple of backpacks from our store, the `line_items` array would look like this:

```
[
  {
    "adjustable_quantity": {
      "enabled": true,
      "minimum": 1
    },
    "price_data": {
      "currency": "EUR",
      "product_data": {
        "name": "Backpack",
        "images": [
          https://media.graphcms.com/U5y09n80TpuRKJU6Gue1
        ]
      },
      "unit_amount": 4999
    },
    "quantity": 2
  }
]
```

We can now start writing the Stripe checkout session request by using the `line_items` array and a bit more information:

```
export default async function handle(req, res) {

  // ...

  const session = await stripe.checkout.sessions.create({
    mode: 'payment', // can also be "subscription" or "setup"
    line_items,
    payment_method_types: ['card', 'sepa_debit'],
    // the server doesn't know the current URL, so we need to
    write
    // it into an environment variable depending on the current
```

```
// environment. Locally, it should be URL=http://
localhost:3000
success_url: `${process.env.URL}/success`,
cancel_url: `${process.env.URL}/cancel`,
});
```

```
res.status(201).json({ session });
}
```

We're almost there. Now, we only need to get the shipping information and store it in two different Stripe session properties: `shipping_address_collection` and `shipping_options`.

We can create two new variables outside the `handler` function. Still, as you can imagine, this can be completely CMS-driven.

To keep it simple, let's create the first `shipping_address_collection` variable:

```
export const shipping_address_collection = {
  allowed_countries: ['IT', 'US'],
};
```

As you can see, we can restrict shipping by manually selecting the countries where we ship to. You can simply avoid passing the `shipping_address_collection` property to the Stripe session if you want to ship worldwide.

The second variable is more complex but allows us to create different shipping methods with different rates. Let's say we offer free shipping, which takes 3 to 5 business days for delivery, and express next day shipping for €4.99.

We can create the following array of shipping options:

```
export const shipping_options = [
  {
    shipping_rate_data: {
      type: 'fixed_amount',
      fixed_amount: {
        amount: 0,
        currency: 'EUR',
      },
      display_name: 'Free Shipping',
```

```
delivery_estimate: {
        minimum: {
          unit: 'business_day',
          value: 3,
        },
        maximum: {
          unit: 'business_day',
          value: 5,
        },
      },
    },
  },
  {
shipping_rate_data: {
      type: 'fixed_amount',
fixed_amount: {
        amount: 499,
        currency: 'EUR',
      },
display_name: 'Next day air',
delivery_estimate: {
        minimum: {
          unit: 'business_day',
          value: 1,
        },
        maximum: {
          unit: 'business_day',
          value: 1,
        },
      },
    },
  },
];
```

The shipping objects are self-explanatory. We can finally add those two new properties to our Stripe checkout session:

```
export default async function handle(req, res) {

  // ...

  const session = await stripe.checkout.sessions.create({
    mode: 'payment', // can also be "subscription" or "setup"
    line_items,
    payment_method_types: ['card', 'sepa_debit'],
    // the server doesn't know the current URL, so we need to write
    // it into an environment variable depending on the current
    // environment. Locally, it should be URL=http://
    localhost:3000
    shipping_address_collection,
    shipping_options,
      success_url: `${process.env.URL}/success`,
      cancel_url: `${process.env.URL}/cancel`,
  });

      res.status(201).json({ session });
}
```

And we're done! We're now replying with a session object that contains the redirect URL to be used on the frontend to redirect the user to the Stripe-hosted checkout page.

We can do that by moving back to our pages/cart.js page and adding the following function:

```
import loadStripe from '../lib/stripe';

// ...

export default function Cart() {
```

```
// ...

async function handlePayment() {
  const stripe = await loadStripe();
  const res = await fetch('/api/checkout', {
    method: 'POST',
    headers: {
      'Content-Type': 'application/json',
    },
    body: JSON.stringify({
      items,
    }),
  });

  const { session } = await res.json();
  await stripe.redirectToCheckout({
    sessionId: session.id,
  });
}

// ...

}
```

As a very last thing, we only need to link this function to the **Pay now** button in the returning JSX for the `Cart` function:

```
// ...
<Button colorScheme="blue" onClick={handlePayment}>
    Pay now
</Button>
// ...
```

We're finally ready to test out our checkout flow! Let's boot the development server, add a couple of products to the shopping basket, then go to the **Cart** section and click on the **Pay now** button. We should end up on this beautiful, Stripe-powered checkout page, where we can insert our shipping information, choose the desired payment method, and modify the quantity for each product we put in the cart:

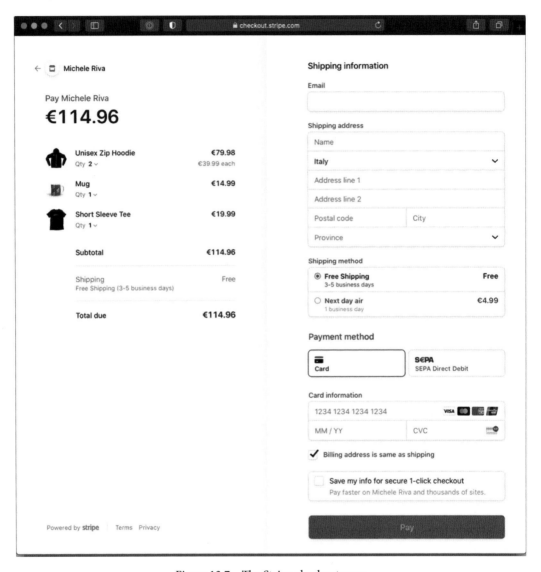

Figure 13.7 – The Stripe checkout page

In my case, you can see that I've been redirected to a **Michele Riva** store (upper-left corner), as I opened my Stripe account using my name, but if you did the same and want to customize the store name, you can edit it on your Stripe dashboard.

By clicking on the store name in the upper-left corner, we will be redirected to the `cancel_url` we set in the `pages/api/checkout/index.js` page; if we successfully complete a purchase, we will get redirected to `success_url`. I'll leave you the task of creating those two pages as a little homework to complete before moving on to the next chapter.

Summary

In the previous sections, we saw how to create a straightforward e-commerce website using GraphCMS and Stripe, two incredible products that can help build scalable, secure, and maintainable storefronts.

Even though we've made some significant progress during this chapter, we're still missing some features that would deserve an entire book on them exclusively.

For example, if we now want to navigate back from the Stripe checkout to the cart page, we will see that our shopping cart is empty, as the cart context is not persistent. And what if we want to allow our users to create an account and see the shipping progress, order history, and other helpful information?

As you can imagine, these are complex topics, and there's no way we can manage them in one chapter exclusively. One thing's for sure: once we know how to handle users and authentication via Auth0, product inventory and order history on GraphCMS, and checkout on Stripe, we have all the elements we need to create rock-solid user experiences and development workflows.

The Vercel team also announced Next.js Commerce in the latest releases, a template ready to be attached to Shopify, Saleor, BigCommerce, and a few more e-commerce platforms to create a custom UI instantly for your storefront. The reason why we're not digging into that template is simple: it is compelling, but it abstracts most of the work that is needed to connect different systems (such as Stripe and GraphCMS, or PayPal and WordPress), and we want to understand how to do it ourselves for the sake of learning more.

In this chapter, we saw how to integrate a headless CMS into our Next.js frontend. But if you found it easy, that's mainly because GraphCMS has been wisely built with the developer experience in mind, allowing us to take advantage of well-written GraphQL APIs built for the modern web era.

We can't say that the same applies to other CMSs, born when the web was still young and evolving, maintaining a full-stack approach, where we used the CMS itself to build both the backend and the frontend of our applications. But today, even those older CMS platforms are evolving thanks to an incredible community effort, aiming to provide a great developer experience by allowing us to adopt Next.js (or any other framework) as a frontend. For example, there's a fantastic WordPress plugin that generates excellent GraphQL APIs from an existing website; that way, we can use WordPress as a complete headless CMS, creating a robust, performant, custom Next.js frontend. You can learn more about this plugin at `https://www.wpgraphql.com`. The same applies to Drupal, another popular, open source CMS that can expose GraphQL APIs thanks to the GraphQL module: `https://www.drupal.org/project/graphql`.

In the followingchapter, we will briefly recap what we've seen so far and see some example projects that we can build to practice more with Next.js.

14
Example Projects and Next Steps for Learning More

We're about to reach the end of our journey, and it has been a crazy ride so far.

We've learned so many things about Next.js; we're now ready to create the next big website or just have fun on our own with a framework that gives us endless possibilities.

In this concluding chapter, we will see what the next steps are for learning more about Next.js, and we will also give a brief recap of what we've discovered so far.

We will look at the following in detail:

- A short recap of what we've learned in this book

- What are the next steps for learning more?

- Some projects ideas for practicing with Next.js

By the end of this chapter, you will know the next steps in your journey as a Next.js developer.

One framework, endless possibilities

Since the beginning of our Next.js adventure, we've seen many different features that the framework gives us to build a better, faster web.

One thing we should consider when talking about a framework is that it is not just about the technology. The community, ideas, and ecosystem are essential and deserve to be discussed in more detail.

Next.js, in fact, is not just a web framework. We've already seen how it revolutionized the way we build our apps on the frontend and backend by providing exciting and unique features that make our lives easier without compromising our love for our work as developers.

It isn't easy to talk about Next.js without mentioning how good and clever Vercel has been in creating something so unique.

Not only does Vercel provide an incredible platform for deploying our applications, but it also puts a lot of effort into enhancing the web framework and its ecosystem.

With the announcement of Next.js 11, the Vercel team also announced Next.js Live, a web browser-based environment for collaborating in real time with your team while coding any Next.js application.

It is still in beta, but it's incredibly promising. I must admit that I was extremely excited the first time I tried it, as I can clearly see how this could boost a team's productivity when debugging, designing, and testing any Next.js-based website.

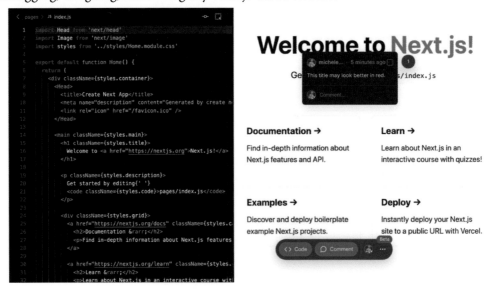

Figure 14.1 – Live coding with Next.js Live

Other than Vercel, there's an entire community of companies and individual contributors creating incredible extensions and libraries to simplify our job when building real-world Next.js applications.

We have already used some of them in our journey, but there are many packages that can help us achieve great results with ease.

There are also great GitHub repositories listing a selection of tools, tutorials, and libraries, such as `https://github.com/unicodeveloper/awesome-nextjs`. Here, you can find an exhaustive list of high-quality packages for every need.

When browsing all those libraries, articles, and tutorials, you'll eventually see that the power of Next.js relies upon many different features. It might have been born as a "full-stack React.js framework," but now it's something more significant and diverse.

In fact, we can clearly see how Next.js is more of a general-purpose framework that we can use for building any kind of application.

In the past, we used to distinguish web frameworks and technologies according to their main domain of interest. For example, if we needed to build a complex and interactive product, our choices usually boiled down to Ruby on Rails, Symphony, or Spring Boot, just to name a few.

Suppose we needed to build a simple company website. In that case, we might have chosen a static site generator, such as Jekyll, or a simple CMS, such as WordPress.

I'm not saying that Next.js changed all of that. Still, it replaced a vast number of technologies and frameworks with a simple approach to web development, where an entire team can easily collaborate on a single project when building REST APIs (via API pages), React components, backend logic, **user interfaces** (**UIs**), and so on.

Another thing that we should consider when adopting Next.js as a web framework is its impact at the architecture level.

In *Chapter 11*, *Different Deployment Platforms*, we discussed how to make decisions regarding how to host a Next.js app depending on its features and purpose.

Some years ago, standard practices mandated deploying any web application on a hosted server. Today, we have many different opportunities to enhance our users' browsing experiences by choosing several alternatives for serving our apps. With more classic tech stacks, such as Laravel or Ruby on Rails, we have just a few choices; we could deploy them on an AWS EC2 cluster or a virtual private server hosted by any company. Next.js allows us to consider many alternatives for creating better deployment pipelines and user experiences by statically rendering certain pages at build time or server-side rendering other pages at runtime. This is a game-changer.

To summarize, there's not just a single kind of web application where Next.js can be a good fit. It can be used for building any app thanks to its flexibility, robustness, and vast ecosystem.

As of the time of writing, I can't tell you a single scenario where using Next.js is the wrong choice.

Talking about possible scenarios, it might be the right time to introduce some little projects for practicing our Next.js knowledge before diving into production website development. In the next section, we will see some excellent ideas for little projects that can help us to practice real-world scenarios.

Real-world applications for practicing with Next.js

The best way to learn is through first-hand experience. In this book, we have covered several topics of increasing complexity and described various approaches for building real-world Next.js applications.

Now it's time to get our hands dirty and start writing some great apps!

When I started my career as a software engineer, I had difficulty finding suitable example applications to build for further learning; now, I want to give you the opportunity to practice by creating something worth sharing with your colleagues or friends, or even in your next job interview.

Streaming website

Streaming applications have become a massive part of our lives and changed the way we watch movies and TV shows forever. They're also an excellent use case for someone wanting to create a real-world application when learning more about a given technology.

As a first real-world project, I'd like you to build a clone of your favorite streaming service. It must respect the following rules:

- It must show a list of movies taken from the `https://www.themoviedb.org` database. This website exposes some beautiful free REST APIs; you can find the documentation here: `https://www.themoviedb.org/documentation/api`.

- To complicate things (just like in real-world scenarios), a user must be authenticated to see all the movies available in the application.

- When a trailer is available, the user should be able to watch it on the movie page.
- All the images must be served using Next.js' `<Image/>` component.
- Users can log in and out.

Before starting to write the code for this application, I suggest you try to answer the following questions:

- What kind of rendering strategy should I choose for the individual movie pages?
- Where should I deploy this application?
- How can I ensure that the user is logged in when browsing the website?
- How would the application perform if there were hundreds (or thousands) of concurrent users browsing it? Would that change my answer to the first question?

Of course, there are many other things to consider when building an application, but this is a good starting point.

In the following example, we will see a different kind of application. You will have fixed technological requirements that you need to meet, as will be the case when you're working for any company.

Blogging platform

Let's pretend that you're working for a company and you're required to build a blogging website by attaching Next.js to a headless CMS, in this case, GraphCMS.

You must observe the following requirements:

- You must use TailwindCSS for styling the UI.
- You must use TypeScript for coding the application.
- Every blog page must be statically rendered at build time.
- The UI must be as similar as possible to your favorite blog.
- Users can log in and save articles into a reading list.
- All the images must be served using Next.js' `<Image/>` component.
- SEO is essential. It must achieve a 100% Lighthouse SEO score.

If you're new to TypeScript, don't worry! Next.js allows you to adopt it gradually. Once you're used to it, you will never go back to vanilla JavaScript, I promise!

Bonus point: if you feel confident enough, you can also build a simple editing page where users can write their articles and share them on the website.

In this exercise, you're supposed to follow some strict requirements (the CMS to use, styling methods, and the language). In the next one, you will have complete freedom over any decision regarding the tech stack.

Real-time chat website

This is probably one of the most compelling examples of how powerful Next.js can be. For this exercise, you're required to build a real-time chat application with the following features:

- There must be multiple chat rooms.
- People can join any room by just inserting their name; no login is required.
- When people enter a room, they can access the full chat room history.
- Communication must be in real time.
- Bonus point: allow users to create new chat rooms.

This is a fascinating exercise because there are many different things to consider. For example, what if a user knows a given room URL and tries to join without entering their name? Where should all the messages be stored? How can those messages be sent and retrieved in real time?

To answer these last two questions, there are multiple great products that can help build secure, real-time software; the most interesting one is undoubtedly Google Firebase. It provides a free real-time database with end-to-end encryption that makes creating any chat app possible with ease.

Next steps

In the previous sections, we've seen some tiny ideas that can contain everything you need to practice and enhance your Next.js knowledge.

Even though we've covered many different topics, there's still so much to learn! But this time, you have all the information you need to bootstrap any Next.js project, and after reading an entire book on the topic, the best way to proceed is by implementing real-world applications.

From now on, you know how to start a Next.js project from scratch with TypeScript or vanilla JavaScript, how to customize its webpack configuration, how to add any external UI library, how to choose between rendering strategies, where to deploy it, and many other great concepts.

Next.js is a fast-evolving framework, and the best advice I can give you right now is to follow any news regarding it by following the Next.js core developers and Vercel (and me, `@MicheleRivaCode`, of course!) on Twitter, by participating in the Next.js Conf (the online event), and by reading the official Next.js blog at `https://nextjs.org/blog`.

You will be surprised to see how fast Next.js moves and transforms the web.

For that reason, once again, the best thing you can do when you start working with Next.js is to stay informed about its newest releases and features.

Summary

This summary marks the end of a book that I wish would never end. Not only because I truly enjoyed writing it, but also because I believe there is so much more to say regarding this beautiful framework.

This book covered all the essential knowledge needed to code real-world Next.js applications starting from scratch. As a result, I firmly believe you'll feel comfortable writing fast, reliable, and maintainable websites with Next.js, the React framework for production.

In this specific chapter, we've seen how Next.js is a game-changer in many different situations and how it has transformed the way we write web applications forever. Given that it is an ever-evolving framework, we also discussed how important it is to follow its latest and frequent releases and take advantage of its new features and enhancements.

We've also seen three real-world applications that we can implement to practice with Next.js, which is an essential part of anyone's journey for learning how to write production-grade applications.

It's now time to close the book, start coding, and enjoy the time we're living in, where Next.js exists and makes our developer experience just beautiful.

Index

Other Books You May Enjoy

If you enjoyed this book, you may be interested in these other books by Packt:

Simplify Testing with React Testing Library

Scottie Crump

ISBN: 978-1-80056-445-9

- Explore React Testing Library and its use cases.
- Get to grips with the RTL ecosystem.
- Apply jest-dom to enhance your tests using RTL.
- Gain the confidence you need to create tests that don't break with changes using RTL.

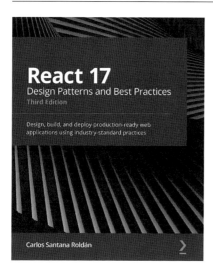

React 17 Design Patterns and Best Practices

Carlos Santana Roldán

ISBN: 978-1-80056-044-4

- Get to grips with the techniques of styling and optimizing React components.
- Create components using the new React Hooks.
- Get to grips with the new React Suspense technique and using GraphQL in your projects.
- Use server-side rendering to make applications load faster.
- Write a comprehensive set of tests to create robust and maintainable code.

Packt is searching for authors like you

If you're interested in becoming an author for Packt, please visit `authors.packtpub.com` and apply today. We have worked with thousands of developers and tech professionals, just like you, to help them share their insight with the global tech community. You can make a general application, apply for a specific hot topic that we are recruiting an author for, or submit your own idea.

Hi!

I really hope you enjoyed reading *Real-World Next.js* and found it helpful in increasing your productivity and efficiency when writing React applications for production!

It would really help me (and other potential readers!) if you could leave a review on Amazon sharing your thoughts on *Real-World Next.js*.

Go to the link below or scan the QR code to leave your review:

`https://packt.link/r/180107349X`

Your review will help me understand what's worked well in this book and what could be improved upon for future editions, so it really is appreciated.

Best wishes,

Printed in Great Britain
by Amazon

78325601R00205